Building Innovative Teams

BUILDING INNOVATIVE TEAMS

Strategies and Tools for Developing and Integrating High Performance Innovative Groups

Chris Harris

palgrave
macmillan

First published 2003 by
PALGRAVE MACMILLAN
Houndmills, Basingstoke, Hampshire RG21 6XS and
175 Fifth Avenue, New York, N. Y. 10010
Companies and representatives throughout the world

PALGRAVE MACMILLAN is the global academic imprint of the Palgrave
Macmillan division of St. Martin's Press, LLC and of Palgrave Macmillan Ltd.
Macmillan® is a registered trademark in the United States, United Kingdom
and other countries. Palgrave is a registered trademark in the European
Union and other countries.

ISBN 1–4039–0386–7 hardback

This book is printed on paper suitable for recycling and made from fully
managed and sustained forest sources.

A catalogue record for this book is available from the British Library.

Library of Congress Cataloging-in-Publication Data

Harris, Chris.
    Building innovative teams : strategies and tools for developing and
integrating high performance innovative groups / Chris Harris.
        p. cm.
    Includes bibliographical references and index.
    ISBN 1–4039–0386–7 (alk. paper)
      1. Teams in the workplace. 2. Creative ability. I. Title.

HD66.H3744 2003
658.4'02—dc21

2002193097

Editing and origination by Aardvark Editorial, Mendham, Suffolk

10 9 8 7 6 5 4 3 2 1
12 11 10 09 08 07 06 05 04 03

Printed and bound in Great Britain by
Creative Print & Design (Wales), Ebbw Vale

In loving memory of my grandmother,
Lillian Blore, whose love and compassion
inspired me to truly choose what I want
to be, what I want to do, what I
want to know, and where I want to go

CONTENTS

Contents

LIST OF FIGURES AND TABLES

Figures

Tables

ACKNOWLEDGEMENTS

I wish to thank the long line of people who have influenced or directly helped me to build innovative teams over the years: Bruno Bettelheim, Charles Handy, Gary Hamel, the late Soichiro Honda, Douglas Hofstadter, Fumio Kaodama, Stuart Kauffman, Kevin Kelly, Vincent Nolan, Marvin Minsky, the late Akio Morita, Rosabeth Moss Kanter, Ken Ohmae, Tom Peters, Howard Rheingold, Peter Senge, Dennis Sherwood, George Stalk, Jim Taylor, Alvin Toffler, Jim Utterback, and Watts Wacker.

I'd like to thank the companies I have worked with over the past two decades for their generous time and support in the development of the content of this book: American Airlines, British Airways, the BBC, Boeing, Bank of America, Capital One, Cisco Systems, A.P. Besson, Concord Lighting, Hewlett-Packard, IBM, McDonnell-Douglas, Matra Satellites Systems, Rockwell-Collins, General Electric Corporation, Raytheon and Toyota.

Many thanks to Aardvark Editorial for their diligent work in the book's overall layout and editing (once again your work is outstanding). Last, but by no means least, I am indebted to my publishers Jacky Kippenberger and Steve Rutt at Palgrave Macmillan, whose guidance during the completion has been invaluable.

Building Innovative Teams

This book is based on my experiences of working within, and hands-on building of, innovative teams over the past 20 years. It also draws on the knowledge of executives, consultants and scholars, who have helped me develop and lead high performance innovative teams over those years. It gleans from the successes and indeed the deficiencies in real-world innovation programmes in some of the most competitive environments imaginable.

Aim of the Book

The aim of this book is to provide a *practical* blueprint for building innovative teams. I emphasise the word 'practical', because this book is designed as a *tool* that you may apply and refer to over the years ahead. It is written for executives, managers and senior staff in the business world, as well as the world of governance, education and public service institutions.

Why a Book on Building Innovative Teams?

In the business world, innovation has become the bedrock of competitive strategy, and a major key to competitive advantage. More to the point, *all* organisations today need to innovate to survive, let alone thrive. Yet innovation is by far the most challenging and complex issue that any organisation faces. Innovation, as this book will make clear, is an activity driven by *uncertainty*, *risk* and *chance*. In fact, most innovations flounder. For every innovation that succeeds, says the inimitable Peter Drucker, there are

99 inventions that fail; 99 of which nothing is ever heard. Further, in their recent survey, the American Management Association asked 500 CEOs what their top priorities were for business survival in the twenty-first century. Almost all 500 claimed that innovation was at the head of their list. But when asked how well they were doing in this area, a mere 30 executives said they were making any headway. In another study, despite the growing recognition that innovation is the only sustainable source of growth, competitive advantage and new wealth, an Arthur D. Little survey of 669 global company executives found less than a quarter of companies believe innovation performance is where it needs to be if they are to be successful in the marketplace.

The Need for Constant Innovation

The question is, why is innovation now such a hot issue? Why, all of a sudden, has innovation shot up the agenda? There are many reasons; rapid commoditisation, time compression, demand-based markets, intense international competition and more.

Commoditisation

The first reason for innovation is the clear fact that the worth of once superior value goods and services now falls ever quicker towards a commodity. In the past, to add value meant exactly what it implied: to create an added return over the investment, and to do that an innovation had to offer an advantage over the competition's alternatives in the eyes of the customer. But adding value is now abruptly neutralised by a number of intensified market forces.

Visit any shopping mall, for example, and you'll experience an overwhelming abundance: everything from the latest high-tech gadgets, to instant service provisions catering for your every whim. We're up to our neck in copious bounty these days. And as a result, markets are soaked and choked ever-more quickly. Every family owns two or three cars, five or six watches, eight different phones, two dozen suits. We've all become magpies, stocking our nests with material effects. Yet even though we aspire to an abundance of choices, even though we stack our nests sky-high with stuff we don't need, the market saturates ever-more swiftly. And as the market is saturated, and as everyone increasingly gains instant access, the process of commoditisation accelerates.

Everything loses value faster today. Whether a cutting-edge competitive advantage or leading-edge pool of knowledge, to the most advanced apparatus available, everything drops in worth as an abundance of alternatives hit the market. As more acquire a particular piece of information or product or service – whether a top qualification, like a PhD, or a top pair of jeans, like 501s – the quicker it loses its value. In a phrase, the more there is, the less the worth.

Time Compression

As if that wasn't enough, time compression further exacerbates commoditisation. In an age of copious choice, the only scarce commodity is time and attention span – we all suffer from attention deficit disorder (ADD) these days – and in a time-compressed world, ADD (perceived or otherwise) means we crave for the to-go convenience of everything, everywhere, every time. We now live in a three-minute culture: video games, football games, educational games, news games, political games, even war games need last no longer than 180 seconds.

And as perceived time contracts, cramming takes over, demanding more experience in less time than ever before: 24-7-365 shopping, banking, TV and news; pubs, clubs and restaurants open all hours; late-night race meetings; gyms and sport complexes open all night; 5 a.m. cinema shows; theme rides at 2 a.m. New products appear, then disappear faster than an express train, new markets emerge and vanish with the life of a butterfly. Buyer habits shift daily, tracking trends becomes real time. Shoppers expect something new every time they shop, so retailers move in and out of markets like there's no tomorrow, discounting and dumping stock like there's no today. Just-in-time is embedded in every movement of the physical and the conceptual. Knowledge lives and dies in a single day, news agencies sell and bid for information with a half-life of 20 minutes. For those that can't skip ahead, let alone keep up, core products and services further shrink in value.

Customers Take Control of Markets

Abundance, commoditisation and time compression only reinforce each other, it seems, and as a result the customer begins to take hold of the market. And this is happening on two levels.

Firstly, extensive choice means a surplus, and when you have surplus on the supply side, you get another pull down on price – the customer gains a handle on what you do. The customer sees, feels, lives among abundance, and actively senses that he's in control. He buys anywhere, demands anything, rejects almost everything too. Abundance means that the customer wins every time, he is now in power.

Secondly, when you have a shortage on the demand side, you enter into keen price competition, and when you do that your margins atrophy, and as your gross margins shrink the customer perceives you as a lowly commodity, whether a top brand or not. Again, the customer is in control.

Global Competition

Next, international competition intensifies. Rapidly industrialising countries, like Mexico and Pakistan, are selling in your local home-grown backyard. The most productive, high quality factories in the world can be found in Mexico. Mexican factories – big auto factories – have achieved world-class levels of quality and productivity, at $4.00 an hour, for well over a decade now. Pakistan is constantly advertised on Japanese TV. With over 114 million people and a GDP growth of 6.5 per cent, even in the light of recent events, the commercial Pakistan has a foothold in the twenty-first century, with established manufacturing ventures with Coke, Phillips and GE, and looking high-tech, high-spec and a million light years away from the poverty-stricken nation we have come to know.

And as the infrastructure and knowledge to assemble and maintain such ventures grow, all rapidly industrialising nations the world over will build the capability to design, make and market anything and everything you care to mention. Remember, knowledge and ideas now cross international borders at the speed of light. The cold war boundaries have gone, old geo-national borders are fading fast. The lessons here is that even if your business innovates at bullet speed, even if you hold all the intellectual capital, rapidly developing nations, by hook or by crook, will one day soon copy your latest inventions. And crash, down goes your value again.

So, in total, market saturation and an abundance of choice force prices down; everything becomes a commodity sooner rather than later. Choice further compresses time – we all become time poor and expectations rich. In turn, the consumer takes control of the market. International competition and clones of everything devalue further. Altogether, once-high-value products and services rapidly disintegrate in worth as all these market dynamics become more deeply entwined. The race to innovate to maintain value is now being fought on multiple fronts, by multiple strategies, in multiple wars.

The Need for Public Service Innovation

In the public domain, it's a similar story. Innovation has become *the* watchword. Presidents and prime ministers alike, social systems innovation is on the tip of their tongue. As society becomes an ever-more complex, rapidly changing, technologically driven place, new kinds of institutions and public services are needed to meet unique kinds of circumstance and the ever-increasing expectations of the public at large. And public expectations have rocketed. Today, consumers of public services simply demand the levels of world-class performance they experience in the private sector.

But again, the numbers show that most innovations in the public arena fall way short of expectations, or never in effect make it into practice. And that's a potential calamity. As populations in urban areas grow, there's little choice other than to bring in radically new ways to manage such expanding demand and complexity. Whether it be transportation, heathcare or education, governments require an order-of-magnitude improvement. In the end, efficiency drives can't provide the answer, as all efficiency gains eventually diminish. The only sure way to effect such continuous stepped development is to significantly increase the success rate of public service innovation.

Innovative Teams: A Key to Future Success

If the future of any business and the public service sector depends so much on innovation, and if, as the reports above show, that performance in innovation is way below what is needed, then perhaps successful innovation is the business world's, and indeed the world of governance's most pressing challenge. So what to do?

By far the most significant factor in achieving successful innovation (I will define what successful means in the context of innovation in Chapter 1) is the very group of people that conceive, develop and commercialise or commission a given innovation. This sounds obvious at first, yet the building of a group of people into a true high performance (again I will define high performance later) innovative team, that can deliver successful outcomes, is all too often misunderstood and, in the extreme, completely neglected.

The main reason why this crucial issue is misunderstood and often neglected is that most – and I mean most – management teams do not have any developed model to work with to build true, high performance innovative teams – until now.

Outline of *Building Innovative Teams*

This book is presented in four parts, each one following on as a system of ideas. Each part describes key insights, building blocks and strategies and tools for building innovative teams in times when the demand for ever-more complex and rapid innovation is required.

Part I – The Dynamics of Innovation: Innovation has a unique nature, in that it is driven by uncertainty. To navigate such uncertainty, there is an acute need for so-called 'innovative teams'. The first part outlines the dynamics of innovation in terms of its distinctive nature and the special qualities an innovative team must have to successfully bring about innovation.

Part II – The Dynamics of Building Innovative Teams: There is much more to building innovative teams than merely putting people together in a group and then demanding that they deliver successful innovation. Unfortunately, this seems to be the mainstay approach to building teams today. But teamwork, and in particular innovative team building, is a developing science with a body of knowledge that can be applied to significantly enhance team performance. The second part of this book outlines the key factors and systems of the dynamics of building innovative teams.

Part III – Innovative Team-building Performance: Practice is essential to all team building. In fact, it is often the missing link for team performance. The third part of this book outlines why exercise is essential, and details a framework of real-world strategies and tools for developing and integrating high performance innovative groups.

Part IV – Appendices: Contains team-building exercises, questionnaires and other material to supplement the text.

In sum, *Building Innovative Teams* is a comprehensive application model that can be employed in any setting, commercial or public, where new ideas have to be turned into reality with greater reliability. As a result, *Building Innovative Teams* will remain a dependable asset over the years ahead, as the demand for innovation becomes ever-more heightened.

CHRIS HARRIS

PART I

The Dynamics of Innovation

Part I of this book takes an in-depth look at *why* innovation and in turn *how* innovative teams vastly differ from conventional practices and organisations. It outlines the key principles of why and how innovation and innovative teams are so extraordinary in two related chapters.

Chapter 1 – The Unique Nature of Innovation: The premise of this chapter begins with this: If something – anything – is new, you can be sure that you and your peers – no matter how smart, insightful or experienced – are not going to understand it that well. And because of this a different set of management philosophies and principles are needed to negotiate successfully this unique nature of innovation. Furthermore, a great many more innovations are increasing in complexity. They are now made up of vast and diverse systems of ideas, technologies and processes that have to function as one integrated whole. In view of this, Chapter 1 outlines the peculiarities of such complex systems innovation, and the secrets to how such idiosyncrasies not only can be overcome, but used to advantage.

Chapter 2 – The Unique Nurture of Innovative Teams: If a potential complex systems innovation project is managed and organised in the very same way as a mainstream operation, then you can bet the potential innovation in question will remain only a question. But this conclusion has a much deeper consequence inasmuch as it is counterintuitive. It goes against the hardened grain of traditional management style and organisation. Simply put: to move an invention effectively through the various stages of technical conception/development and eventual commercial/public adoption, a particular kind of organisation needs to form – the *innovative team*.

CHAPTER 1

The Unique Nature of Innovation

There is nothing more difficult to carry out, nor more doubtful of success, nor more dangerous to handle; than to initiate a new order of things. MACHIAVELLI

Innovation is a competitive necessity today. Yet this competitive must-do is unlike any business activity I have come to know. It is an enigmatic endeavour that few have mastered. And those who claim to be masters of the dynamics of innovation secretly tell that they are still subject to the same peculiarities of innovation as any novice. Innovation can be, and often is, a cruel venture. It can put out the flame of a budding business in an instant, it can send a giant corporation reeling down the stock market and off the chart (permanently) and of course it can cause confusion and utter distress in already overburdened public services. For it is easier for an innovation to flounder, than to fall off a log. And believe me, my colleagues and I have the wounds to prove it.

But we also have the rewards and esteem that come from the many successes we have had. We do not claim to have mastered all the dynamics of innovation, nor do we profess to have penetrated all the depths of its unique nature. But we have learnt a trick or two on our journey thus far, and I would like to share some of them with you here.

Leading Definitions of Innovation

So what does innovation actually mean? Here are a handful of definitions from leading thinkers in the world of innovation. Cap Gemini Ernst & Young Consulting, Centre for Business Innovation calls innovation:

'The realisation of value from a new solution to a problem, changing the rules of the game.' Jim Utterback, Professor of Management and Engineering at MIT calls it the 'Reduction of an idea for first use or sale'. Colin Clipson, formerly professor of architecture and research, University of Michigan, says it is a 'Commercially successful use of a new solution'. Peter Drucker defines innovation as 'Change that creates a new dimension of performance'. So, in short, technically speaking, the word 'innovation' means the *successful introduction of new ideas*.

However, these definitions are qualitative. Accountants often raise an eyebrow (or two) when they hear such nebulous definitions, often asking for more concrete interpretations. Yet, unless you are talking about one particular innovation, at one particular moment in time, attempting to tie down the quantitative definition of successful innovation to some unified objective measure is an elusive task.

Nevertheless, the most significant measures that have turned up again and again over the years are based around three strategic precepts: exceeding the customer's unsatisfied, unarticulated and/or emerging needs and expectations; creating a new market space; and creating a superior value return:

■   *Exceeding the target customer's unsatisfied, unarticulated and/or emerging needs and expectations*: All success, or indeed failure, starts with an expectation, that is, whether an outcome goes the way you anticipate, and so it is with innovation. There is no more important expectation than the customer's expectation that the innovation is meant to satisfy. If the innovation does not at least meet the expectations of the customer, then it is not an innovation. Furthermore, in both the commercial and public domain these days, the goal has become to exceed the customer's emerging or unarticulated needs and expectations – wants and whims that are just beginning to develop or indeed have not yet been identified or served. And don't forget that this is no easy challenge, as all customers now demand top quality levels of service as standard.

■   *Reinventing or creating a new market space*: Change in the business world is no longer gradual or continuous. Change today happens in sudden, disruptive leaps that can radically transform the rules of the game. In a discontinuous world, things don't simply happen faster, different things happen faster. Consequently, continuous improvement and efficiency drives no longer provide competitive advantage alone. Innovation is the key not only to keeping one step ahead of the competition, but provides completely new categories of competition.

Innovation is about creating a difference, creating new means over and above old modes. Here, so-called radical, category-breaking innovation, such as brand new business concepts, can create completely new markets, even entire new industries. This is fundamentally about new concepts that create new segments outside traditional markets.

■ *Providing superior value return on total investment*: Of course, in the business world this is pivotal. But again, the measure is all to do with expectations. What is deemed a superior return is industry relative, and depends on who is doing the anticipating. Often, expectations are set against historical financial performance of both the company and industry. In the public sector, best value is now a key yardstick for gauging successful innovation. In Chapter 2, I'll give up some of the secrets of how teams can deliver best value innovations.

There are other criterion for success that are important these days, such as safety, ecologically sound, regulatory and legal issues. But all these fit into the three criterion in some way.

What Innovation Is

Beyond the definition of successful innovation, it is important to grasp the deeper nature of innovation. As with all processes, there are peculiarities here that must be mastered if successful innovation is going to take place.

The starting point to determine the specific nature of innovation is that it is a *deviation from the norm* – whether in business, technology or social systems. And that means getting away from conventional practice and wisdom. And when you are in such *terra incognita*, you are in a world of novelties, uniqueness, original things and often the downright strange and complex. Such novelties can occur in everything from new products to processes to new business platforms; to popular culture, the arts and sciences; and in modern day social systems and institutions. Innovation touches all.

Embedded in innovation's unique nature are various underlying dynamics and distinctive traits:

■ *Uncertain*: Anything new, we do not know that well, and if we do not know something that well, we are unable to predict its behaviour and how it will interact with the real world before output. Furthermore, the inputs of any given innovation cannot be predicted accurately either. What resources are needed, the timing and the length of use are at best ambiguous. Together, uncertainty in inputs and outputs makes innovation the most unpredictable, tricky endeavour an organisation can take on.

■ *Risky*: Risk is related to uncertainty, but it is quite different. Risk is about attaching probabilities to a predicated outcome; where uncertainty is more to do with going beyond what we know. One of the major associated risks with innovation, such as a new product or service, is that once the investment has been made there is little or no residual value left, until the innovation is launched into the market and reaches the financial breakeven point. For many financial institutions, this 'absence of residual value after investment' is too much of a risk, and the number one reason why many fiscal institutions won't pursue radical innovation.

■ *Stressful*: Because innovation is uncertain and risky, it is certainly not for the faint-hearted. It takes grit and determination to innovate – anything. Unless you are lucky, innovation is a toil of sweat and tears. Beyond the visceral stresses are the emotional and psychological stresses. Because when we are acting in unknown territory, we are at our most vulnerable. As I'll explain in Chapter 3, when we're working in the unknown, the oldest primitive emotions and reflexes start to kick in, to a point where, for some, changes in behaviour and interactions can be quite dramatic.

■ *Intellectually taxing*: One of the most challenging elements of innovation is the solving of problems that have not existed before, because, for the most part, there is *no* pool of knowledge or experience in the areas of breakthrough that innovators can draw upon. Innovators have to be both intuitive and analytical in their creative endeavours.

What Innovation Is Not

It is also worth describing what innovation is not, because many managers and professionals mistakenly force conventional practices on innovation activities, which actually only impedes progress:

■ *Not a repeatable process*: Indeed, there will be transferable knowledge and processes that can be used the next time around. But, for the most part, an innovation, particularly rule-breaking innovation that contains many radical ideas, will require unique ways and means to bring it to market. Again, this means novelty and uncertainty.

■ *Not a linear process*: The activity of innovation is not like a sausage machine, where you input some information and materials and out comes a new computer chip or fast-food brand. It simply doesn't work like that. In fact, in the manufacturing world, the standard way to bring new ideas to market is to follow a so-called project life-cycle model, a serial, step-by-step process (sausage machine). But most manufacturing companies find it almost impossible to bring new products and services to market on time, budget and specification; and many run three or fourfold over plan. This is partly due to innovation's habit of morphing, at the drop of a hat, from something that we thought we knew well into something that we don't understand. Solutions to problems don't arrive in any particular order, don't turn up when we expect them to, or behave as we predict. The point is that innovation is a non-linear activity, and it's best to use a system – such as high performance innovative teams – to manage such non-linearity.

■ *Not efficient*: The number of times executives have asked me to make their innovation activities more efficient I could count on the stars above. Because innovation is a non-linear activity full of novelties, uncertainties, risk and so on, it is just not possible to make the activity efficient. In fact, the late Akio Morita, co-founder of SONY, often said that the best innovations appear out of a process that looks something like a demolition derby.

■ *Not driven by common sense*: At one level, common sense is the application of experience and knowledge that worked well in the past. But what of innovation, where there is no bank of cumulative knowledge? Again, innovators have to invent solutions as they go. But more than that, many of the solutions to new kinds of problem fly in the face of conventional wisdom, because the problems themselves are unique and original. For innovation, common sense may be the worst teacher in town.

What Successful Innovation Can Be

Paradoxically, despite what innovation is and what it is not, teams can bring in an innovation with high levels of operational performance:

■ *Productive*: Productivity is not the same as efficiency – an all too common misunderstanding. Productivity is quite different to efficiency in that you can be quite inefficient, but have high levels of output and results over time. My office, for example, is not an efficient place, it looks like a playground, full of gadgets, tools and toys, new product concepts, seminar scripts, training programmes and schedules. But I put these out at a rate of knots, because of the very fact that my office is set up for so-called non-linear activities. Later, in Chapter 8, on high performance goals and metrics, I'll explain how to build teams that are highly productive under such chaos.

■ *High speed*: Rapid innovation cycle-times are now a competitive entry requirement. That is, what used to take years to develop is now often brought to market in a matter of a few months. As noted above, innovation teams are set up for the non-linear nature of innovation, and therefore are the best organisational unit to deliver quick innovation cycles.

■ *Leaner operational expenses*: High levels of productivity and speed dramatically reduce operational expenses. Futhermore, innovation teams are leaner (as you will see in Chapter 9), again reducing costs.

■ *Higher product/service performance*: This is how well a new service or product conforms to the intended technical and market specifications. Again the interactivity of innovative teams enables better design solutions to meet such challenges.

■ *Leaner product/service costs*: Because design solutions often achieve improved performance, the actual build cost of a product or service innovation is often reduced. This also goes hand in hand with high productivity and speed.

Failed Invention and Deep Uncertainty

As touched on in the Introduction to this book, most inventions fail to make it to innovation, most ideas don't make it successfully to market and are never heard of again. There are umpteen reasons why innovations fail, but in the end, the reason why most innovations fail is that teams do not understand the magnitude of the task at hand. Therefore, one of the most important issues to address is to define the type of animal a team is dealing with. And the best way to do that, I have found, is to define an innovation in terms of uncertainty. Once the uncertainty factors have been defined for a given innovation, a team can begin to understand how far they are going *beyond* cumulative experience and knowledge, and in turn begin to get a feel for the magnitude of the risks and issues they will face.

But you may ask: How much uncertainty does an innovation contain? How do you define the uncertainties? How do you then measure these uncertainties? These are substantial and important questions.

The most general definition of uncertainty I've developed thus far goes by how much *novelty* and *complexity* a given innovation exhibits. Yet this general definition turns out to be a powerful tool for determining and managing uncertainty within innovation projects.

The degree of novelty (newness) and complexity (diversity of ideas) embedded within any particular invention sets the level of uncertainty. In short, the higher the degrees of novelty and complexity, the higher the degree of uncertainty.

Novelty can appear in many guises, from new technologies, to new processes, to unique market introductions, even novelties in cost. For example, Southwest Airline's innovative strategy to develop the lowest cost structure in its industry has given it best-in-class net income and growth. Its no frills, almost austere service system has given major competitive advantages, enabling Southwest to operate at two to three times the gross margin of its nearest three competitors (Standard & Poor).

Complexity is represented in terms of the diversity of ideas, and can appear in forms such as the number, sophistication and resolution of core technologies, to the performance of the innovation such as reliability, durability, finish, level of service and so on. For example, a television in the 1970s had a six-month mean time between failure (MTBF), with of course backup by a not so keen maintenance crew. In the 1980s, this went up to three years, and by the turn of the millennium, five years was the standard MTBF for the TV.

Innovation Uncertainty Matrix

Innovation uncertainty is best viewed in the form of a two by two quarter (Q) matrix, showing complexity along the X-axis and novelty along the Y-axis. The further one goes along each axis, the greater the uncertainty becomes (Figure 1.1).

There are, of course, many ways to define a given innovation, and indeed many systems of categorisation. In this case, each quarter (Q) box of the matrix has four very different categories of innovation, represented by different levels of novelty and complexity and therefore uncertainty:

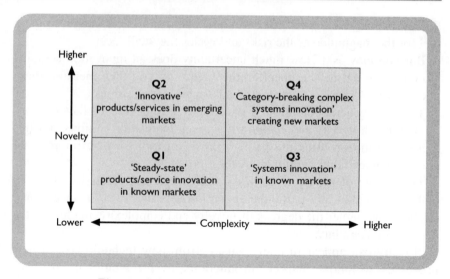

Figure 1.1   Innovation uncertainty matrix

■ *Q1 – new steady-state products/services* in known and well-defined market segments. This category is the least uncertain, and in turn least risky. Examples would include: office equipment such as lighting, seating and carpeting; fashion items such as off-the-shelf sports shoes; popular music such as yet another rock album. These are standard commodities with little or no novelty and lower levels of complexity in terms of core technology and processes and/or market distribution and communications.

■ *Q2 – innovative products/services* in new or emerging markets. Examples would include; the geographic introduction of AppleCola into China; a brand extension such as a Cadbury's Coffee Shop; even a new domestic appliance such as a bath overflow alarm. Novelty may appear in the form of core technology or market logistics and communications. Complexity, however, would be lower in terms of the number and sophistication of the technology.

■ *Q3 – systems innovation* in known and well-defined markets. One example might be a new palmtop personal computing device. Such an innovation might stimulate new demand in a saturated market, or change the competitive context of established markets. Novelty would be lower in terms of the market communication and technology, but higher in terms of the technical complexity.

- *Q4 – radical category-breaking systems innovation* creating new/ emerging markets/industries. Examples include in-flight entertainment systems, or a radically new concept for a fast-food outfit. Such radical category-breaking systems innovations often create entirely new markets, even industries. Everything from the core technology to the market communications and distribution need to be constructed. This is by far the most uncertain, risky and chancy innovation an organisation can take on. Expect high uncertainty, basic blunders, acts of nature and booby traps on the road and in the market if your innovation fits in this category.

And so, a rule of thumb for innovation: the more novelty and/or complexity an innovation exhibits, the more uncertain an innovation becomes, and, in turn, the more challenging and risky an innovation is. Clearly the uncertainty an innovation exhibits has significant impact on the potential success for a given innovation.

Successful Innovation and Accelerated Learning

So, what to do? Clearly, teams need a way of driving out uncertainty within given innovation projects, in the least possible time, and with the least contingent effort. What drives out such uncertainty is accelerated real-world learning and cumulative knowledge. Essentially, the faster the rate of learning occurs, the faster the rate of feedback for adaptation, the faster uncertainty drops.

As noted in the Introduction to this book, most innovations fail. But that's not all bad news! Tom Peters says the essence and engine of innovation is failure, because it is in failure where we learn most. Failure, then, is part of the culture and nature of innovation. The quicker you trip, the faster you push your innovation to its limits, the more learned about a given innovation you're going to be. As the late Soichiro Honda, co-founder of the Honda Motor Co., often said: 'My success comes from ninety-nine percent failure and introspection.' He lived by the belief that a failed innovation can tell you what direction to go next, or how a design could be improved. Furthermore, if you don't sometimes or ever have that naive feeling, that feeling of slight stupidity and of being out of place, then you will never learn. Again, it is when we experience that feeling of naivety, that we are learning most.

Clearly, there is a need to apply the most effective methods to drive out uncertainty in the least time. Here are some principles that do just that:

- *Portfolio of diverse experiments*: There is a principle in innovation that asserts that the potential future success of your organisation is directly proportional to the number and diversity of new experiments taking place. Therefore, how intense and assorted is your experimental innovation programme? A few kick-starts in the pipeline? Or a rich zoo of experiments? Remember, most inventions fail to become innovations. So uniqueness and novelty in experiments are key here.

- *Accelerate learning before output*: The primary objective for any experiment is to effect high levels of understanding about how an invention (physical equipment or people-based services) behaves in its working environment before launch (output). This is all the more important today, as more innovations contain so-called 'disruptive technologies and processes' that are not very well understood. In too many cases, this kind of learning is achieved after a new product/service is launched. For large-scale projects (for example aerospace, automotive, internet banking and so on), this causes acute learning disability and is the number one reason why we see quite poor performance in many large-scale projects.

- *Real-world learning*: Make sure that the applied rules promote learning with real prototypes, in real markets, with real customers. Prototype experiments are also essential to risk management in any innovation process, because learning is the single most effective way to derisk – anything. Furthermore, prototyping is the single most significant activity within innovation, in terms of the value-adding information it gives up. So centre the learning around the customers and providers who will purchase, use, abuse, transport, make, serve, maintain, and recycle the contraption. Too many firms ignore the customer when experimenting with prototypes. At the end of the day, it's the customer who is both the judge and jury. The message here is to get the prototype into the market, today.

- *Experiment differently than the competition*: To create new value, you must innovate in ways the competition are not or cannot. To maintain differentiation from the competition, there is a vital need to enrich with radical ideas and learning experiments. The bottom line here is that to truly innovate, you must not only learn faster and better than the competition, you must learn different things than the competition.

- *Quantitative performance measures*: Performance targets must be identified, and the tests to qualify those targets must be defined. These include such measures as component technical characteristics performance, process characteristics performance and end-process controls performance. Equally, operational and field performance and test criteria now come from an increasing number of international technical and safety qualification standards. These give a baseline for performance, that is, they set the minimum performance requirement. In many situations, it's important to exceed these standards to achieve competitive performance advantage.

■ *Get-out strategy*: Don't get stuck on a single idea. Innovation is also a game of probabilities. You need to play the numbers. To do this you must define the minimum technical and market performance that you must meet for the innovation to be successful. After several failed attempts to reach the performance targets, you must be prepared to walk away. Furthermore, as noted above, a key to derisking a project is to fail quickly. The earlier you fail, the faster you derisk and/or learn. As James Dyson says: 'If it works, and especially if it works first time, you learn nothing!' So, treat all prototype failures as learning experiments.

Any innovation that contains significant amounts of novelty and/or complexity will have elevated levels of uncertainty. Learning is route number one to driving out such uncertainty, and in turn levelling risk and increasing the chance for a successful outcome. The above guidelines will accelerate learning and are a major set of application ideas that any innovation team can use to make successful innovation happen.

(NB: The main points of this chapter are outlined in Exercise 1 in Appendix A in an easy-to-learn team-building format.)

CHAPTER 2

The Unique Nature of Innovative Teams

If the rules of engagement are changing you can bet that your team will be innovating.
M. LANG, CONSULTANT

As with innovation itself, innovative teams also have a unique nature, in that they are a skilled, creative group of people who need to make an uncertain activity certain and successful – the challenge of challenges. This chapter outlines how and why innovative teams are necessary to reduce inherent uncertainty, accelerate learning and in turn produce successful innovation.

The Difference Between Innovative and Steady-state Teams

A quiz: Set out below is a list of different teams (of sorts), seen in everyday life. The objective of the quiz is to determine which teams are innovative, and which are steady-state. Put a tick beside either definition (innovative or steady-state) to indicate your opinion.

	Innovative team	Steady-state team
Football team	( )	( )
Dental surgery	( )	( )
Production team	( )	( )
Engineering research group	( )	( )
Ministerial war cabinet	( )	( )
Advertising development team	( )	( )

It is a teasing quiz. Because unless you know the key factor that differentiates an innovative team from a steady-state team, you will be hard pressed to know which is which. But that is the point of the quiz, to get you to think about which *is* which, because it is vitally important to know what the key difference is between an innovative and a steady-state team when it comes to innovation.

So, to put you out of your misery, the key difference between an innovative and a steady-state team is in the rules of engagement that each kind of team face.

Steady-state teams work within established rules, regulations and routines – a steady-state environment. The next day's schedule, game or format is much the same as the last. The football team, for example, may be extraordinarily creative whilst playing a game, but that is not the point. A game of football has fixed rules of engagement. The football team is a steady-state team which does not change the rules of the game. In a dental surgery, tooth problems may vary dramatically, but a dental surgery is primarily a place of precise procedure. Again, the rules of engagement are in place. A production team is a steady-state team. Even in the modern day flexible service operation, where continuous improvement is vital, the change in routine is evolutionary and gradual. In fact, the first three groups in the quiz are steady-state teams.

In stark contrast, for any given innovation team, the rules are yet to be written or rewritten, as by definition the team is innovating new ways and means. Engineering research groups, for example, explore new areas of knowledge for capture in real-world applications. And so, by definition, the rules of engagements may change at any time. Whether it be the research methods, or even the objectives of the end results, changes can be dramatic over time. It is well known that ministerial war cabinets follow well-thought-out strategies and scenarios pre-empted by military strategists. But any modern war can change dramatically in real time. Again, the rules of engagement are dynamic. Equally, advertising teams have a vast body of knowledge about buyer psychology and so on, but how they apply such knowledge is ultimately creative, resulting in changes in the rules of engagement. So, the last three groups in the quiz are innovative teams.

Perhaps it can be seen that the idea of routine is senseless to a truly innovative team. Innovative teams deal with unique situations. They have to solve problems that have not existed before, and literally having to create something out of nothing is the nearest innovative teams get to the luxury of fixed, routine rules and ideas.

Innovation is not about consuming a body of information or following a linear set of well-defined rules fixed by some higher authority. It is a dynamic process set by progressive learning, adaptation and breakthrough. Look at the contrast between the two working environments:

Steady-state environment	*Innovative environment*
Certainty	Uncertainty
Routine	Novelty
Meditated	Spontaneity
Order	Chaos
Planning	Learning
Procedure	Induction
Experience	Naivety
Best	Different
Continuity	Discontinuity
Efficient	Creative

From this we can find another rule of thumb for innovation. The more fixed and in place the rules, the greater the certainty, the more steady-state the environment becomes, the more steady-state a team can be and the less a team has to learn. Clearly, then, there is a huge difference between the dynamics of a steady-state team and an innovative team, because innovative teams work in unknown territory, and therefore often have to invent the rules of the game as they play. This fact will become clearer as you read on.

Multifaceted Change and its Impact on Innovation

The old world order that supported steady-state rules and routine is giving way to a new sphere of rapid change. In fact, change has become such an issue within the world corporate governance and public service strategy, that 'change' has now become an industry in itself. Change is a business today. Yet change is no easy challenge, neither is it easily understood. Change is a multifaceted phenomenon which arrives in many forms.

The most basic form of change is *serial change*, where issues simply move from one state to the next in a straight line. Examples of serial change include: if interest rates go up, spending goes down; or Newton's second law of motion, that says 'Every action has an equal and opposite reaction'. These kinds of serial change are highly rational, connections are simple and cause and effect is discernible. Serial change is most people's idea of change.

A major feature of change these days is the *rate of change*. I first came across this feature 20 years ago, when I read Alvin Toffler's book *Future*

Shock. One of the main messages was that change was not only happening more rapidly, change was happening faster and faster. Toffler proposed that there was a 'rate of change in the rate of change'. Back then, I found it exciting. Today, I find it unnerving, because Toffler's projection has leapt from the inanimate pages of a book into hard reality. In fact, Toffler goes so far as to say that more change will take place in this decade than in the last 50 years. So something is afoot.

The most inclusive way to look at change is through so-called *systemic change* – change as a system. In this way, when something changes here, something will eventually change over there. However, in systemic change, cause and effect begin to break down, because the interactions are so complex. Consequently, it is often difficult, if not impossible to trace why a change occurred in the first place. For example, why did Enron Corp. go out of business? Too much risk? Too far too quickly? Incompetent management? Greed? Too high expectations? What? Who really knows, because each of these are tied up in a complex network of causality. Systemic change is all too often non-deterministic.

As a result of serial change, accelerating change and systemic change comes the most jarring form of transformation – so-called *non-linear* or *discontinuous change*. This kind of shift can completely replace the present, and often in dramatic ways. For example, a new breakthrough in technology can literally make conventional technology obsolete in a short time. The car replaced the horse-drawn buggy, the telephone replaced the telegraph, the microchip replaced the valve. A discontinuous innovation can dramatically change the competitive context within a market too. Clearly then, in a world of increasing interconnections across cultures, economies and technology, discontinuous disruptive change becomes the norm.

Gary Hamel, visiting professor of strategy and international business at the London Business School, goes further, saying: 'We've reached the end of incrementalism, and only those companies that are capable of creating industry revolutions will prosper in the new economy.' In support of this, a report in *Fortune* magazine (12 June, 2000) claimed that only non-linear, non-incremental innovation will produce long-lasting value creation. That is, (Q4) radical breakthrough systems innovations, often inconsistent with the existing portfolio of skills, knowledge and expertise, are no longer a nice-to-do, but an essential must-do strategic issue. These kinds of discontinuous change now continuously knock out well-honed business and public service strategies.

Perhaps we can see why strategy and innovation are now synonymous to the point where they are indistinguishable. As the rate of change accelerates, and the non-linear forces knock out well-honed strategies, complex systems innovation has become the linchpin for sustainable value creation.

Such non-linear innovations are made up of a huge diversity (complexity) of disruptive (novel) core technologies and processes, that need to be developed and integrated into a functioning whole. In turn, such complex innovations are often introduced into markets that are either embryonic or, indeed, being created from scratch – the highest levels of uncertainty and risk an organisation can face.

Examples of Complex (Q4) Systems Innovation

To give an insight into the levels of complexity and novelty faced here, let us start at the extreme. The most complex self-contained systems innovation I know is the US Navy's Seawolf attack submarine. It is made up of over 10,000,000 components, integrated in 6000 subsystems, via 32,000 kilometres of electric cable! The combat computer's software is one of the most sophisticated systems the world has seen, with a software code length approaching 40,000,000 lines. The complexity the Seawolf exhibits is on an extraordinary scale.

In the inner-space direction, Dr Nagayama Kuniaki, a Japanese research scientist, is pioneering the field of so-called molecular self-assembly. His latest products include synthetic molecules and new nano-scale engineering materials. What this means is a new level of technological complexity. Products such as semiconductors, sub-microelectromechanical devices and molecular materials are beginning to proliferate. In fact, Kevin Kelly, author of the treatise *Out of Control*, has said that we are entering an age where technology is so complex that it can be compared to natural living biology.

This new level of biological-like complexity is the stable diet for industries such as aerospace, defence and chemicals. Corporations like British Aerospace, Lockheed-Martin and Du Pont are well used to such deep complexity contained within their innovations. Admittedly most organisations don't come even close to such complexity in their innovation. However, because of such dramatic discontinuous changes that we are seeing, more and more organisations are climbing the ladder of complexity as the need for category-breaking systems innovation becomes more of an issue.

Another example that shows the level of complexity is the rapidly emerging in-flight entertainment industry, depicted by disruptive, hyper-competition. One competitor here is the world renowned Rockwell-Collins

Corp., which has brought its eTES in-flight entertainment system to market in record time. eTES is a true category-breaking (Q4) complex systems innovation. It offers carriers, such as American Airlines, Qantas and so on, any combination of overhead video, in-seat audio and video on demand (AVOD), interactive games, telephone, seat-to-seat and World Wide Web internet access from 10,500 metres in the sky. The digital media server stores up to 80 full-length feature films that may be randomly accessed by all passengers at any time, and in a range of languages.

Again, think of the radically innovative technologies and processes that needed to be designed, developed and integrated to create such a mega-platform. Take the passenger control handset, for example, that enables interactivity with the eTES. It consists of telephone functionality, a credit card reader, liquid crystal display for messaging and a Nintendo-like game controller. The control handset is made up of 17 different core technologies, requiring 14 different engineering disciplines for development and integration – all in an itsy-bitsy handset! But it doesn't stop there. Each of the systems that make up the eTES has to be designed for reliability, durability, safety and maintainability. Next, the eTES has to be qualified and certified to the highest airborne equipment standards. Then once that's been achieved, the eTES has to be integrated into the aircraft's in-flight cabin system, for full commissioning and acceptance testing.

Of course, if you are wondering 'Well, my innovations aren't even close to the level of complexity this book is rattling on about', think of this. Think of the gains your organisation will reap if you take on board the capacities of the organisations I mention here. All of a sudden that new rotor blade or photo booth is no longer the daunting task it seemed.

Difficulties with Complex Systems Innovations

There are several difficulties with such complex (Q4) systems innovations that may potentially affect the successful introduction of an invention.

Firstly, and most obviously, systems innovations encompass a huge diversity of issues, including technology, processes, market and customer demands, and regulatory and political issues – whatever is needed to produce a successful outcome. As a result, the sheer scale of a project can be overwhelming. Confusion about what technical or market performance is required is all too common in these kinds of project.

Secondly, because systems innovations can be complex, they often result in counterintuitive behaviours and outputs. In fact, biologists tell us that we cannot totally understand a truly complex system. But that is the way man-made contraptions and systems are going. So yet another difficulty is that such systems are impossible to control in all their dimensions. This will again entail achieving the desired performance around systems reliability, timing of introduction and issues of cost and quality. These issues are not insurmountable, yet often stretch individual and team talents to the limit.

Thirdly, complex systems are difficult to optimise. There is a law in systems dynamics that says it is possible to optimise either the whole system, or each subsystem, but not both! Here, the best optimised systems innovation often comes at the expense of a sub-optimised subsystem. I have found many a manger who will not accept this basic law of systems dynamics, demanding that the whole system be functioning perfectly. But the real world moves so quickly today, that any attempt to optimise every aspect of a complex system will be out of touch with these changes.

The Need for Innovative Teams

Clearly, successfully delivering such non-linear (Q4) complex systems innovations requires rapid rates of learning across a multiplicity of highly uncertain issues. But learning – let alone accelerated learning – has always been a major problem for traditional organisations. Few know how to effectively learn, capture and apply new knowledge under such dynamic uncertainty. But this does not have to be the case. There is a special kind of organisational unit that is set up for accelerated learning: the innovative team. Learning is especially swift, even amplified, in such teams. Moreover, there is much evidence that a true innovative team has the potential to learn at exponential rates.

This is because when there are a higher number of connections between people (see Chapter 9 for optimum number), the creative thinking space goes up dramatically. This in turn is due to the network-like structure found in such teams, which ultimately takes on the topology of the supreme learning machine: a brain. Teams are a special kind of neural network, which accelerates and amplifies learning in a wide variety of ways. In fact, there's a technical term for such networks, so-called *hypernetworks*, which refers to the many-dimensional connections. As a result, as the number of people in the network increases (up to a critical point), the number of possible interconnections goes up dramatically, so the potential scope for creative thinking and problem solving goes up proportionally. These many-dimensional connections are the secret behind the ability to learn across diverse, uncertain problems at a rapid pace.

As noted above, complex (Q4) innovations have ultra-diverse issues and far-reaching problems to solve. Clearly, the day of the true polymath is over, so teams made up of many people from different backgrounds with equally diverse sets of skills, knowledge and talent are required to tackle a given systems innovation holistically. In this way, innovative teams bring together such diverse skills and expertise in a way that multiplies each other's effect. Furthermore, innovative teams can adjust their approach and address issues in real time. As new issues and facts emerge, innovative teams swarm around problems instantly, and therefore learn spontaneously without top-down command and control. In fact, traditional top-down directed learning is the dumbest form of learning. It is jerky and reactive, and only hinders progress. Consequently, it can be seen that innovative teams are the best organisational unit to cope with complex uncertainties, risk and chance, because they are indeed the best organisation for rapid learning and adaptive behaviour.

As one example, the burgeoning biotechnology industry is chock-full of complex innovations which require true innovation teams. Projects have immense complexity and novelty, demanding an ultra-diverse set of professionals – everyone from chemical engineers, to molecular biologists, process engineers, brand managers and so on.

The Seven 'Cs' of Innovative Teams

In my experience, most teams tasked with innovating (radical or otherwise) are anything but a team. In fact, as I will outline in Chapter 7, the pseudo-team is widespread within both commercial and public service innovation projects.

However, with the appropriate strategies and tools, and serious attention and time committed to building innovative teams, high performance teams which reliably deliver successful innovation can emerge. As an indication to whether a team *is* a team, there are usually seven structural capacities or 'Cs' that will be noticeably present:

1. *Collaborative*: A capacity to think and learn as a team across intellectual borders is fundamental to both original concept generation and the solving of complex and uncertain problems that such original concepts give up. Decisions, implementation and feedback must also be made as a collective, otherwise complex, often divergent issues will quickly overwhelm a team.

2. *Consolidated*: This is a team's combined outlook and expectations. This really all boils down to the values a team holds. Without such mutuality, individuals will not function as a team. In Chapter 7, we will explore the development of innovative team values.

3. *Committed*: Team members are both committed to the successful outcome of an innovation and committed to one another. In Chapter 8, we will address the issue of high performance teams and successful innovation in detail. We will learn here that successful innovation is the result of a virtuous circle: successful innovation can be the result of high performance teamwork, and high performance teamwork can be the result of successful innovation.

4. *Competent*: Of course, without some level of competence related to intended outcomes, a team could not begin to produce and perform. However, team competence is a matter of time and effort, as any sufficiently novel innovation will break new ground, and therefore, by definition, distinct areas of competence will be lacking. Again accelerated team learning is essential here.

5. *Complementary*: This is the capacity to bring together a wide variety of skills, know-how and talent that complement each other in the execution of tasks and the pursuit of goals. In Chapter 12, we will explore the issue of selecting individuals who complement each other's talent for the task at hand.

6. *Confident*: A high performance team has a positive can-do attitude. Furthermore, extraordinarily high performance teams have an untethered tenacity. One thing psychologists note about teams (and individuals) in virtually every discipline where a degree of competence is required, is that performance drops dramatically when confidence is lacking. Confidence, again, is a product of time and effort through collaborative learning and producing results. The work of leadership – outlined in Chapter 10 – has much to do here, as confidence goes up, so does competence.

7. *Camaraderie*: *Esprit de corps* is as important as all the other capacities. Without that sense of fraternity and empathy towards each other, mutual support and commitment will never arise, and, in turn, team performance will drop, especially when a project hits a difficult patch or falls short of expectations. Furthermore, when there's a high degree of mutuality, pushing the boundaries of what is thought

possible – which is part and parcel of innovation – is likely to happen more frequently. In contrast, without such team camaraderie, risk taking is likely to be non-existent, and with it innovation.

Of course the seven Cs all remain a pipe dream without the capacity to build such high performance innovative teams. In Part II we will be looking at the dynamics of successfully building such teams.

(NB: The main points in this chapter are outlined in Exercise 2 in Appendix A.)

PART II

The Dynamics of Building Innovative Teams

Part II outlines the dynamics of building innovative teams, through the philosophies, practice and insights into the strategies and tools that actually go towards building such teams.

The strategies and tools outlined in each chapter are accompanied by detailed step-by-step exercise templates (Appendix A) that can be used within a full-blown innovative team-building programme (or as stand-alone exercises).

Chapter 3 – The Brain, Learnt Behaviours and Human Interaction: The rudimentary study of the basic human brain is where we begin our team-building effort. It is, after all, where we do our thinking, and therefore where we take in, process and spit out information, and because of this it is central to how we interact with our peers. This chapter examines the function of specific parts of the human brain that affect how we behave and communicate with other people, and in turn how it influences team performance.

Chapter 4 – Creativity and Innovative Teams: Creative people by their very nature do not always integrate well within teams. In fact an innovative team is a contradiction in terms, because inventive types tend to be independent thinkers who often go against standard practice and procedure. This chapter explains how we may gain the best of both worlds: higher performance teams and creative people working in harmony.

Chapter 5 – Developing an Innovative Team's Whole Mind: We all see the world in special and different ways. We all tend to fragment the world into personal, even idiosyncratic categories and distinctions in our thoughts, determined by our own experiences and life lessons. However, it seems that we are held captive by these biased distinctions, wholly forgetting that we constructed them in the first place. As a result, attempting to bring together people from diverse and disparate backgrounds into a group and then developing such a contrary range of people into high performance team is an extremely challenging endeavour. This chapter demonstrates why this is so, and outlines strategies and tools that begin to develop and integrate such a sweeping range of personalities into holistic innovative teams.

Chapter 6 – Collaborative Learning Beyond Knowledge: All innovation lies just beyond what we already know. Again, new is new after all. To go beyond what we currently know and bring together complex systems innovations, people with diverse talents, knowledge and experiences need to learn together in highly dynamic and collaborative ways. This chapter explains why this is so, and gives examples, strategies and tools for collaborative learning beyond knowledge.

Chapter 7 – Innovative Team Values: The values that a team holds relate directly to how they perform. This chapter describes why this is so, and outlines the key values that an innovative team must hold, and how such values can be developed and embedded within a team's culture.

Chapter 8 – The Need for High Performance Goals and Metrics: Team goals and their performance measurements are key to high performance teamwork; not merely because they give a team direction and focus of effort, but because they mould a team's behaviour and drive motivation as well. The reasons for this are explained in detail, with the methods for the design and application of such high performance goals and metrics.

Chapter 9 – Organising Innovative Teams: Size matters when it come to teamwork. How teams are structured and how the individual within a team is organised matters too. This chapter outlines the key issues in organising innovative teams.

Chapter 10 – Innovative Team Leadership: By definition, innovative team leaders lead differently than leaders involved in more steady-state processes. The unique characteristics, roles and selection of such special leaders are overviewed in the last chapter in this part.

CHAPTER 3

The Brain, Learnt Behaviours and Human Interaction

Most of what you are thinking about you are unaware of, most of what you do you are not thinking about, and most of what you are aware of you are not thinking about. PROF. R. WINSTONE

All conflict begins and ends in thinking. From global level corporate disputes to hostility within a local group, thought is at the heart of all discord. Yet human thinking is perhaps the most complex process of all. Civilisation has for millennia endeavoured to tie down the fundamental mechanics and processes of human intelligence in the disciplines of psychology, neurology and philosophy. And for at least the last century and a half these cognitive sciences have burgeoned into a body of applied knowledge that we can use to enhance the processes of team building, and indeed the very processes of team thinking itself.

The Basic Structure and Physiology of the Human Brain

The human brain is the most complex self-contained system we know. A mere 1.4 kilograms of grey matter that can understand itself, love, hate, create and destroy, and perceive a galaxy 10 million light years across. It is perhaps the most wondrous artefact of nature we know.

Even though the human brain is so unbelievably elaborate, much headway has been made in understanding its structure and functions.

Multifaceted in plan, it is a complex interconnected network of 100 million nerve cells capable of producing in the region of 100 billion simultaneous electrochemical system impulses. Self-contained within this amazing organ are at least 400 so-called 'bulbs' (pea-to-peach stone in size), each evolved for specific processing functions, ranging from physical utilities such as sight, to visceral processes such as emotion, to wholly intellectual functions such as reasoning.

For our work here, there are two major subsystems we are interested in: the old wired primitive brain which gives rise to our most basic emotions and reflexes; and the modern brain that gives rise to our ability to think. The old brain we shall refer to as the 'primitive brain', and the new brain we shall refer to as the 'cortex'.

The primitive brain is based on a construction dating back millions of years to prehistoric times. The primitive brain is irrational and easily angered, and can take control of our thoughts in an instant. The cortex is the rational part of the human brain, and is stacked on top of the primitive brain, with a thin layer in between called the limbic system. The limbic system is newer that the primitive brain, but much older than the cortex. For our purposes here, when I talk of the old primitive brain it includes the limbic system.

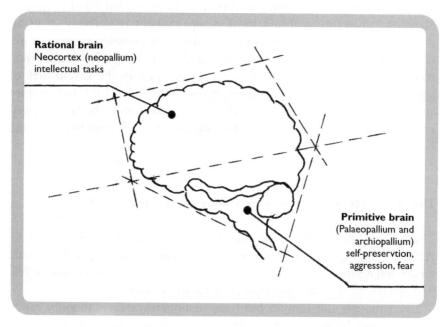

Figure 3.1   The basic structure of the human brain

The Ideas and Habits We Learn

The cortex is the part of the brain that makes us human, the area in which recall, association and reasoning happens. Specifically, this is where human thinking takes place, and actually occurs in the so-called prefrontal lobes. Psychologists believe that there are two major kinds of thought, *explicit* and *tacit*. Explicit thought is actually knowledge expressed as language in the cortex. Without language, and in turn knowledge, the process of thought is limited to tacit thought; thinking that needs no words.

Explicit thought is carried out via so-called 'representations of reality'. These are simplified models of what is actually going on outside the brain in the real world. A drawing, for example, is a kind of representation. A drawing is obviously less than the actual object it represents. But the abstraction is advantageous because it focuses on what is important, with all the inconsequential details left out. In other words, representations organise in ways which may help and are relevant. However, because such representations are simplified models of reality, they tend to be less than accurate. In fact, as such representations are recalled over time, they tend to become more and more distorted. Each time a memory is recalled, our imagination adds a little bit of information. In turn, as new information comes in through the senses from the outside world, it mixes with old representations, and consequently can lead to inaccurate representations of people and events. The point is that human thinking is not objective, but ultimately a subjective imprint of reality.

The Emotions and Reflexes We are Born With

In contrast to the cortex, the primitive brain is wired in such a way that it has evolved purely for survival. It does not think, it just does. Hunting for food, finding a mate, defending territory, social hierarchy and aggression all stem from the old brain.

Specifically, the primitive brain is the source of our unconscious emotions and reflexes; we are all too often unaware of our irrational actions as a result of such emotions and reflexes. In fact, such unconscious feelings and reflexes are not really thoughts or verbal processes in the mind at all, but visceral, bodily responses. Again, we don't think, we just do. We know such unconscious emotions and reflexes exist because of the behaviour patterns and automatic responses that derive from them.

Psychologists call this unconscious motivation; doing things for reasons that we are unaware of. These behaviour patterns often defy all common sense, as people don't learn or choose a particular behaviour via the primitive brain, rather, these primitive behaviours are burnt into the brain from birth. Like the instinct a newborn foal has to immediately suckle on its mother, or the hard-wired instructions an ant has to track its swarm, the reflexes in the old brain are fixed in as well. The old primitive brain also contains our primitive and irrational emotions, such as anger, fear and lust.

Now, it is important to understand that the explicit thoughts in the cortex manage the emotions and reflexes in the primitive brain. As noted above, memories, in the form of simplified representations, may become distorted over time and can, and often do, affect primitive reflexes and emotions in all sorts of random and arbitrary ways. These so-called 'misrepresentations' can actually lead to quite erratic, wholly unmerited patterns of behaviour. Think of a conversation between two people, for example. There forms in both minds a simplified representation of the conversation, which homes in on the most important points of that conversation. But the representation will not be an exact reflection of the actual conversation, it will only highlight the key points that the receptor will hold as important – not good for coherent teamwork.

Because the primitive brain is unconscious and driven by the cortex, it cannot tell the difference between fantasy and reality. In other words, all that the primitive brain experiences comes through the cortex, therefore it can never know if what is being input is real or imagined. Do this little test:

Imagine you are holding a slice of lemon. A big yellow juicy lemon, spurting with citrus. Now imagine bringing that juicy lemon up to your mouth – closer, closer, closer. Now imagine taking a big bite out of that juicy lemon and sucking!

Notice anything? Wait a few moments ... I wager that you can taste the citrus flavour in your mouth. I bet your mouth is flowing with saliva. And I will venture that this response will hang around for the next few minutes.

Why? This is a so-called 'phantom' response produced by your primitive emotional-reflex brain. It has recalled past experiences in the form of representations from the cortex – biting into a lemon – and has produced a phantom response based on those misrepresented experiences. Amazed? Most are. And most are even more amazed when they begin to understand the deeper effects of phantom responses produced by the primitive emotional-reflex brain. And what is more, the more a phantom response occurs, the more the imaginary experience reinforces itself. People have shouted with rage at colleagues, thrown plates at a spouse, even maimed a loved one all because the emotional-reflex brain became overactive, self-reinforcing and took control of the situation.

The problem here is that the old brain has evolved to deal with unfinished or continuous situations. This is great for survival, as we have to pick up on what we were doing if we are distracted from chasing that rabbit. The problem here is that human relationships are never done until we say they are. So we can, and often do, run negative memories over and over in our minds to gain closure. As a consequence, we reinforce the negative images, which tend to increasingly arouse the primitive brain, only making the situation worse. The more we think about an old negative memory, the more significant it becomes. Each time we rerun the memory, we change it a little, based on our internal representations (or misrepresentations) of the world. In the end, we can completely blow the original situation out of all proportion, which can lead to out-and-out conflict. Again we cannot tell the difference between the phantom response and reality.

The primitive brain has no ethic or moral code, it just does what it has evolved to do. For example, if the primitive brain has satisfied its survival needs and there is no further possibility of a threat, it goes into standby mode, ready to home in on whatever is loudest or most complex at the time (that is, a predator is usually more noticeable than the background it is lurking in). If the environment changes while the brain is in this mode, attention will change without a single thought occurring. Do this second little test. Look at the symbols below. Quickly glance at each of them in turn:

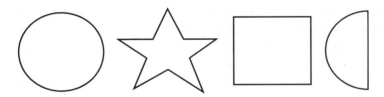

Now quickly pick a shape. Nine out of ten people pick the second shape. As noted above, we are all predisposed to whatever is the most complex, colourful, loudest or brightest. Which one did you pick? Still feel the lemon juice in your mouth? Your primitive brain is at work.

The primitive brain also regards issues as black or white. There is no grey area, no capacity for creative or multidimensional thinking. All questions are expected to have a succinct and to the point answer, even one known in advance of an outcome.

A third test. Pick a number between 1 and 10. Most people say 7. But what about the number 1111? Can you see that number between 1 and 10? Let your cortex go to work and you will eventually see the number 1111 embedded in the word 'and'. It is not trick question, it just goes to show how the primitive brain puts us on a black or white autopilot when we are expected to answer such a common question. Innovation can be an ambiguous activity. There is no right or wrong, black or white, only limitless amounts of choices and options on the future. The primitive brain is under-developed for such a task – another reason why innovation is so tricky.

Finally, when the primitive brain dominates the cortex, all reason flys out of the window. The primitive brain is focused on the short term, with high emotional involvement. No prudent reasoning is present to think about the longer term. By definition, all innovation is about the longer term, as innovation affects the future like no other human activity.

The Fight/Flight Response

One of the most significant reasons why teams do not gel as a high performance unit is that the primitive brain, and the emotions and reflexes that come with it, simply gets in the way of team unity. This is mainly because the primitive brain sees the world in terms of potential threats. In the workplace, for example, primitive brain responses can switch on at a moment's notice when a predicament arises that makes one look inferior in front of others. The old brain has a built-in self-protection response for such situations. For example, if someone challenges our position in the workplace hierarchy or moves in on our territory (our desk, say), we will snort and grunt like some prehistoric beast. Again the old brain's primitive emotions and reflexes really do stop cohesive teamwork.

Wired throughout the body is something known as the sympathetic nervous system. It is the nervous system that works to arouse the body for action, stimulating all the major organs, such as the heart, lungs and adrenal glands. The sympathetic nervous system is involved in all the primitive brain responses. The system gives us the ability to instan-taneously react to sudden threatening changes. Psychologists have identified two main responses associated with the sympathetic nervous system, called the 'fight or flight' response.

The first is fight. When we are in fight mode, there is no positive-sum, no chance of compromise. Forget everyone else, everything is a competition. Whatever we are doing, we want to win. If something or someone gets in the way, we get angry. In fight mode, we become particularly sensitive to threats, everything, no matter how insignificant, is upfront and personal.

The second is flight. When we are in flight mode, we deal with situa-tions by avoiding them; not just running away from a problem, but tangible actions like putting off a meeting, avoiding a particular topic in conversations, being too busy to solve that nagging problem, forgetting to book an appointment and generally being indecisive. We have all met the manager or subordinate who will not face up to a problem, no matter how hard you try to convince them that it is a priority.

Frankly, we are all predisposed to both responses, with different intensities, depending on (a) the given situation or environment, (b) our history of responses, and (c) how aroused the old brain is. The rest of this chapter will focus on each of these reasons and provide appropriate exercises to alleviate the symptoms that derive from each of them.

Uncertainty and the Fight/Flight Response

Faced with something we don't understand and working beyond the predictable, we often suffer enormous emotional stress. In fact, nothing gets the fight or flight responses going better than uncertainty. As noted above, the primitive brain cannot deal with ambiguous situations. It wants black and white answers. And if it cannot get objectivity, then fight or flight is the answer. Whether the uncertainty is caused by hunting for prey, or, here in the modern day setting, caused by the high levels of uncertainty contained within a (Q4) complex system innovation, the fight or flight response is equally present.

Over time, individuals in groups develop their orientation towards each of the responses. The more aroused our primitive brain becomes, the more anxious we become. The more anxious we become, the more our primitive brain is aroused.

Like the lemon taste in your mouth (is it still there?), the anxiety you experience is a phantom, one of nature's tricks to keep you on your toes. But if anxiety is prolonged, the anxiety tends to become a crippling experience for an innovation team, blocking out the cortex, and people's intellectual capacities and social graces and skills fly out of the window. In short, heightened anxiety comes from self-reinforced phantom experiences.

Shaping Up the Individual's Mind for Teamwork

The more aroused the primitive brain is, the more extreme the two responses are likely to become. As a result, flaming anger or crippling fear hinder our ability to think through taxing situations, inhibit creative thinking, and wholly limit individuals from building relationships and understanding within a group. Clearly, an aroused primitive brain is no good at all when it comes to building innovative teams!

So, the question remains, are your people's minds in shape for team-work? Is your own mind fit for the kind of group dynamic necessary for systems innovation?

There are a multitude of factors that excite the primitive emotional-reflex brain in ways that impede innovative teamwork: prolonged work hours, fatigue, unhealthy lifestyle, monotony and so on. Over time, these factors only tend to reinforce one and other, amplifying each other's effect. So, in the light of these factors, there are seven initiatives you and your people can apply to slow down the primitive brain:

1. *From eating to survive to eating to thrive.* Being overweight is not only a problem for your heart and mental alertness, you will also store more toxins in your system, which will bring down that feeling of well-being. And when that happens, your old brain is more aroused. So what should you do here? A colleague of mine, sitting across a table from me, once asked how I kept so slim. 'Do you have some magic potion?' he asked, as he stuffed a home-made cake into his mouth. I replied, 'why do you eat?' He was surprised to hear such a question. 'Eat! Why for the same reason everybody eats, because I get hungry!' Well, we all respond to a rumble in the tummy, but my question had a deep point. So I then asked him about his relationship with his food. He gave me an even more surprised look. The point is that my colleague and I have a completely different relationship with food. He eats to satisfy his short-term responses telling him that he is hungry, 'so stuff in some food'. But I eat food for a very different reason. I love food, but I eat food that keeps me healthy and fit. My relationship with food is to stay healthy, and that is the secret. Adjust your relationship with your food to keep healthy and you will turn from eating to survive to eating to thrive. And when you are physically healthy, your reflex brain is more inclined to relax.

2. *Limit alcohol intake.* As with the wrong kinds of food, alcohol will flood your body with toxins and oxidising chemicals. You will get older more quickly, feel lethargic, even tired more of the time. It will negatively affect your concentration. You will even bring down your immune system so that you are more susceptible to viruses and bugs, even terminal diseases such heart disease and cancer. In the extreme, alcohol will affect your nervous system in all sorts of bad

ways. Scary. But the affect on the old brain is equally bad. It will make you grumpy, even angry for extended periods. It will degrade your relationships with team members, and people outside work too. So, stick to under 42 units of alcohol for men (21 shots of spirit) and 28 units for women in any given week. High days and holidays are a different story, we are all entitled to let our hair down from time to time. Again, like diet, it is about your relationship with alcohol. Is it a genuine two glasses of social lubricant and/or enjoyment of a fine wine? Or is it the way you wind down after work, or worse still, relieve boredom? The difference is telling.

3. *Regular exercise.* 'Oh boy. Not the exercise thing', I hear you say. Regular exercise not only and obviously keeps you fitter, it releases your body's natural endorphins and stores up the happy chemical in your brain known as serotonin. And just watch your old brain equalise. If you find it hard to get motivated here, seek physical activities you enjoy, set short-term goals within long-term objectives and reward yourself when you meet those goals.

4. *Take time out to relax.* Doing nothing is hard work these days. It is hard to find the time to down tools and flake out on a beach or park. It is often difficult to juggle family responsibilities and get that extra half-hour lie-in. So, is there a magic formula here? Yes, most certainly. The secret is to work at a steady pace, not too fast, but not too slow, finding a balance. Over the longer term, this turns out to be more productive and less tiring. This sounds so obvious, but in my experience most people work in spurts, punctuated with bouts of boredom and lack of concentration. The second is to cut out the chaff and do less. What is value-adding work and what is really taking away value? Third, go on holiday. In spite of the increase in holidays abroad, less than 50 per cent of people now take an annual holiday away from home!

5. *Serious play.* All work and no play makes Jack a ... The answer is to integrate work and play! Moreover, view play as an important part of work life. In fact, play is now well understood to be an integral component of creative and innovative work. Play calms the old brain and stimulates the cortex in original and often quirky ways, which is, of course, essential for creativity. Play is also good practice for processing simultaneous, complex information, which is essential for systems innovation work. So, if you are an executive, you must actively be seen to be playful. Design your company's work day with elements of playful activities. Extend the lunch break

from half an hour to an hour. Organise lectures and clubs which people can join during the day. Organise company get togethers and fun weekends.

6. *Changes in routine.* Change is as good as a rest, but more, a change in routine cleans and oils the mental cogs. Change in routine can be broken into the short and longer term. Short-term changes in routine are a must. Working long hours in front of a computer screen can indeed make the computer operator agitated. Long hours, without respite, will wholly affect performance. The rule of thumb is two-hour stints, punctuated with 20 to 30 minutes of doing something completely different. Equally, the longer term is important. So, do you have a hobby outside your normal day job? Do you make sure you do something at the weekend other than sit in front of the TV and vegetate with a bottle of red wine? Do you play with the kids anymore, even though they are 18, 34, 46? When was the last time you went off for a weekend with your partner? When was the last time you contacted your best friends at school, or entered a competition of some kind where you had to practise to win? When was the last time you changed your role at work? What classes have you taken lately? The list is endless.

7. *Worry.* It's the biggest killer. Anxiety takes more people out of circulation than any other disease, and it is classified as a pathology if it carries on for too long. Worry is a self-feeding loop that turns up the old brain, and when the old brain is turned up, you worry more. So what to do? All of the above will help significantly, but beyond technique, there is attitude. Developing a positive attitude to life and work will stop anxiety dead in its tracks. And how do you develop a positive attitude? Four things: pursue what you love, that is, find ways to make a living out of what you love doing most; surround yourself with people you like, who have a positive outlook on life; have lots of sex; and you only live once, so make the most of it.

In the Far East (particularly in Japan), people are expected to keep the mind and body in shape. Nissan, for example, state as employment policy that people must be fit and healthy. Especially in the West, this can be seen as an invasion of privacy (what right does my company have telling me to get fit?). But, on reflection, a fit mind can and does significantly add to teamwork performance. In fact, a fit mind is the first step in building an innovative team, because the subsequent team-building strategies and tools outlined in this book will be, to a large extent, nullified by an unfit, overaroused primitive brain. And besides all the logic, who on earth wants to be unfit and unhealthy anyway? The answer, I am afraid, is given by the statistics: over 40 per cent of people in the USA, and over 30 per cent in Europe, are classified as overweight.

Control and the Fight/Flight Response

One of the secrets to tempering the primitive emotional-reflex brain is to instil a perception of control over the environment. Control is, in fact, at the heart of the flight or fight response (or at least the perception of control). Again, for reasons of evolution, the primitive brain switches to a heightened flight or fight state when it senses it might be losing its ascendancy over its territory or is under attack from a predator. Remember, the old brain cannot tell the difference between reality and imagination, so any sense of losing control, whether it be an attack by a sabre-toothed tiger or project manager, will only heighten the flight or fight response. In turn, all kinds of negative effects can emerge. Well-being, concentration and the feeling of security disappear into the ether.

There is a famous case study that illustrates the power of the perception of control, or lack of it, and its impact on people's emotions and performance. Time and motion studies have shown that the productivity of factory workers goes up significantly when they are given a degree of control over the production process. The surprise, in the example I am referring to, was that the control was given by the ability to stop the production line – via a little red button – when a production problem arose. Not only did production output and quality go up, but the well-being of the production workers improved, in turn absenteeism went down, and relationships between workers generally improved.

So what happened here? Again, when the primitive brain is losing control over its environment, it is in threat or survival mode, with all the anxiety and hostility that comes with it. Think about it. You are trapped for eight hours or more a day, in an environment in which you have little or no control. It is bound to make you tense up.

So, putting this in the context of systems innovation and team building, there are many lessons that can be gleaned:

■ *Autonomy de-stresses and builds trust*: Ownership and control from within the team reduces fear and increases trust in uncertain environments, so starting a virtuous win–win cycle. When individuals and teams lose ownership and control, fear builds and trust evaporates into the ether. This is because a relationship between control, fear and trust exists, revealing that trust and fear are symptoms, but lack of localised control is the core precipitant of anxieties. And without trust relationship building becomes quite limited.

■ *Localised control enhances confidence and, in turn, well-being and concentration*: It is clear that confidence will fly out of the window if people do not have a sense of control over what they are doing. A big boss with a big stick will instil a fear that will take away any chance of building confidence. But more, when one has lost confidence, concentration flies out of the window as well.

■ *Localised control enhances creativity*: Once people build a level of confidence, the creativity within a group usually goes up. This is mainly because the whole brain is working better as a more balanced system.

■ *Localised control enhances responsiveness, flexibility and adaptability*: People tend to become more adaptable to changing situations if they have a level of control over the situation. Again, the confidence that comes with such control gives the impetus to adapt.

There are a number of team-building exercises that, firstly, illustrate the power and necessity of autonomous control within innovation teams, then move on to actually enhance the perception of control, for all the above reasons.

(NB: The text above is outlined in Exercise 3 in Appendix A.)

Tolerance Building and Communication Stress Scenarios

The military knows that to condition an army to extreme battle fatigue, trauma and uncertainty, soldiers must experience excruciating, even humiliating levels of discomfort. This is about bringing the threshold of tolerance to a level where even the worst scenarios in war will seem relatively bearable. However, I'm not suggesting for one minute that civilian innovation teams need, or indeed should, undergo such strife, but we can take the spirit of the philosophy and apply it to the building of high performance teams.

The goal of tolerance conditioning is to put individuals in groups through high stress conditions, which produce high levels of uncertainty. Almost any basic team-building exercise can be used here, but it needs to be carried out with extremely difficult goals and targets. An example may be to finish a subproject that usually takes weeks within 24 hours. What happens is that individuals will go through what psychologists call an 'adjustment condition', where the experience framework dramatically shifts. Once this occurs, tolerance to natural anxieties goes up.

To be reasonably effective here, you will need a leader that will push each exercise quite hard. As this happens, you will witness confusion, panic, frustration, anger, even a few tears. But that is the desired effect. Believe me, once these kinds of extreme exercises have been completed with a degree of success, you will find your people walking on air (with a can-do attitude that they actually can walk on water too) (see Appendix A, Exercises 4–7).

Example of a Tolerance-building Exercise

Here is the outline of a programme that I have facilitated on several occasions. This kind of conditioning programme usually happens over a period of four days.

Day one begins with group games that limit what the individual can contribute to the group, all under time pressure. Each member, for example, has a role to play and cannot do anything beyond that (for example if tying ropes is on your list, then that is exactly what you can do, if not, you cannot). The day is designed to show that: (a) having people in narrowly specified roles is inherently restricting, (b) multidimensional roles are more suited to complex innovation, and (c) the means to achieve an objective depends on interactive communication and collaboration. The team spends most of the day fording rivers, climbing over rocks. By late afternoon, people are stressed out, personalities show. After dinner, there is a team discussion led by a facilitator. The idea is to review the past day and discuss team dynamics, such as what helped, what hindered, who participated most and other issues about team dynamics.

Day two is the same routine and time pressure with a variation over the course, with some new exercises to fulfil and slightly different roles. But this time no one is permitted to communicate verbally. Stress results and, even though they are not supposed to talk, expletives to suit. Then a repeat of the night before, a group review of the day. But this time, points start to hit home (that is, the cyclic learning nature starts to take effect).

Day three and it is getting harder. But there's a reward. Today they're about to find treasure island or something as near to it with a bit of imagination. The objective of the day is to highlight the benefits of whole team problem solving. The rules are simple. There are three items of hidden treasure, with three different sets of clues. Each person is randomly given a one-paragraph clue on a piece of paper to keep. But no one is permitted to ask for anyone else's clue in any manner. The treasure hunt is spread over something like three or four square miles of unfamiliar territory. They have a time limit of six hours. The first hour usually turns out to be quite amusing, as information can only be volunteered, which restricts communication to a one-way street. At the end of the day, often wet, cold and very tired, usually at least one item, if not all the hidden treasure, is found. In the evening, some quite important points are aired in terms of teamwork: 'What was it like *not* to be able to ask or have information available at a particular point in the treasure hunt (problem) and what was its effect on time?' 'What was the effect of pressure and stress on performance, what was the effect on anxiety?' Collaboration and problem-solving issues often raise their head.

Day four often turns out to be one of the most challenging days of all. The aim is to explore something called 'control-flight/fight-trust cycles'. The day includes abseiling down a 200-metre cliff face, over a rapid river, in a pitch black pothole! Actually, the drop is only 9 metres, with no river at the bottom, just a tape recorder. But when they set out in groups of six and begin the descent they don't know this. This is a game of fear versus trust, in uncertainty. The dark alone is enough to scare the wits out of anyone. The financial director or technician at the top has your life in their hands. People go through enormous personal barriers of fear. Some break into tears, people begin to see each other as they really are. Relationships begin to bond, as each discovers the need to collaborate in order to solve tough problems. Often, people who haven't seen eye to eye realise they have something in common after all, and that previously disliked person is quite a resourceful guy. All of this is done in complete safety with experts swarming all over the place.

Then on the last night it's back to a watering hole for a group review session. The lessons of control–flight/fight–trust cycles are aired. An open debate ensues about how the development of ownership and control from within the team reduces fear and increases trust in uncertain environments, so starting a virtuous win–win cycle; and about how when individuals and teams lose ownership and control, fear builds and trust evaporates into the ether. Issues about the relationship between control, fear and trust usually emerge, revealing that lack of trust and fear are symptoms, but lack of localised control is the core precipitant of anxieties.

Then, at last, it's time for a well-earned beer. But then what happens? Singing, brothers in arms and a feeling of unity; and at that moment, the team begins to bond.

(NB: The tolerance and communication stress scenarios above are outlined in Exercises 4 to 7 in Appendix A.)

CHAPTER 4

Creativity and Innovative Teams

*Getting an innovative team to work together
is not unlike herding a pack of lions.*
ANON.

The vital essence of invention is creativity. Yet creative people and teamwork are potentially uneasy bedfellows. By their very nature, creative people are different – different in their expectations, temperaments, even their beliefs and values. And it is these very distinctions in disposition that can lead to difficulties in team performance development. This chapter looks at the many obstacles and points of discussion here, and reveals insights into how it is possible to have the best of both worlds: creativity and teamwork.

Creativity and Creative People

Creativity is the ability to connect the unconnected that breaks through to something new, the ability not only to see what others cannot see, but to think what others have not thought. It is the capacity to redefine boundaries so that new ways and means can occur. In fact, cutting-edge innovation theory tells us that there is an infinite white-space of possibilities for original insights and eventual innovation. And entering into new strategic white-space always comes down to creativity.

In truth, there are many kinds of creativity. Dr Irving Taylor, the renowned psychologist and former Pratt Institute professor, asserts that there are five distinct levels of creativity:

1. *Expressive*, the unskilled and spontaneous sort seen in children.

2. *Productive*, where people have become fairly conditioned and have developed rules in their efforts to produce things.

3. *Inventive*, where people have some degree of ability in connecting usually unrelated matters or objects.

4. *Innovative*, when people have reached a higher level of understanding of a principle or issue and can progress into unforeseen developments.

5. *Emergent creativity*, the highest level and extremely rare, wherein individuals or teams create a completely new principle or archetype concept.

The great Leonardo da Vinci had truly emergent ideas that were way ahead of his time. He had little reference from which to build on, and few people of a like mind with which to build a dialogue. Yet in between painting the *Mona Lisa* and studying the motions of the planets (as you do), he came up with the concept of the helicopter, in 1507!

The key to unlocking this potential is, of course, the creative individual. These people bring unparalleled value to an organisation. What pours out of their heads will in due course have a profound impact on people's lives. Their ideas will create the new wealth and jobs, even the value systems the market tends towards. And because of this, they are not only the golden egg, they are the goose as well.

Beth Rogers, the Cranfield management consultant, wrote in her book *Creating Product Strategies*:

> Curiosity has been acclaimed by many researchers in the field of creativity as the trait which is singly important to idea generation. The creative individual is also independent, able to break out of old mind-sets such as 'the way we do things around here'. He or she is optimistic, enjoys humour and likes to be humorous. The creative individual can defer judgement, take risks, use imagery, tolerate ambiguity and think impulsively. The very best of breed will also be able to test their assumptions and be prepared to persist in seeing their ideas through to implementation. The creative individual of most value to an organisation will also have skills relevant to their activities, supported by knowledge, experience and motivation. This person will be committed to the truth, willing to root out the ways in which we limit or deceive ourselves, able to integrate reason and intuition, and be willing to take responsibility.

I have to totally agree. All of my mentors, my best friends and partners personify Beth's description. All of them are highly successful in life and pursue highly ambitious, highly creative careers. Yet none of them follow the same path. They are all very different people, with their own ideas on where they are going and how they are going to get there. This is the underlying power of creativity and innovation: there is room for everyone if we are all creative, conversely there is room for no one if we all think and do the same.

Left and Right Brain Functions

We need to take a look at the brain again. Back in the 1960s, Roger Sperry, the neuroscientist, won a Nobel prize for his so-called 'split-brain' theory, deducing that the human brain consists of two major cerebral hemispheres – left and right (as opposed to the up and down of the cortex and primitive brain). The seeds of this discovery were sown in a California hospital, where patients with severe epilepsy underwent radical operations. In grasping hope, the surgeons attempted to prevent the seizures by severing the patients' 'corpus callosum', the band of fibres that connects the left and right hemispheres. On analysis, Sperry found that each side of the brain behaved as two independent brains when disconnected. One typical result of this was that a patient would tie up his lace on his right shoe, only to find that he would untie the one on his left shoe. In turn, these split-brained people enabled Sperry to observe the left and right-hand functions of the whole brain. He proposed that the two hemispheres are responsible for very different thought processes: the left hemisphere for logical, analytical thought functions; and the right hemisphere for imaginative, conceptual and associative thought functions. Intriguing.

Left brain	*Right brain*
Logical	Intuitive
Sequential	Holistic
Verbal	Visual
Analytical	Aesthetic
Explicit	Spatial
Convergent	Divergent
Categorising	Unifying

Clearly, creative people tend to be right-brained. That is, their dominant thought functions are a result of right-brain bias. So it is no wonder that highly creative, right-brained people can be very forgetful. Their mental arithmetic and verbal recall are often quite poor. But they can often visualise in their mind's eye three-dimensional representations of quite complex systems, which even the smartest left-brained individual cannot.

The Whole Brain and Creativity

Like the right hemisphere, the primitive brain plays a significant role in creativity as well. Creative people also have a bias to emotional-reflex responses. It is well known that many of the most creative types are highly emotionally charged people. It often comes with the personality package.

Basically, the primitive brain is telling you to move to the next meal, and keeps a constant look out for territorial invaders. The task at hand is secondary. Specifically, creative people tend to have an easily aroused limbic system (see Figure 3.1). Indeed, the limbic response is the switch that enables creative people to absorb, interrelate and see meaning in a vast range of seemingly disparate issues and ideas. This is because the enhanced reflex response short-circuits convergent or linear focus. At the same time, too much short-term focus can easily lead to spreading concentration too thinly, whereby nothing gets done.

In short, the cortex on its own is quite rational, and often a bit dull. The old brain is provocative and irrational, and can evoke quite creative and inspiring thoughts. In turn, the right brain does the creative divergent stuff, and the left brain does the convergent stuff. Consequently, when the whole brain works together, a quite amazing level of creative and practical work can be achieved.

The General Nature of Creative People

Creativity has its price. As a rule, creative types live by their own particular codes and tenets. The most extreme, and often the most outstandingly creative, are seen as mavericks and dissenters. By definition, they are nonconformist and at times rebellious. They think they are right much of the time, view their knowledge as superlative and believe that they have exceptional thinking capacity.

Creative people tend to wade into the problem without thoroughly defining what the question is in the first place. They often conjure up solutions that are either not really what was asked for in the first place, or indeed not practicable. This is not always the case, however, some creative types, such as design engineers or architects, are great at conjuring up practical ideas and solutions.

Many people who fret for control, stability and efficiency, think that such maverick types are a right royal pain in the neck. Some people I know cannot stand such characters. On the other hand, to some, they are much loved, the spice in their life and, on occasion, they surprise, sometimes amaze with what they produce. Read what Frances Horbie has to say in her book *Creating the Innovation Culture*:

> research has shown that groups think better with a dissenter in their presence. They tend to come up with more original ideas if a dissenter challenges their views ... Interestingly enough, the dissenter doesn't have to be right to foster more independent thought and less groupthink. In fact, he could be completely wrong, but the act of reacting to his prodding seems to be enough to generate better ideas.

We see new ways not only by a deeper understanding of what we already know, but by looking beyond the boundaries of our current understanding and world view. To be different we have to think differently, and this kind of thinking comes in the main from creative people.

Creative people are often divergent thinkers, some are even multidimensional thinkers. Divergent thinking always leads the dialogue away from the main issues, often resulting in conversations going off at a tangent. Multidimensional thinking is the ability to connect a range of disparate issues or ideas into a coherent whole. Again the difficulty here is that multidimensional thinkers often lose sight of the objective. Divergent and multidimensional thinkers are great for creative, original thinking, but all too often poor when it comes to following things through and producing an end result as required.

As a result of a creative temperament, mavericks don't easily blend into close-knit groups. Creative people are prone to cause tension and conflict within organisations. Their unorthodox thinking and approach to problems often causes rolling waves for those of a more steadfast disposition. I have even seen a whole department upset just because one creative individual wanted a different colour computer. Furthermore, creative people are the ones likely to get pushed out of the door first in times of crises. They are the ones managers try to avoid confronting, because they are the ones likely to speak up and out over the incumbent's view. After all creative people create, don't they? This is not only a dilemma for managers and the organisation as a whole, it is a real issue for team building too.

Individual Autonomy and Teamwork

The whole idea of an innovative team is contradictory. Innovative teams consist of many kinds of creative and practical people. Indeed, revolutionary ideas would not arise without the creative individual. But innovation – the successful introduction of that new concept – could not take place without an innovative team (see Chapters 1 and 2). The complex, radical category-breaking innovations that are needed to create new markets and value can only be realised and introduced successfully via a coherent high performance team of diverse individuals.

A key to unleashing the power of a diverse high performance team, whilst utilising the creative individual's abilities to the full extent, is paradoxically to create an environment where both high degrees of autonomy and teamwork are present. Here is what Vincent Nolan, Chairman of Synectics, has to say:

> Teamwork, like motherhood and apple pie, tends to be regarded automatically as 'a good thing' ... This pro-teamwork bias is, I believe, dangerous, because it tends to discount the importance of personal autonomy for the individual. People work with maximum commitment and energy when they are doing what they have chosen to do, and are doing it in a way they believe is best for them. If they have no emotional ownership of the task, if they are doing it only because they have been told to, or because it is merely a means of earning a living, they cannot bring their full energy and enthusiasm ... As well as valuing one's own personal autonomy, people also like to work with others; they like to be helpful, be supported and to identify with a whole (preferably successful) that is larger than themselves. It is natural, therefore, for people to work in a team, specially if it operates in a way that values and encourages individual autonomy.

The key here is orientation, I think. An orientation where individuals can come together for complex tasks that require a variety of skills and knowledge; but just as easily work on solo tasks that need highly specialist skills and focus. This orientation can be achieved via acknowledging and practising the following issues:

■ *Valuing difference*: Different cultures can give rise to different values and beliefs. In the United States, people's individual rights and freedom are given credence above all else. In Japan, loyalty to the group is sacrosanct. It is often said that this deeply held belief about the individual is the single, most important reason why the USA is the most entrepreneurial nation. If a team is to value difference, then individuals have to learn to listen to and understand the values of *difference* and all the benefits that spring from such diversity. Prejudice here will shut down the powerhouse that is the source of innovation, as truly original and higher value innovation comes from a diversity of people and their ideas.

■ *Goal duality*: Individuals must be comfortable with working towards both individual and team goals. Individual goals need to work in parallel to achieve a collective outcome. However, over time integrated goals must be put into place if complex systems innovation is to occur. See Chapter 8 for insights here.

■ *Mutual accountability*: Over time, as creative individuals develop new skills and capabilities, they develop new sensibilities and abilities (see Chapter 7). They see the world in a different way, they interact with people in different ways too. But we don't want to tame them too much. Creativity, after all, is the product of the unorthodox. The key to integrating the creative individual to a level where they become an effective team member is in the value of shared accountability. Doug Smith and Jon Katzenbach say no team has ever become a true high performance team until they have reached a level of mutual accountability. They say that team accountability is about the sincere promise individuals make to themselves and others, promises that underpin two aspects of a team: commitment and trust. I discuss this further in Chapter 7.

■ *Win–win*: For a team to truly reach high levels of performance, the whole must develop a mind-set of a positive-sum, where it is seen that everyone wins, everyone has a chance for growth. Some of the most innovative teams I know are composed of highly ingenious, outspoken people, who not only get on, but in fact create something far in excess of the individual – a wonderful, mutual, fun loving and productive work atmosphere. Much of this is due to the presence of a win–win atmosphere. Again the value of mutuality is central here (see Chapter 7).

■ *Common working methods*: A box of intellectual tools and methodologies is essential for autonomous teamwork. Tools are a little like snap-on clips that slide up and down a metaphorical curtain rail, giving a team and individuals both continuity and flexibility to work together or alone when need arises. See my book *Hyperinnovation* for examples of such tools and methods. The design and/or selection of such methods and processes is way beyond the scope of this book. But there are a handful of issues that relate directly to team performance here. Firstly, common working methods give a certain amount of objectivity to defining problems, gathering and analysing information, solving problems, making decisions and taking actions. There are non-exhaustive lists of methodologies that can be applied to innovation, from customer expectation analysis to technical problem solving to carrying out experiments in a systematic way and so on. Common processes are a little more tricky than method. As noted in Chapter 1, innovation is, in the main part, not a repeatable process, therefore static or even re-engineering processes are difficult to define.

One-man band companies and public committees can get locked into a one-dimensional world view, and cannot imagine radically innovative concepts and models. But it is at the intersections of difference that we find the avenues for creativity, for new beginnings, for new insights and conceptions. Diversity and difference are *the* vital source of the new. To be truly innovative, a team has to be unconventional, in terms of its approach to learning, the way it is organised, even in the way it thinks. On the other hand, without autonomy within a team, the realisation of such dreams will not take place. The paradox of team autonomy, then, is central to building a high performance innovative team.

Surfacing Conflict as a Source of Learning and Innovation

Clearly, creative thinking is often confused with conflict, and conflict is often seen as bad, no matter what the issue. Yet conflict itself can be a healthy source of fresh insight. In fact, radical ideas will almost certainly be at odds with established organisational rules and procedures, they might even challenge the fundamental values upon which the organisation is built. As a result, creative thinking can be seen as cynical dissent. Frances Horbie, again:

> The very qualities that make for great innovation – passion, drive, out-of-the-box thinking – are viewed as arrogance, unreasonable and compromising behaviour by those hell bent on efficiency.

In short, what the old guard sees as rebellious, the vanguard sees as progress. Where a creative individual might buck the system in order to achieve a breakthrough, an incumbent manager would tend to do exactly the opposite. And so, at the border between the old guard and the vanguard, conflict or creativity emerge, and it all depends on how one looks at it. So what to do here? Well, there are, in fact, many kinds of conflict:

■ *Functional conflict*: This is the most basic conflict, where two or more simple ideas are contested. For example, two different ways of approaching a problem from two distinct parties can cause deadlock in actually solving the problem. This can derive from many sources – the group or individual's background, expectations, knowledge and working methods, and the organisation they represent. However, such functional conflicts are nearly always caused by one or more of the four types of conflict outlined below.

■ *Conflict of personality*: Discord between personalities can arise from outlook on life, disposition, character, nature and the like. John and Rob just do not get on, Judy simply does not like the way Mary acts and so on.

■ *Territorial conflict*: Conflict between people's boundaries, whether physical (like land or a desk) or organisational, like scope of role and authority. This is the most common kind of conflict, it happens absolutely everywhere, every day, in the most subtle ways.

■ *Political conflict*: Friction between people's own agendas can occur, ranging from personal ambition, to deviant manoeuvres, to keeping back information for personal gain and so on. Competition between businesses can cause conflicts of interest, and indeed may lead to a game of cat and mouse, if each organisation is working in an alliance but, ultimately, at the end of the day, is striving for the same business value.

■ *Cultural conflict*: Disharmony between values and norms is quite common at the individual level, the corporate level, and indeed the nation-state level too. This is the most difficult kind of conflict to resolve, as different value systems often lead to the most acute misunderstandings and hostility.

Conflict can emerge from one or a mix of the above. The further one goes down the list, the more difficult, explosive and protracted a conflict can become.

But conflict is not merely an adverse manifestation, but a division that can be a source of creativity and eventual innovation. As I say, it depends on how one looks at it. Here are three strategies that either make the most of the dispute amongst adversaries, or make use of a conflict in a way that creates the original and new. These are building a win–win position, standing in the other person's shoes and difference as inspiration.

Building a Win–win Position

There are ultimately only five positions each creative group or individual can find themselves in, after a conflict has arisen and run its course (whether it be a functional, personality, territorial, political or cultural conflict).

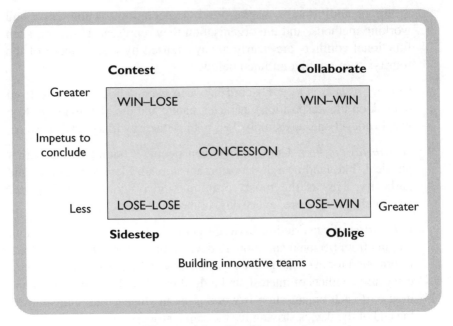

Figure 4.1 Conflict matrix

The first situation is one of compromise, where both parties finally give up ground and ultimately both come away with less than they wanted (a position of concession). The second is an avoidance situation, where both parties sidestep the issue, brushing it under the carpet. Here, unless the issue dies its own natural death, ultimately both sides lose (a lose–lose position). The third is a situation of accommodation, where one side gives way to the demands or needs of the other group or individual (a lose–win position). The fourth is a situation of competition, where the group or individual with the most at stake, or with the most power, digs in and will not let go of the situation and ultimately through attrition secures its own way (a win–lose position). But it is the fifth situation that is always the most desirable. The goal of any conflict resolution should be a positive-sum outcome (a win–win position for all). That means that both sides of the equation obtain something equal to, or more than they expected.

The fifth position is ultimately a game of synergy, where the whole output is greater than the input of the individual parts. The most effective way to achieve such a synergy is through collaboration between each party, and that, as this book makes clear, mainly comes down to building high performance innovative teams. However, there are a handful of strategies and tactics that can be directly applied to building a win–win situation:

■ *Define and communicate what win–win means:* Innovative teams can only triumph if the whole succeeds, thus a win–win situation means less head-to-head competition, and a move towards a positive-sum game. The goal then is to move the emphasis away from I win, you lose; to a win–win for all situation. And this needs to be communicated from the very top down and throughout the organisation.

■ *State win–win as a strategic goal:* Win–win must be viewed as important and therefore set as a strategic organisational goal. To underpin this, the win–win strategy must obtain management attention and sponsorship. Further, the importance of win–win can be amplified if put into the context of long-term goals. The development of such win–win goals gives credibility and begins to embed win–win into the organisational culture (more on this in Chapter 8).

■ *Define what is at stake:* Objectively (as much as possible) mark out what is at stake. Explain why win–win is so central to successful innovation and high performance teams. Outline the different kinds of competitive–collaborative positions (lose–win, win–lose, compromise, lose–lose and win–win) within a team, and the gains and losses that are at stake.

■ *Relative mutual benefits:* By far the most important requisite for developing a win–win situation is equality in reward. Of course this is relative, depending on the magnitude of effort and resource of each party put into the win–win situation.

■ *Clarify the tactics to gain win–win:* Beyond the organisational strategies there are various tactics that can assist in building a win–win organisation:

1. *Quid pro quo.* I give you something that you need and you give me something that I need. For example, I once needed some highly specialist and very rare expertise for a particular project. The only place I knew that held such talent was another department miles away across the vast systems integration site I was deployed at. When I approached the department's head and made my request, I didn't go in on a wing and a prayer, I actively went and found out if this department had a particular problem my department could solve. The head of that department was over the moon with my offer. The message is just do your homework first, find out what they need first.

2. *Seek, work and build relationships with natural collaborators.*
    There is another way to build a win–win situation. It comes from
    the infamous syndrome 'the prisoners dilemma' – the principle that
    says that somebody will eventually want to run away with the pot
    of gold. The secret here is to look for people who have a natural
    tendency to collaborate, who understand that to receive they must
    first give, who even enjoy putting other people first.

So, in all, what does such a win–win for all position mean for creativity and
innovation? Firstly, it starts a virtuous circle of trust, which is important,
because without trust, as you saw in Chapter 3, risk taking just will not take
place. Secondly, win–win gives longevity within relationships (whether a
strategic alliance, a local team, or a working relationship), and that is important too, because all innovation is a matter of persistence and patience over
the longer term. Thirdly, and most important of all, a win–win for all situation opens up the space of possibilities for innovation, because win–win
means people and organisations will be prepared to learn and explore
together, as all parties eventually receive something greater than they put in
at the beginning. Hence win–win is wholly important for surfacing conflict
as a source of learning and innovation, but this is just where it begins.

(NB: The main points of the above text in this chapter are outlined in Exercise 8
in Appendix A.)

Standing in the Other Person's Shoes

This is where the cortex's imagination comes in very useful. The goal is
to get each side (individuals or groups) to imagine what their rival(s) is
experiencing. In graphic detail, what are they actually feeling and
thinking? What are their own unique circumstances? What are their
expectations? What is their agenda? Can you gain an insight into their
value systems? What are their political constraints? Identify the key
issues and concerns and then determine what results would be acceptable.
The experience of all this often proves to be enlightening.

To add further to standing in the other person's shoes, there is a technique called 'the theatre of the mind' developed by the late Dr Maxwell
Maltz, an American psychologist who specialised in human mental high
performance. This technique amplifies the power of the imagination and is
used in all sorts of competitive situations – sales, combat, sport and so on –
where one needs to improve mental achievement. The theatre of the mind
is constructed in your imagination, much like a real theatre, with a

big projection screen and comfortable chairs. You own the theatre, so you can run any film you like. When you go into your private mental theatre, make the images about your opponent's circumstances as vivid and as detailed as you can. Then, any time you want to, you can stop the film, and actually jump into the opponent's shoes and become your opponent's character. The more you run the imaginary film with you playing that part, the more vivid and detailed the film becomes. In time, you will enable yourself to stand in the opponent's shoes in such an animated and elaborate way that it will be difficult to tell the difference between what you imagined and what was real. Again, the old brain cannot tell the difference between the imagined and the actual.

(NB: 'Standing in the other person's shoes' and 'theatre of the mind' are outlined in Exercises 9 and 10 in Appendix A.)

Difference as Inspiration

When two or more distinct ideas or disciplines come together, there is a potential for conflict. After all, unique concepts frequently emanate from distinct cultures and belief systems. We know, from everyday life, that when two distinct belief systems collide, it can have dreadful repercussions. But difference is also a source of creativity and eventual innovation. To mediate between two or more contrasting ideas, we need an arbitrator, a way of thinking that seeks a synergy between the many different ideas.

Essentially, we need to move to an orientation and mind-set that sees difference as a source of inspiration. Here, different perspectives broaden the view on innovation, offering up wider options on the future. The goal, then, is *not* to find what's negative about the discord, but rather to find positions that are complementary. Therefore we must not strive to demolish each other's ideas, precepts or values, but find a synergy amongst them. To begin to do this, bring out the positive; at what point does each idea complement the other, even if each notion is at loggerheads? I suggest that you consider any one of the following techniques when doing so:

- Pick out three good things about each conflicting idea and three issues that might be seen in a different way.

- Pick out three aspects of conflicting ideas that you have observed to work together elsewhere.

- Pick out three fundamental themes from each conflicting idea that should be incorporated into an innovation.

- Pick out three attributes of difference that affect internal (those who work within the company) people positively and directly.

- Pick out three attributes of difference that affect external (those outside the company) people positively and directly.

- Pick out three measures of success that are germane to each of the conflicting ideas.

For example, take the archetypal conflict between oil and water molecules, stubborn foes that don't like to mix. Below are three aspects of that conflict working together:

- Emulsion paint.

- Beautiful oily iridescent patterns on the surface of a pond.

- Machine lubricant.

Here, oil and water coexist in harmony, and if it can be done with these two adversaries, it's quite possible to find areas that work in the most controversial conflicts in business, politics and innovation.

(NB: 'Difference as inspiration' is outlined in Exercise 11 in Appendix A.)

CHAPTER 5

Developing an Innovative Team's Whole Mind

It is not the individual elements that control the whole, but the whole that controls the elements.
PROF. C. CAPRA

Questions: Why do people tend to become hostile when confronted with difficult situations in formal meetings? Why are conversations by the coffee machine so much more open, creative and fruitful? Why don't the copy department sort out their differences with editorial, and just talk? Why don't the Republicans agree with the Democrats? The answers to these agitating questions have a common thread.

Mental Models

Innovative teams perform best when they think, learn and act as a coherent whole. Yet I find such coherence is an all too rare thing in the corporate world. As noted in Chapter 4, creative types often make such team unity challenging, but not impossible. Nevertheless, beyond the creative attributes and issues of team building lies the question of personalised, and therefore divergent, perspectives and perceptions. As more innovative teams are international, multilingual, multicultural and multiskilled in their make-up, such an extensive variety of viewpoints is yet another barrier to building high performance innovative teams.

At the heart of such diverse perspectives and perceptions lies what cognitive psychologists refer to as the 'mental model'. Mental models are the simplified, highly personalised representations, assumptions and ideologies that we all carry in our heads, which make up our own particular version of reality. And because such mental models are simplified and personal, they are all too often distorted reflections of actuality. These mental models, in their simplified plan, inform and guide what we see and pick out in any given situation, and this is a major reason why different people often see and prioritise quite distinct issues and facts from the same issues or situations.

Conflicting mental models frequently inhibit the building of a whole team mind. In particular, new ideas fail to make it into practice because of a discord between the different internal mental models we hold. Here, mental models can go so far as to limit creative thinking; and even to the making of unfounded assumptions and generalisations. In fact, mental models can affect assumptions so much so that they grow to be a real threat to team collaboration.

The earliest reference to mental models is that of the work of Kenneth Craik, the Scottish psychologist. As far as I am aware, Craik coined the term 'mental model' back in 1943. Since then, the field of mental model research and application has been widespread, ranging over artificial intelligence, clinical psychology and, lately, organisational learning and team building. A latter-day proponent of mental models is Johnson-Laird, the cognitive psychologist. He says that:

> Mental models play a central and unifying role in representing objects, states of affairs, sequences of events, the way the world is, and the social and psychological acting of daily life. They enable individuals to make inferences and predictions, to understand phenomena, to decide what action to take and to control its execution, and above all, to experience events by proxy; they allow language to be used to create representations comparable to those deriving from direct acquaintance with the world, and they relate words to the world by way of conception and perception.

Examples of mental models range from the tangible (such as a car, an apple, or a fire-breathing dragon), to more symbolic (such as a brand like Virgin or beliefs such as Buddhism), to the abstract (such as money and time). Mental models always turn out to be much simpler than reality. Clearly, we all have limited mental capacities, such as concentration span, memory and basic information-processing capacities and so on. These limited mental capacities are in fact our editors on reality.

Furthermore, mental models are known to exist below our conscious thoughts, and therefore are tacit and mostly invisible to our thinking. Most people's mental models have in fact been influenced and, in the extreme, wholly constructed by other parties (a family for example) and formal systems of learning (schooling for example).

So what are the basic elements that furnish individuals with such distinctive cognitive archetypes of the world? There are seven key factors:

1. *Functional or local context*. The context in which different people live has a profound impact on constructing mental models. For example, the functional context of a medical doctor is quite different from that of a hospital administrator. The dominant functional issues for a doctor are likely to be the application of medical science, and the patients' immediate and longer term well-being. For the hospital administrator, local issues might be resource efficiency, patient throughput and costs. Local context deeply colours our mental views of the world.

2. *Scope of context*. The scope of context can dramatically vary the mental models we hold, and therefore the way we see the world. A vice president of new product development, for example, has a significantly wider span of issues to deal with than, say, a design engineer working within a project team.

3. *Experience*. Over time, out of the scope of context comes our cumulative experiences. Whether it be our family or social background, the educational systems we encounter, or, in particular here, the professional and functional organisations we work within, the experiences we gain deeply colour our mental models.

4. *Knowledge*. The element that has the greatest potential to instantly change people's mental model is knowledge. Equally, knowledge has the potential to blind people to events and facts, and therefore limit their model of the world. People who come together for the first time, who have accumulated knowledge from quite disparate fields, all too often see the world in very different ways.

5. *Personality*. This is a tricky one. Psychologists tell us that personality is made up of many distinct components, ranging from physical elements such as the detailed physiology, chemistry and hard-wiring of the brain (sometimes called psychobiology), to the basic intellectual intelligence and emotional mentality that an individual develops. However, when it comes to innovation, there are personality types that either see innovation as significant or a problem to be avoided. Person-

ality types are built either for bringing about successful innovation, or not. Later in Chapter 12 we will be looking at these innovative personality types in more detail.

6. *Expectations.* From our experiences, knowledge and personality grow our expectations in life. Expectations, again, either help or hinder the activity of innovation. For the most part, bold activist types generally have different expectations than, say, a shy conformist. But it is not as easy as that. I've met many an individual with an introvert personality who wanted to move mountains. In fact, many TV stars are quite retiring offstage. But at the end of the day, if the expectation is that of the status quo, the world view is going to be one that hinders innovation.

7. *Beliefs.* The ideas we inherit from our family and peers during our formative years significantly mould what we see as meaningful in life. What we value as important shapes our mental model of the world too. In the workplace, the culture of acceptable norms and practices also adds to what we think is important and right. In the steel business, for example, it is an acceptable norm to display aggressive tendancies, as steelworkers are expected to be tough guys. This belief and resultant behaviour would simply not be acceptable in a bank or hospital. Thus, beliefs dramatically shape our mental models.

Collectively, each basic element moulds and frames the mental models we carry around.

Dominant Mental Models

We all feel that our particular view of the world, whether an opinion, a perspective, or a point of view, is the right one. In fact, without that sense of self-belief, we tend to feel unsure of ourselves. It is as though we have to believe we are right, even at the cost of being wrong. However, when it comes to innovation, this stance can have a detrimental effect on team performance. If each team member doggedly defends his or her account of a given situation or issue, innovation of even the simplest system will not occur.

This is exaggerated because individualised models of the world are tacit and subconscious. People often have little self-awareness, let alone an awareness of other people's mental models. An individual often feels that his or her own view or opinion is so right that he or she cannot help but try to convince his or her colleagues that his or her opinion is the one and only right view. But if every one has his or her own distinct opinion and is not ready to hold up their ideas for open critique or comment, then the situation is merely a battle of convictions.

This is exacerbated still further when a strong personality is present within a group. Managers and peers with strong personalities and a clear view of what they want to achieve can really cause unrest within an innovation team, especially if there are several managers or senior staff of this disposition. Dominant personalities often hold the dominant mental models of the group, which not only causes friction, but also stops dead any level of dialogue, and ultimately brings a narrow, often shallow, sometimes totally wrong and static view.

Beyond strong personalities, there are other reasons that might enforce a dominant and askew mental model, ranging from self-interest (such as ambition), an impulsive nature (such as quick to judge), to misunderstanding (such as pure, unadulterated ignorance).

The goal, then, is to realise the difference between assumptions and clear facts, to inquire into people's suppositions and beliefs. If this is not done, sticking points with further potential conflicts will occur and reoccur, which will be absolutely dire for innovation of any kind.

There are two main ways that entrenched, dominant mental models limit innovation. First, basic and all too common conflicts arise between competing mental models within close-knit groups. Second, entrenched and long-held mental models can limit new ways of seeing the world.

(NB: The main points of the above text in this chapter are outlined in Exercise 12 in Appendix A.)

Transforming Mental Models

Mental models tend to be self-reinforcing, as learning new knowledge and gaining new experience are often encumbered by our existing mental models. It is a kind of feedback-loop, a kind of self-selection of knowledge, where like selects like. Essentially, mental models precede what we pick out, think and do next. Like a well-trodden path, mental models guide us to the next notion or assumption. Mental models thus give a confined range of thought. The more we pay attention to ideas and information that support our own world view, the more entrenched our mental model becomes, which in turn limits our ability to think and see differently.

Clearly, if innovation of the category-breaking (Q4) kind is going to happen, individuals must first abandon the existing components of their mental archetypes, do away with anything that does not have integrity. This has to be the case because it is virtually impossible to fundamentally innovate without first expanding and then totally transforming perennial mental models. In fact, the more successful a team has been in the past, the less likely that it will be successful in the future, unless it makes a concerted effort to grow and transform its dominant mental models. In essence, the newly constructed mental models must leave the past behind and reconstruct new beliefs and insights that create the new competitive space of tomorrow.

Here are five ways to begin to transform dominant mental models so that category-breaking (Q4) systems innovation can occur:

1. *Define your existing mental models*: The starting point is to know the borders of your beliefs. Ask yourself 'what are the limits of my constructed reality?' 'What are the key ingredients and precepts that define my mental models?' Think about the political climate, the kind of customer wants that need to be fulfilled, the technology, competitors, distribution channels, the product and service concepts and so on. How are they defined? Are they old linear abstractions, based on years of serial learning and innovation? Most are. The point is that when you are aware of your mental models in terms of their outlines, you will start to see how restricting your mental models really are.

2. *Look beyond the boundaries of your mental models*: Many of the ideas, issues and challenges that will define the future will not be conceived or even born within your current line of sight. That is, the issues and key factors that will shape your tomorrow will come from outside your own mental models, to the point that they might even be invisible to you right now. To encourage this, Watts Wacker and Ryan Mathews say firms need to employ deviants and the mental models that come with them, as deviance is the source of all innovation. They say it is the wellspring of new ideas, new products, new personalities and ultimately new markets. Things that we found on the edge, things that we often found repugnant yesterday, we lionise today. What starts out as weird and dangerous morphs into the company's latest successful product. However, the corporate world hates the deviant. And government institutional culture works to eliminate deviants, and thus the insightful and rebellious mental models that go with them.

3. *Seek the underground fringe*: What's new? I mean really new and on the edges of life? Most people follow highly conservative patterns in life. But how on earth are you going to transform your own and other people's mental model and in turn truly innovate if you don't do outlandish things from time to time. Too dangerous, you may say. But that is your rational cortex brain, with its high ethical sensibilities, telling you that doing

things differently is a bad thing. Marvin Minsky, Professor of Artificial Intelligence at MIT, says that many people's creative powers are limited because they have an overexaggerated sense of what is right or wrong. Even Tom Peters says honour thy cheats, because it is the boundary pushers who make the best innovators. I am not suggesting for one moment that we should develop an unscrupulous mind-set, far from it. What I am saying is that to see and think differently, we need to cross the normal boundaries from time to time, and one of the best ways to do this is to go out and actively seek the underground fringe.

4. *Visit far-off places*: If you want to find the fringe, go off the beaten track. Again you will experience a moral dilemma here, as we are often told not to go off piste as it can be dangerous. But what is life about anyhow? So get out, way out, from time to time and you will find the fringe, and believe me it will stimulate the old emotional-reflex brain in all sorts of positive ways.

5. *Innovatively interconnect with adjacent mental models*: What new insights, near and far, can you interconnect to your current mental model outline that would begin to create a new mental model definition? What unarticulated and unsatisfied customer demands or challenging issues could you fulfil by expanding your mental models with ideas outside the current fold? What emerging ideas in other industries could you interconnect with to reinvent your world view?

(NB: 'Transforming mental models' is outlined in Exercise 13 in Appendix A.)

The Sharing of Great Minds

A team may function quite well within a routine environment (see Chapter 2), but when confronted with complex, novel tasks, team spirit seems to disappear into the ether. Given the high levels of uncertainty, and the natural anxieties that rest with such ambiguity, friction around values, knowledge, experience, personality, approach and so on can easily arise. So unless teams share – at some level – mutual realities, discord will most certainly occur, the experience will be emotionally painful, complex innovation projects will be tardy and, in the extreme, not make it to market or commission.

There are two principal tools that can be applied that help bear, share and, to a degree, attune individual mental models, and in turn begin to build that whole team mind; the techniques of open exploration and getting a new perspective by asking original questions.

Open Exploration

Route one to shared mental models is the capacity and scope to explore the many different issues at hand for an extended period. Essentially, if a group assiduously measures up even the most unlike for long enough, a shared kind of sense emerges. Deep comparison is about having the room collectively to explore what is on the mind of each individual, taking time to see what others do. It is a straightforward method, but takes time and practice to master. Here are the basic methodological issues:

■ *Make a legitimate space*: Without setting up a formal time and space for open exploration, it will be hard to carry out. Set aside a full hour to examine a critical issue at hand. Switch off your mobile and lock the door if you can. Quiet is important, and a tranquil setting will stimulate the most open exploration.

■ *Multiway reflection*: If we are *unable* to listen, take in and reflect on other people's ideas within our own mind and within a wider group, then there will be little or no chance of collectively exploring emerging, unformed, or indeed the deepest, most fully shaped thoughts, ideas and beliefs. People from all walks of life suffer from an incapacity to reflect on what other people are saying, feeling or thinking. Instead of hearing what is being said, they have a tendency to have already made up their own mind on what their peers mean or intend. So what to do here? Here is a simple, nine-step process to begin to develop the ability of multiway reflection within a team:

1. Pick a real issue to reflect on.
2. A colleague defines and states the issue at hand and gives their views and ideas.
3. Practise pausing before you answer a question or even think of a retort. Count to three (1,2,3) then reply.
4. Ask your peer(s) to elaborate (I'd like to understand more ...) on their views or ideas.
5. Pause once again (1,2,3) before you reply. Let your subconscious, and indeed your conscious cogs turn in the mind.
6. Ask your peer(s) to consider what you feel and think (I'd like to give my views/experiences/issues relevant to this if that's OK with you ...).
7. Be constructive.
8. Stop and listen to the response.
9. Repeat 1 to 6.

■ *Stop the show/start the show phrases*: There are thousands of words and phrases that stop the exploration and sharing of mental models. If we continually use such terms in our daily discourse, what chance is there of mental model sharing and development? On the other hand, there are words and phrases that open up conversations, get the open exploration show rolling between two or more people. Here's a handful:

Stop the show:	*Start the show:*
We've tried that before	That's a good question
It costs too much	Let me see it
Put it in writing	That might be fun if …
It's impossible	How could we do it?
That's just stupid	What other ideas do you have?
You can't do that here	I like that, please elaborate
Our team's too small	How could we improve?
That would take too long	Let me ask you this …
If it ain't broke, don't fix it	If it ain't broke, improve it

■ *Reiteration over an impasse*: Go over and over the same ground (detectives do it all the time) if an impasse is reached. This is in fact a central tenant of complexity theory, the deeper one looks the more complex the system becomes.

(NB: 'Open exploration' is outlined in Exercise 14 in Appendix A.)

Get a New Perspective by Asking Original Questions

An answer to sharing (and developing) current mental models is in the questions that you ask. Questions enable reflection and inquiry, the sharing of ideas and notions, and the beginning of collaborative development. Here is an outline of some of the kinds of question you need to encourage your people to ask:

■ *Controversial 'what if' questions*: Some say that what if is the most powerful question anyone can ask (maybe it is). But controversial what if questions are designed to bring out our peers' deepest thoughts and feelings. Controversial what ifs are mental tin-openers that often bring out the deeper underlying motives, meanings and ideologies that drive people's actions and behaviours. Some examples:

What if – We worked a four-day week, but with the same weekly hours?

What if – The whole company worked in one big room?

What if – We all worked from home?

What if – We all wear a company uniform?

What if – We have an informal dress code?

What if – We could have extra days off without pay?

What if – We increased working hours with more pay?

The idea is that such questions are provocative, which often switches on the old primitive brain, and when that happens we begin to recall our deepest fears, anxieties and dislikes. At first this may seem like an antagonistic approach to revealing and sharing our mental models. But in fact it quite often reveals our deepest motives and meanings, which in turn gives up information into how individuals and groups think and therefore behave.

■ *Not 'why', but 'how' questions*: The manager's favourite question is *why*. But not only does this question get people's back up (it nearly always comes across as a challenge of competence), it does not get to the heart of the matter. On the other hand, *how* is a surprisingly powerful question in terms of digging out what is important. Asking peers how they are thinking, how they came to that conclusion, how they managed to achieve that and so on reveals the underlying motives and meanings at the time. Again, powerful, but simple stuff.

■ *Out-of-the-box questions*: An out-of-the-box question is a question outside the norm (whether conceptually, technically, culturally or politically). These questions make known how a peer or a group of people think in terms of how far they are prepared to share knowledge and informtion. How? Well, people who find it easier to think out of the box generally (but not exclusively) have broad knowledge, and that means that they have been in contact with a lot of different people in one way or another. So are your people asking out-of-the-box questions? If not, practise it. Actively get them to ask out-of-the-box questions. Here are two examples.

1. *Metaphorical questions.* Einstein once said that the mark of true genius is the ability to describe the world in metaphors. It is the same with such questions, I suspect. Metaphorical questions break down conditioned mind-sets, opening up channels to a higher level of inspiration. Metaphorical questions break serial thinking by

transferring ideas from remote and often conflicting knowledge spaces, which would not readily be accepted or seen as a logical path to an original idea. A metaphor is a powerful mental model sharing tool because it can jump literally thousands of linear and logical thought steps in a single bound. The number and kinds of metaphorical questions are endless. Search and connect unlike circumstances, even unrelated objects, which if drawn into your own area of technology/markets/customers would impart a breakthrough. Look for contrasting parables, stories, fables, yarns, which if brought into a new and remote context would lead to new insights and original inspirations.

2. *Lateral questions.* For example, ask a question about a situation or problem. Now get hold of a sheet of paper and write the question in the top left-hand corner. Now ask a peer to write down the first associated word that comes into their head. Then the next peer must write down a word connected to the second word. Now do it for a third, fourth and continue to do this for a whole minute. What you have is a list of words leading out of the box from a single question. Now take each of those words and attempt to interlink each of them to make up a sentence. Let's have a go: car tyres, for example, are an expensive items to replace. So how could we reduce the replacement cost of car tyres? Start by picking one of the parameters related to the problem. Let's start with the word 'expensive':

EXPENSIVE	> DIAMOND	> HARD	> LATIN
AMERICAN	> COP	> CAR	> TYRE
RUBBER	> ELASTIC	> BAND	> TRUMPET
BRASS	> POLISH	> WAX	> SPRAY
RAIN	> UMBRELL	> COLLAPSE	> DISPOSAL

Now make up an answer with the connected words, even if it sounds a bit odd. In fact, the stranger the better: Diamond rain wax polishing a disposable rubber tyre stops the collapse of American cars! Nonsense? Maybe. Now try to interconnect that sentence to the given customer problem to come up with a new concept. What about a diamond impregnated rubber tyre to reduce wear! Nonsense? Maybe. But the point is that, within just a few minutes of using this technique, it's quite possible to arrive at a totally unique concept through a strange string of words, that would not have been achieved by hours of sequential thinking.

Once people start asking out-of-the-box questions, they begin to seek ideas, information and knowledge out of the box too. And if they are doing that, you can bet that they are engaging with people they would not readily have in the past. And if they are doing that, they are developing and sharing their mental models.

(NB: 'Get a new perspective by asking original questions' is outlined in Exercise 15 in Appendix A.)

Getting to the Heart of the Matter

This group thinking technique helps to get into the head of your peers; to probe into what they are really feeling and thinking about, instead of what they are merely saying aloud. Often, far too often, what we say and what we think are two completely different things.

There are two steps to getting to the heart of the matter: firstly, *drawing out generalisations and assumptions*, and then to be *constructively honest*.

Drawing Out Generalisations and Assumptions

Generalisations can force us into narrow, quite distorted perspectives. Assumptions can lead us to false conclusions about the people and tasks that we have to work with. Thus, drawing out generalisations and assumptions for reflection can open single point perspectives towards diverse but shared world views. Here is an example discussion:

Kim's drawing out:	Where do you stand on Ann's qualification as Thunderbolt project manager?
John's assumption:	Ann's far too young to head the Thunderbolt project.
Ali's generalisation:	Yeah, a greenhorn.
Kim's explanation:	Wait a moment, didn't she write that report on Thunderbolt Topology ... and wasn't she captain of the basketball team at Princeton/ Oxford/Open?
John's open reflection:	Got to admit I didn't realise she had those kind of talents.
Ali's open reflection:	Maybe a young team manager would break new ground.

The key here, is to hold up the main points, expand upon the assumptions and then reflect on those assumptions.

Constructive Honesty

Once again, what we think and what we say are often two very different things. We keep our deepest thoughts private for many reasons, not least because of office politics. But politics, after all, is often a matter of timing. During discussions or meetings, ask team members to write down what they actually say and what they actually think underneath. Then ask them to reconsider what they say in light of the private thoughts they have written down. The result is often quite astounding. Here is an example discussion:

Kim's idea:	Most of our customers are 50 years of age and over. What about bigger text size on the display?
Ann's direct reply:	Yes, bigger display text seems like a good idea.
Ann's concealed thought:	It'll never work because the 5000 series chip only has a 5k memory.
Ann's reconsideration:	We'll need to upgrade the 5000 series chip, to an 8000 series; this'll up the cost by $1.87 per unit.
Kim's admission:	At 50,000 units, that's just over $93,000, we can just about absorb that ... Anything else we need to consider Ann?

The keys to constructive honesty: write down private thoughts and reconsider the consequences, then acknowledge those consequences. This is simple, but potent stuff.

The Wheel of Reinforcement

Almost all radical ideas in the form of novel concepts or original solutions to problems are greeted with some scepticism, even outright suspicion and contempt. Sometimes such resistance comes down to a perceived threat to a position. Mostly, however, rejection, or indeed acceptance, is based purely on a supposition, which in turn is based on a past, often unrelated experience. Such rejection (or acceptance) happens because people, in general, think that their assumptions and experiences are some objective truth based on concrete information. But, as we have already explored in Chapter 3, our memory, in the form of representations of reality, is distorted in all sorts of conflicting and confusing ways, therefore our mental models of reality are always somewhat askew, yet often we continue to believe that what we believe is absolute gospel.

In fact, Rick Ross, of Ross Partners Inc., the learning organisation consulting firm, says that we live in a world of self-generating beliefs which continue to be mostly untested. We take up these convictions because they are based on judgements which are implied from what we observe, coupled with our past experience and knowledge base. Our capacity to accomplish the ends we aspire to is hindered by our feelings that our beliefs are the truth, obvious and based on genuine facts.

To expand and understand that most of our beliefs are based on more than shaky assumptions, I often use something I call the wheel of reinforcement (Figure 5.1). It is a simple diagram that illustrates the basic thought processes that lead to the rejection of an idea as bad, or its uptake as good. The diagram shows that all too often we make decisions based on unsound reasoning, rather than objective data, and often reasoning that is not really common sense, but imagined events or emotional bias.

The wheel has seven segments defining each stage of the thinking process:

1. *Assert idea*: The basic idea is stated, affirmed in many forms. An idea may be a whole new concept for a public service, or a detailed solution to a task, it may well be an opinion of a matter at hand, or indeed pure meaningless gossip.

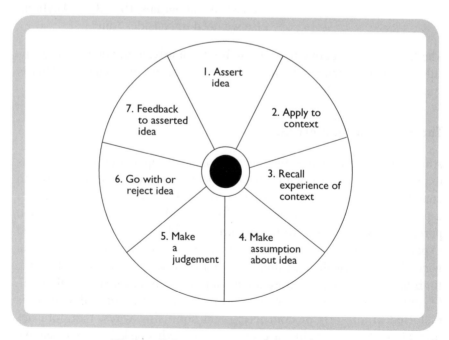

Figure 5.1   Wheel of reinforcement

2. *Apply idea to context*: Ideas can be applied in many different contexts. Examples include a particular challenge within an innovation project, to a formal management meeting, or even an informal social gathering.

3. *Recall experience of context*: Often, and especially within the field of innovation, the experience of context will be limited, as the context itself may be new or different. In fact, all context has its own unique and particular circumstances surrounding it. After all, it is a complex world.

4. *Make assumption about idea*: A supposition is made about the idea within that unique context, through our tacit representations, assumptions and ideologies of the world (our mental models).

5. *Judge idea*: An unconscious conclusion or judgement is made about the idea in question within its context.

6. *Go with, hold or reject idea*: It is then either rejected, retained as a maybe, or taken on board as fact, and good.

7. *Idea reinforcement*: It is the seventh step in the thought process that is the most significant. If we see an idea as good or bad, we tend to reinforce our view of the idea as we go around the wheel. That is, if we reject the idea as bad, the more we think about it, the more we go around the circle of reinforcement, the more the idea seems like an even worse idea.

The central problem with the whole reinforcing wheel of thought is that data is not always around when it is needed, especially for novel concepts or solutions to unique problems. Furthermore, surreptitious information and ideas are more likely to be believed, rather than hard facts from an official source. Again, it seems to be part of the human psyche to hold a belief as a universal truth. Consequently, we tend to fall unconsciously into a reinforcing circle of thinking that keeps us from actuality. The goal, then, is to be more aware of our tacit thought processes and mental models that give rise to decisions about new ideas and solutions.

(NB: 'Understanding the wheel of reinforcement' is outlined in Exercise 16 in Appendix A.)

Stopping and Opening the Wheel of Reinforcement

It is possible to use the wheel of reinforcement to make our thought processes more visible. Each step in the wheel can be slowed for analysis and debate. Once this happens, it is possible to see how conflict between

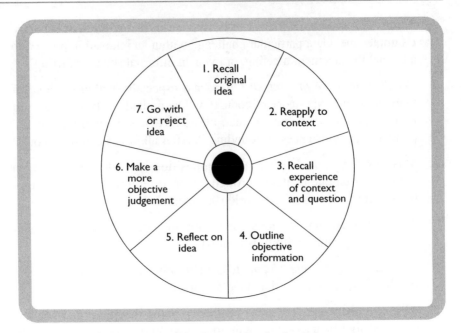

Figure 5.2   Objective wheel of reinforcement

tacit assumptions can be overcome. Again there are seven stages in stopping and opening up the wheel of reinforcement:

1. *Recall original idea*: Paraphrase the idea or notion, so that all parties are clear about its content.

2. *Reapply idea to context*: Again this helps to clarify.

3. *Recall experience (if any) of context and question*: What mental models are present that may distort actuality? Are there any experiences (good, bad, indifferent) colouring the thinking. Remember a recalled experience is not hard data. What organisational cultural norms are present (for example status in the hierarchy, departmental scope, what is most important and so on)? What loyalties are present? What legacies have your people inherited?

4. *Outline objective information*: What information is a hunch, guesswork or political work? What facts are real or mere fiction? What quantitative studies have been carried out to verify the data?

5. *Reflect on idea via open exploration and getting a different perspective:* Open reflection is made about the idea in a more objective context.

Then reduction of earlier assumptions is made via inquiry and comparison with real data.

6. *Make a 'more' objective judgement based on reflection and comparison*: A new, more impartial conclusion is made about the new idea.

7. *Go with or reject idea*: It is then either rejected or taken on board.

(NB: 'Stopping and opening the wheel of reinforcement' is outlined in Exercise 17 in Appendix A.)

Perception Orientation

Perception is one more area of the mind that can get in the way of teamwork. Human perception is in fact highly fungible. It changes depending on where we stand, it shifts depending on our mood, it distorts depending on our levels of stress, but most important of all it modifies depending on the series of experiences that lead up to a particular event.

Try this experiment. Get hold of a cup of hot water, a cup of cold water, and cup of water at room temperature. Now grab hold of two colleagues, and ask the first to put a finger in the hot cup, and the other colleague to stick his finger in the cold cup. Count to 50, then ask each of them to stick their respective finger in the room temperature cup, and ask each of them whether the room temperature cup is hot or cold. You can be sure that the one who put his finger in the hot cup will say the room temperature cup of water is cold, and the other will say it is hot! The lesson is that the incidents we experience leading up to an event influence our perception.

There are many other similar experiments that show that past circumstances colour our perception and in turn colour our judgement and outlook. Ask a child from a impoverished background to draw a penny, and then ask a rich child to draw a penny and what do you get? Time and time again, the poor child draws a giant penny and the rich child sketches a relatively small penny. History, experience, life's twists and turns, all go towards colouring our perceptions, and since we all have different legacies, we all perceive the world in slightly, and sometimes hugely, different ways.

Yet another reason for different perceptions is that we often take the line of least resistance in our memory. That is, whatever is easier to recall, often the last thought we had on a given situation, is what comes to mind first. Again that's an issue, because complex systems innovation requires a diversity of knowledge recalled from a diversity of people with a diversity of memories. Conflicts and chaos again.

So for innovative team performance, perception, or rather perception orientation, is an issue. If we are to bring together people from diverse backgrounds, with an array of divergent mental models, then you can be sure that perceptions of the world will be equally diverse. Therefore, another aspect of building innovative teams is orientation perception so that there is some degree of alignment. Here are three ways to align perception:

1. *Bring about parity through learning together.* Where you end up often depends on where you start. As above, a rich child with a privileged education is likely to see the world very differently from, say, a child from a poor background with a poorer education. Notwithstanding opportunities, the rich child will probably end up in a professional career and the poor child with fewer prospects. The poor child and the rich child are locked into an outcome from the beginning. In psyche speak, this is known as 'anchoring'. Again, where you end up often depends on where you start. Likewise, if a team is to collaborate they must have some level of parity in their anchoring. Such parity comes once again through learning together over time. But this must be accelerated with in-class exercises – such as the example in Exercise 25 – to bring about such parity as early as possible.

2. *Setting expectations.* Without doubt, if one individual's expectations are higher or different from another individual's within a team, perception will again be out of sync. The key here is to lay out the lie of the land at the beginning of the project. To state what performances are expected from both individuals and their work products.

3. *Control (again).* Perception orientation again affected by control (or at least the perception of control). If an individual is set in a management environment where he is being herded like cattle, all the anxieties outlined in Chapter 3 will kick in. And when that happens perceptions within the group go askew again (things get blown out of proportion, other people's comments seem unhelpful, even contemptuous, and the boss seems like some awful brute. If, for example, a group is unable to take a task in a direction they think best, each member of that group's perception of the situation will be quite different, so control within the group is key.

(NB: 'Perception orientation' is outlined in Exercise 18 in Appendix A.)

CHAPTER 6

Collaborative Learning Beyond Knowledge

What I suggest is a kind of collective enquiry not only into the composition of what we think and feel, but also into the underlying motives, assumptions and ideology that leads us to do so. DAVID BOHM

Systems innovations are not only the combined end result of many distinct minds and ideas, but the result of learning beyond what is already known. In fact, I would go so far as to say that *true innovation only occurs when learning exceeds current knowledge*. Therefore learning beyond knowledge is at the heart of all innovation.

Now take the premise that complex innovation needs (a) the input of a diversity of minds and (b) learning must take place over and above what is already known. Clearly, there is a distinct need for collaborative learning beyond knowledge (a + b), learning where the whole output is greater than the individual inputs.

However, before we get underway and explore the mechanics of collaborative learning, it may be a good idea for you, the reader, to get a feel for the potential limits of learning and in turn systems innovation.

The Limits of Innovation Possibilities

Question: how many potential permutations exist for combining ideas in novel ways? It sounds like a philosophical question (it is), but at the end of the day it is also a real-world inquiry into understanding the potential for collaborative learning and resultant systems innovation.

In the past, attempts to quantify both the rate and limits of innovation have been frowned upon. After all, how could a subject so nebulous hold any kind of objective measure? The following extract comes from Peter Russell's thought-provoking book *The White Hole In Time*:

> One inspired attempt has been that of the French economist George Anderla for the Organisation for Economic Cooperation and Development. He takes the known scientific facts of the year A.D. 1 to represent one unit of collective human knowledge. Assuming that our collective learning began with literature, it had taken approximately five thousand years for humanity to accrue that first unit. According to Anderla's estimates, humanity had doubled its knowledge by A.D. 1500. By 1750 total knowledge had doubled again; and by 1900 it had become 8 units of knowledge. It then doubled again in the next seven years, and again in the following six years, taking us to 128 units in 1973, the year of Anderla's study. There is no indication that the acceleration had slowed since then. It has almost certainly continued to increase ever-more rapidly. The French astrophysicist Dr. Jacques Valley, for instance, has estimated that human knowledge is currently doubling once every eighteen months.

From this, more questions arise: What are the limits for systems innovation? Do we foresee an end of ideas, a wall for technological innovation? And what possibilities lie afoot for new products and services, markets, indeed whole new industries? The answers may lie within a concept known as design-space.

Design-space

The term 'design-space' is a conceptual thinking apparatus allowing an invaluable insight into the library of all possible systems innovations. From this perspective, we will see that all conceivable design-space for innovation is theoretically infinite (although for practical purposes it is finite). Theoretically, there is infinite interconnected white-spaces for innovation.

We can look to the science of information theory to give us a clearer insight into the potential here. Researchers at Bell Laboratories invented the science of information theory while researching better ways to transmit complex information signals over vast communication networks. From this research, they found a practical limit to the complexity of information that could be transmitted. Here, we can use information theory to reveal the theoretical and practical limits for the complexity and ultimate innovation of ideas, within all possible design-space.

Let's play a game: I want you to seek out all past, present and potential ideas in our universe, from the big bang to the end of time. Start the game just before the universe began.

Picture a TV screen. The screen is switched off, it's blank; we have no universe. Press your remote control and switch on the screen. A picture appears instantly, it's next Thursday's edition of the CNN update! Impossible? Well, theoretically it's very possible, yet, for practical reasons, it's impossible! Confused?

The screen has, for argument's sake, 1000×1000 pixels (the dots that make up the picture). If you could somehow turn on and then turn off each pixel (or atoms and/or ideas in a universe) in any sequence at your command, you could – in theory – generate any picture you desired (or object or process). You could generate the photo finish of the men's 100 metre race at the 2012 Olympic Games, you could preview Stephen Spielberg's next film, before he begins to make it, you could even show next week's winning lottery numbers! The screen, in theory, can give up all pictures of all possible ideas, within all possible design-space. After all, you only have to switch off and on each of those 1,000,000 pixels, in the right sequence, and you'll have the corresponding picture. *Only* 1000×1000 pixels! That really isn't too big a number to deal with, considering the potential stakes here: to know all futures, all ideas, all knowledge! How would you accomplish this? What strategy could you invent to achieve this in the most effective way? Come on, there are riches beyond your wildest dreams on offer!

Okay, the most obvious starting point would be a screen with all the pixels turned off. The second screen would have the very top right-hand pixel turned on, and the rest turned off. The next screen would show pixel 1 and pixel 2 switched on and all the rest switched off. Carry on like this until all the pixels are turned on. But, hold on, surely there must be a faster way?

Let's work out mathematically how long it will take to process all possible pixel sequences in the screen's design-space. There are $1000 \times 1000 = 1,000,000$ pixels; so there are 10 to the power of 1,000,000 combinations. That's a figure with the number 1 and a million zeros after it. This number, 10 to the power of 1,000,000, would cover an area of one square metre (in 12pt). The sobering fact, however, according to astrophysicists, is that the projected life of life is around 10 EXP(70) seconds (stars burnout) and the total life of the universe, from the big bang to the big chill, is only around 10 EXP(106) seconds long. The universe will suffer heat death in the year 100-trillion-trillion-tillion-trillion-trillion-trillion! The universe at present is less than 10 EXP(18) seconds old. If we had begun sequencing at the big bang, we would not have sequenced any significant percentage of all possible design-space by now, and even if we carry on, we could only execute a minute fraction of all possibilities by the end of the universe. In terms of pictures on the screen that make any sense, even by the time the universe ends, we would *not* have had any reasonably intelligent picture to tell of, but, at best, a zillion-zillion fuzzy white noise spaces.

We can carry this abstract game into something more meaningful. Information theory tells us that we'll never have a chance to see all possible meaningful designs under the laws of known physics. Even though most arrangements of ideas are meaningless to us, and by comparison to all possible design-space, the amount of meaningful ideas is infinitesimally small. Under the pretext of the known life-cycle of the universe, we will only see a glimmer of all possibilities. Indeed, the saying 'nothing is impossible given time', is quite correct, but it seems almost everything is quite improbable because the universal clock is so small. Almost all meaningful possible design-spaces will be out of reach.

The point is not that there is a limit to meaningful design-space, it is that there are so many meaningful design-spaces. Idea growth, driven by all possible design-space exploration, is not unlike going for a day out in London, we simply don't have time to visit all the interesting places. Innovation, then, has an immense and unending journey through design-space. Ideas have no destination, from our perspective. If we look forward, shining our headlights towards the future, there are a million, billion, trillion and more ideas that we have not yet found, and a zillion curious and wondrous systems innovations that we have yet to explore.

Accumulative Design Work

More profound still: now think of design-space as a maze, an imaginary maze with infinite connected spaces for innovation. In this imaginary labyrinth, if you decided to move downwards, you would find lesser evolved innovations. If you move horizontally, you would find innovations of the same parity. But if you climb upwards, you would find ever-more evolved kinds of innovation. This imaginary scheme can give us a profound insight into the creation of higher value innovation. Paul Romer, the Berkeley economist, says that the faster a firm can search up through the maze of possible innovations, the better and better ideas become, and, in turn, the higher the innate value those innovations exhibit. The reason for this is that the higher a firm drifts in the maze of possibilities, the more involved and complex the design work is to realise those innovations, consequently the more value it represents. Think of what Daniel Dennett, Director of Tufts Artificial Intelligence Laboratory, has to say on this. He wrote in his seminal work *Darwin's Dangerous Idea*:

> How much design work does a thing exhibit? Automobiles contain more design work than a bicycle, sharks contain more design than amoebas, and even a short poem contains more design than a 'Keep Off the Grass' sign.

Perhaps it can be seen why we are more inclined to throw an empty drink can in the rubbish bin, than, say, an old bicycle wheel with a broken spoke. Each represents different levels of design work and thus perceived value. But beyond the philosophical point, if an automobile exhibits more design work than a bicycle, then it follows that a Boeing 777 exhibits more value than an automobile – which, of course, it does. So still keeping on this track, a bicycle with an integrated information system is worth more than one without. Daniel Dennett calls this the principle of 'accumulative design work', and we can apply Dennett's insights to the strategy of complex systems innovation.

One strong definition of 'design work' is the amount of work needed to achieve a novel proposition. That is, any innovation can be expressed as the amount of new design work above and beyond existing work. Clearly, cloning an existing product exhibits no design work, and therefore exhibits little new value. But blending two different existing concepts to form a new kind of contraption requires some level of design work. And when this happens, you climb a step or two up the maze of possibilities towards a higher value. But to truly blaze up the maze in leaps and bounds towards relative mountain peaks of value takes an enormous amount of novel design work. And that's the trick! Enterprises can achieve higher value by increasing the novelty in and of their design work. Therefore, greater design work equals novelty, which in turn equals higher value.

Synergy: The Nature of Collaborative Learning

Clearly, it can now be seen that any systems innovation, such as a radically new fast-food outfit or a virtual reality gymnasium, is the end result of a vast and diverse pool of skills, knowledge and experience combined in extraordinarily original ways. Briefly, a systems innovation is always the end result of a *synergy* amongst a team's ideas and work.

The term 'synergy' refers to an end result that is made up from many interacting elemental bits, which create a whole that is greater than those constituent members. The synergy is what gives us the greater whole. Synergy can, in fact, be found everywhere. The human mind is a result of synergy, for example. The physical brain is no more than a zillion buzzing atoms. But now interconnect those zillions of atoms in just the right way, and a whole mind emerges that is far, far greater than the constituent atoms. Amazing stuff.

Amazing or not, all innovation is in fact the result of synergy. That is, the output (the innovation) is a synergy way beyond the many component inputs (a team's ideas). The collaborative combination of skills, knowledge and experience can produce unexpected insights and solutions that do not exist in those individual parts. As a result, innovation synergy is not only probable, it is a major source of competitive advantage.

There are five fundamental synergistic processes at work that deliver inventions, and finally innovations, that result in a greater whole:

1. *Creative symbiosis*: When a team sees interconnections and integrates unrelated ideas, they produce an adaptation of those ideas. Further, on rare occasions, and under the right circumstances, teams can breed an entirely new concept through a very intense process of mental cross-fertilisation. Idea 'A' borrows some good features from idea 'B' to make idea 'C', for example. In genetic evolution, this process is called symbiosis, in technological innovation (idea evolution), I call this 'creative symbiosis'.

2. *Creative co-evolution*: When two ideas remain completely separate in the mind, yet at the same time affect each other's development, the two ideas may co-evolve, even though they do not connect: idea 'A' affects idea 'B'; idea 'B' affects idea 'A'. For example, when two people come from completely different walks of life, they carry two very different mind-sets of ideas. But, as soon as those two people come together in dialogue, both mind-sets of ideas begin to affect each other's development – they creatively co-evolve.

3. *Creative strange-loops*: This thinking dynamic allows teams to break rules and givens. A team's whole mind is very good at doing the equivalent of pulling a rabbit out of a hat. A team mind can nest idea 'A' in idea 'B', but also nest idea 'B' inside idea 'A' at the same time. A true higher performance team's whole mind works something like

this: it builds a tangled, multidimensional hierarchy of ideas that connect through a complex, convoluted network, that are nested inside more ideas, that are nested inside other ideas, that are nested inside themselves and the first idea – very complex and some would say strange stuff. Now picture a plate of spaghetti. Can you picture in your mind's eye that messy, convoluted web of pasta? Not so difficult to understand after all, and this is the kind of arrangement of ideas in your mind – it is multidimensional. It is in fact a clearer picture of the messy creative thinking dynamics in the mind. This is why we find it not too difficult to break rules or come up with original concepts. We see, evaluate and reconfigure perceived conditions and rules, and break beyond current ideas through these very complex thought processes.

4. *Creative accumulation*: More complex ideas emerge from a history of lesser, simpler ideas. We see this when a young apprentice, with a head full of fresh, newly formed, yet simpler notions of the job at hand, grows in sophistication and complexity as time goes by – storing more and more ideas and developing ever-more complex interconnections between those ideas. Many years later we see how that young mind matures with a wealth of accumulated ideas, delivering more advanced concepts for new products than s/he could manage as a young apprentice. Of course there is the exception, where we witness a young prodigy who can produce exceptional work. Mozart could compose wonderful musical melodies. But was this pure genius, or was this a learnt ability (creative accumulation)? Yes, he had a very able mind, his creative intellectual selection powers were brilliant in the case of musical pattern-making. But it was his accumulated idea set – his ecology of ideas – through his family and social background that had built his capacity to create great musical works at such a young age. His father was a violinist and chamber musician in the service of the Prince-Archbishop of Salzburg. His musical instruction began at the age of three. So his resultant ability to compose at the ripe old age of five was not merely down to his acute mind, but his very early 'creative accumulation of ideas' (of course there were other elements that contributed to his musical genius, such as charged emotion, passion and obsessive practice).

5. *Creative criticality*: Breakthroughs in concepts also come through a process of creative criticality. This is achieved once again through a process of accumulation of ideas, where a point of criticality is reached, which starts an avalanche of new, unforeseen ideas. This happens to creative people and teams all the time, where for some reason they just cannot think of a new concept, but after months,

sometimes years of thinking and accumulating ideas, all of a sudden the creative floodgates open, with more ideas than they can use. This has happened to me more times than I can recall. Neurologists have studied this creative thought activity going on in the mind, and have actually captured the dynamics of mental criticality on electromagnetic resonance scanning technology. The rate of change in arrangements of the neurological patterns and networks they see is phenomenal, and literally encompasses the whole brain system.

Together, these fundamental synergistic mental processes, either within a team or within an individual mind, are the mechanisms that give rise to new ideas beyond what is currently known. In short, synergy is all about learning, and it is through intense collaborative learning beyond what is current that complex systems innovation arises.

How Learning Reduces Risk and Uncertainty

Increasing the novelty/complexity of an innovation does indeed increase its value, but it also increases uncertainty, risk and chance. Collaborative learning leads to new and unexpected insights. It also leads to unexpected issues. That is, if innovation is more or less a non-deterministic endeavour, then unexpected blips and issues will emerge. In fact, the more complex a system is, the more capricious and unexpected the activity of innovation becomes.

Paradoxically, however, it is the very learning that reduces risk and uncertainty. The faster a team can gain an insight into a problem, the faster that problem heads towards a known certainty. But the kind of innovations needed today, the complex systems innovation described in Chapter 1, require learning beyond knowledge in vastly disparate fields and disciplines and the capacity to unite such learning into a seamless, coherent whole.

To affect rapid team learning, Peter Senge of MIT, as quoted in Rowan Gibson's *Rethinking the Future*, says:

> We have to develop a sense of connectedness, a sense of working together as part of a system, where each part of the system is affected by the other parts, where the whole is greater than the sum of its parts.

Thus learning together as a team affects such connectedness, such synergy, and as that happens, the further and faster we climb up the space of innovation possibilities towards higher value and original outcomes.

(NB: The main points of 'Understanding collaborative learning beyond knowledge' are outlined in Exercise 19 in Appendix A.)

Team Dialogue Development

Learning beyond knowledge drives innovation. Collaborative learning beyond knowledge drives systems innovation. Yet the activity of this kind of collective learning – the exploring, experimenting and developing of each other's knowledge and ideas in open and creative ways – is often unknown in many settings. And here lies the challenge. Systems innovation is a recipe for conflict. Everything from opposing ideals and mental models to basic primitive fight or flight responses can stop dead the dynamic combinational exploration of knowledge. Little wonder that it is an unknown quantity. However, we have no choice here; without such collective enquiry and discovery among disparate ideas, there is little chance that such (Q4) systems innovation will happen.

Fortunately, there is a rapidly growing body of application knowledge that can be utilised to open up and develop collaborative learning. This is the work of 'team dialogue development'.

The goal of team dialogue development is to enable individuals to think and therefore learn together as a collective. To do this, individuals must be able to distinguish between memory and real thinking. And not just in the mode of analysing problems or sharing knowledge, but a sharing of much deeper emotions and tacit notions that drive explicit opinions and assumptions within the group. Dialogue is as much an emotional experience and process, as it is cerebral.

The individual who has contributed most to the field of dialogue development in the modern day setting is the late David Bohm. Bohm began his professional life as a theoretical physicist, where his ideas rocked the foundations of the so-called 'Copenhagen interpretations of quantum physics' (instituted by Niels Bohr and Werner Heisenberg). But Bohm's interests and work stretched far beyond the boundaries of physics to embrace the arts, philosophy, psychology, religion and the future of society. Moreover, he was acutely curious about the nature of human interaction and communication:

> In dialogue a group of people can explore individual and collective presuppositions, ideas, beliefs, and feelings that subtly control their interactions ... It can reveal often puzzling patterns of incoherence that lead the group to avoid certain issues or, on the other hand, to insist, against all reason, on standing and defending opinions of particular issues ... What makes this situation so serious is that thought generally conceals this problem from our immediate awareness and succeeds in generating a sense that the way each of us interprets the world is the only sensible way in which it can be interpreted.

Bohm's belief was that there is a greater whole where true understanding and advance in man's endeavours occurs, that beyond the visible tangible world, there lies a deeper, implicit order of undivided wholeness. Bohm's main concern was that, as the world grows more complex, rather than the world coming together as one whole, there is a tendency for the world to become more fragmented. He was concerned that our world is infested with fragmented thinking. In fact, it is quite natural for people to apply their own particular meaning to a given situation, and by doing so begin to fragment the given reality into categories and distinctions within thought.

But we tend to adhere so slavishly to these divisions that we forget we fabricated them in the first place (see the wheel of reinforcement in Chapter 5). This fragmented thinking limits individuals within groups to quite narrow perceptions of reality. In turn, specialists in one field find it quite difficult to understand and talk to specialists in another field. Instead of reasoning together, people represent and guard their own speciality.

This observation can also be seen in small groups of people, where different mental models concoct a fragmented perspective upon critical issues, which in turn causes conflict. Bohm often said that most communication within a group of people is more like a ping pong match, where ideas are metaphorically batted back and forth, with the objective of the game to win or score a point oneself. Bohm believed that conversation should bring out the tacit thinking behind the explicit thoughts within a conversation.

In spite of the goal to pursue successful innovation, a team's efforts are often coloured with personal aspirations and the weight of opinion, all at the expense of creative collaboration towards a common goal.

Within an environment where high levels of dialogue are present, there is little need for formal, and indeed artificial and cumbersome plans and decision-making processes. Teams begin to act in unison, and don't need formal structures and schedules in order for everyone to know what they should be doing. Each team member simply understands what he or she has to do, in a competent and open way.

Supercool Dialogue

According to Bohm, what makes group situations so difficult and conflicting is that our individual and collective thoughts are invisible, and therefore hidden from our immediate awareness, thereby giving a sense that the way an individual thinks is the only and best way of thinking about a situation. That is, that our own ideas and beliefs are the most important and right. Beyond the fact that individual thinking is invisible, it is also a complicated process, coloured by our experiences, beliefs, ideas, fears and expectations (our mental models), all of which are bounded by our knowledge, general intelligence and culture. And when our thoughts are joined with those of our peers, the process of thinking become exponentially more complex, as we need to consider all these beliefs, expectations and so on in a complex web of interaction within the group.

Bohm made it clear that what is needed is a way to make our thinking more visible and tangible, so that individuals can understand each other's motives and the meanings behind their thinking. In other words, a way to slow down the process of thought in order to observe it while it is actually happening. The answer, he said, is much needed *dialogue*, a disciplined form of conversation within groups. Bohm compared this kind of dialogue to the physics of *superconductivity*, where, at extremely low temperatures, electrons flow without colliding into each other, experiencing virtually no resistance or loss of energy. In essence, at such supercooled temperatures, the individual particles begin to behave as one indivisible whole.

By comparison, particularly within politically entrenched issues, the heat of the conversation can reach boiling point, where people tend to become even more isolated in their thinking, and thus at cross-purposes with each other. Here, the old reflex brain takes the lead, as the fight or flight mode is in operation. However, dialogue is a way of cooling down a conversation within a team so that the team can think and learn as a unit.

Clearly, then, dialogue development is a centrally important mechanism within the building of whole teams and learning beyond knowledge. Bohm laid down some guidelines that promote and help to develop whole team dialogue, which I now build upon:

■ *Overcoming initial resistance and alienation.* When individuals come together, they bring a wide variety of differing mental models, which contain assumptions driven by tacit motivations and thinking. Three things must happen to overcome initial resistance:

1. A continuous programme is the linchpin. A continuous programme must be put into place, so that the stages and tools become an embedded part of the work practice and culture (see Chapter 11).

2. Acknowledgement that there will be initial difficulties.

3. Explicit willingness to explore the tacit structure of thought as a collective whole.

■ *Comfortable settings*: The quality of a dialogue development session depends significantly on the setting. After all, we are what we eat. If a team is put in a dank, dark room, with paint peeling off the walls, then you can only imagine what thoughts are going to emerge. The ideas we experience in the places we carry out sessions feed our thoughts and set the mood. Many experts in this kind of dialogue development recommend that a team sits in a circle facing each other, with no table to block out body gestures. If you are so inclined, beanbags are ideal, as people really do relax and open up. Better still, on occasion, on a sunny day go to the local park or meadow, with a few bottles of wine or whatever. Put some fun and harmony into it.

■ *Suspend assumptions*: This does not mean repressing personal thoughts, impulses and judgements, but presenting ideas, feelings and opinions for reflection and inquiry, in such a way that the whole team observes the deeper, more subtle meanings. The aim is to observe intently, without any preconceptions, the many divergent views that exist within diverse innovation teams; to let concepts, questions and ideas flow, to go down inventive and unusual thought paths towards original insights and conceptions. The outcome is often a collection of open-ended ideas and perspectives. Continued application and practice of suspended assumptions is important, as in time the innovation team begin to understand the power of suspending assumptions.

■ *Treat each other as peers, even friends*: Dialogue is essentially a conversation between equals, so boss/subordinate formalities must also be suspended. The aim is to develop an honest, friendly, even fun kind of atmosphere. This empowers team members to think and talk openly, and see private ideas and feelings in the light of the wider context. Only then are variances in world view held up for review. But you cannot coerce teams into this mode of thinking, teams have to want to move to this arrangement. I find the secret here is to get on and practise. Even if early trials fall short, in time, people learn intrinsically how to suspend assumptions and open the door for collective free thinking.

■ A *facilitator should hold context*: The facilitator's role is to coach the process and context, bringing in different points of view, encouraging open thinking and generally monitor the suspension of assumptions. The facilitator should think about: 'How can I improve my collective listening skills?' He or she should try to see the other person's viewpoint: 'Who is emotionally fragile, who's tough?' The observation of non-verbal language is a must. Don't criticise or make judgements; if you do, suspended assumptions will crash to the ground with a thud. Clarify where needed. Most of all, stop talking, start listening and facilitating.

■ *Starting and ending the session*: There are many ways to start a session, from asking open-ended questions, such as: 'What's the definition of a high performance team?' Another idea is to say 'I was thinking about such and such, what do you think?' Don't ask 'Does anybody have anything on their mind?', because this will lead down divisive paths. The key is to pick on relevant, burning issues which, if thought about collectively, could lead to brilliant solutions. As for ending the session, two hours is the maximum. Once they get going, dialogue sessions are taxing, to say the least. Just remind the team about the time as the end draws nears.

As awareness and experience of true dialogue develops, an understanding of a shared meaning and purpose evolves, where people find that they are neither confronting one another, nor simply interacting. Rather, there is an emergence of whole thoughts that are greater than the sum of the individuals in the team. There is no imposed consensus or attempt to avoid conflict. No single individual is able to achieve dominance, because even the issue of superiority and submission is aired.

Innovation teams find that they are in an ever-churning and learning pool of common ideas and activities. Within dialogue, a shared empathy emerges, which allows a level of creativity and insight not generally available to the individual or poorly functioning groups. As Bohm often asserted:

> beyond a critical point, lies an even more significant and subtle realm of creativity, intelligence and understanding that can be approached only by persisting in the process of inquiry and risk-taking re-entry into areas of potentially chaotic and frustrating uncertainty.

Undoubtedly your own experiences pay testimony that this is perhaps the most difficult change we face.

(NB: 'Team dialogue development' is outlined in Exercise 20 in Appendix A.)

Practice Games for Collaborative Learning

Another key to building whole team minds is to facilitate accelerated team experiences. The greater the pool of shared experiences, the greater the recall of positive (and negative) team outcomes. This is where playing (proto-games) can stimulate and step up the whole mind learning and creative experience (recall Chapter 2). Here are six exercises to speed up team mind-set development:

1. *Team narrative building*: The idea is for the group to write a meaningful story – a tragedy, comedy, whatever – spell-checked, punctuated, printed and finished in a binder, within 24 hours. The team must create a unique story, develop the concept, then each member must write a single chapter, at least one page in length. The rub: narrative alignment and continuity in each chapter requires intensive whole mind collaboration. Quickly members see how the collective whole can build complex, highly creative, in-depth narratives, in shorter cycles and in directions that would not have emerged in isolation. You'll find members physically crawling over each other, skipping lunch, staying late into the night, engaged in holistic creativity. This begins to build the team mind-set further. The whole team learning experience is real, tangible and accelerated breakthrough comprehension (see Exercise 21 in Appendix A).

2. *Role redeployment*: Working in immediate and continual proximity with other, sometimes unknown people, with vastly different backgrounds and skills, can be disorientating. For many people will not have had any close contact will such diverse disciplines before. For example, I consulted on a new platform multimedia project for one of the big publishing houses. The prototype, make or break, had to be ready within six months for review at a major Far Eastern exhibition. The ensemble of skills comprised a playwright, a crime writer, a psychologist, a systems analyst, three software programmers, two graphic designers and a book illustrator. They came together for the six months, full time, then went on their merry way. Few had any real understanding of each other's role, and on the first day you could sense those basic instincts mentioned above – not good for the timeliness and creativity of the project at all. The first week, before conceptualisation proper began, each member swapped their various roles to experience the glamorous life of the so-called other half. Each member's experience was exhilarating and dumbfounding. An experience that accelerated breakthrough understanding at the beginning of the project, rather than via accumulation throughout the real project (see Exercise 22 in Appendix A).

3. *Whole team problem solving*: These kind of games can only be resolved by the *whole* team. If any one or a few individuals limit information and/or knowledge sharing, it will stop the problem-solving process dead.

Picture puzzles are typical, good examples of whole problems. Break the problem (puzzle) up into a dozen or so clues (pieces), then spread them about the group, even hide a few clues, with other clues leading to those clues spread around the group. Throw in a few rules, such as you cannot talk to anyone if you are wearing a yellow hat, and you can only receive information if you are wearing a yellow hat. Remember, rules inhibit creativity and communication. Surprises abound here. These games can be applied in many different contexts and platforms, such as in-class games and outward bound courses (see Exercise 23 in Appendix A).

4. *The synergy game*: Take a poster picture, preferably one with lots of content (say a panoramic city view), and stick it on a wall in front of the group. Give each member an identical piece of card and ask them to write down a description of the picture in their own words. Give them five minutes to do this. Gather up the cards and shuffle them. Now read aloud each description in turn. What you'll probably receive is a diverse array of descriptions about the content and theme of the picture. Again, mental models are at play here. Each individual describes what she or he sees, guided by the distinct models of the world they hold. In the real world, this happens every day, and is the number one reason for the quite senseless conflicts we see between people. Now for part two of the game. On a single large piece of paper, ask the whole team to consider each member's thoughts and expressions about the picture. Ask them to interconnect each individual idea so that a team description of the picture emerges. Ask them to reserve judgement and listen to each comment and view (see dialogue development, above). The outcome is often quite astounding: an expansive, yet integrated description of the picture, a narration greater than the sum of the individual descriptions. The point is that individual views can be a source of synergistic creativity, if personal viewpoints and ideas are aired, and the whole team reviews and looks for connections between those unique insights (see Exercise 24 in Appendix A).

5. *Context perspectives*: This game is for groups that have spent some time together, where people have some level of shared mental models. The exercise is similar to the synergy game, but has a more tangible output (use whichever is appropriate). Copy a one-page piece of text from a book (preferably text with some abstruse insights). Split the group into smaller groups, give each subgroup a copy of the text, then ask each subgroup to think of an individual theme (for example computer programming, market learning, organisational theory, whatever's appropriate). Ask each subgroup to read the text

from the viewpoint of their theme, and write down what they learn. What usually happens is that each subgroup picks out quite unique insights and ideas from the very same sentences. The lesson is that, even though we may have shared mental models when we read from the same hymn sheet, our different context perspectives lead us to see and prioritise things differently. For example, I worked with a team made up of medical doctors, hospital administrators and systems analysts, who were involved in specifying the layout for a new teaching hospital in London. I gave them a piece of text on the self-organisation of ant colonies. What happened? The doctors gleaned insights into new ways of testing vaccines. The administrators saw new ways to organise bed rosters. The systems analysts saw that distributing computers throughout the hospital might be a more effective way to coordinate operations. We then brainstormed to gel these disparate insights together (see Exercise 25 in Appendix A).

6. *The egg game*: A well proven, simple, but effective tool for team building and evaluation. Present the team with a standard box of farm eggs. Ask them to design and make a protective packaging for one egg, which will withstand a drop from three metres onto a hard floor. Set a time of two hours and a modest budget. After the allotted time is up, the team submit their ideas and test the designs. Then evaluate the team's effort, looking for strengths and weaknesses, ranging from quality and quantity of suggestions, range of thinking, focus on results, budgetary management and, most important, team traits such as mutuality, trust, openness and so on (see Exercise 26 in Appendix A).

CHAPTER 7

Innovative Team Values

Our values, especially the ones we hold most dear,
are what make us who we are and how we act.
P.N. FRANCE

When is a team not a team? Too many corporate and/or public initiatives are wrapped up in the language of teams. After all, it is de rigueur to do things in teams – is it not? But just because executives use the language of teamwork, it does not mean that a true high performance team actually exists. Much of the corporate jargon I hear about teamwork, and many of the initiatives I witness, is little more than rhetoric.

For example, putting signs on walls that say something like 'Teamwork Wins', or 'Solos Don't Fly Around Here' is the same as putting up posters that say 'You must break the four-minute mile' or 'You must not have toothache'. The messages in the posters are superficial, mere symptoms of deeper issues. Teamwork and breaking the four-minute mile are the result of underlying issues that have to be in place first.

Force-feeding teamwork, like this, into an organisation can be the death knell for many an outfit. Demanding that 'We all must work together as a team', is simply delusional management. Rhetorical teams abound in the corporate world, as well as in spheres of government, education and social institutions. Leaders must know the difference between a pseudo-team and a true high performance innovative team.

The main message here is that an organisation can only build true high performance innovative teams if they have the requisite mechanisms and systems in place first. And there is no more powerful organisational mechanism for building teams than to develop the right kind of core values.

The Idea of Core Values

Values are another kind of mental model. They are a set of mental representations and ideas that guide our beliefs, inform and direct how we behave, the way we communicate, our expectations in life and, yes, even what and how we think. Because of all this, values are an intensely powerful influence on the development of innovative teams.

Values include issues like norms, such as protocols, customs and totems; and convictions such as a bias towards a set of principles or a philosophical doctrine. Values can be what we think is most important in life, such as freedom and equality. They can be outlooks, such as expectations, goals and viewpoints. They can be the words we use most frequently, that help us to express ourselves. Values help us to prioritise and balance things, such as work, family and friends. But most of all, at their most fundamental, the values we hold are what gives our life meaning, what is significant and of consequence in our existence.

Values and a Team's Meaning

Values underpin the essence of a team's meaning, the vital sum and substance that govern a team's behaviour.

A common meaning is a deeper level of shared consciousness. If everyone in a team sees and shares a single or similar meaning, the content of consciousness is essentially going to be the same. Whereas if there are different values and therefore meanings within a team, then the content of conversation is going to be quite different across the group. If teams can share a common meaning, then the team will be participating together unconsciously – and this is where and why the most extraordinary high performance innovative teams emerge, because the thinking is so connected: communication, expectation, outlook, beliefs and priorities and all the rest are set in some holistic team harmony.

So, to get to the root of this, what are the actual values expressed in the form of words (values are best described in simple nouns and adjectives) that the team uses to describe itself (or needs to describe itself) as a team? What are the assumptions and statements upon which the members take the greatest pride? Ask your team to pick the single most important word that describes the team, and that will be the meaning of the team. If they cannot agree upon a single word, the team will be limited in having a shared meaning. More-over, if, for example, the word is something like efficiency or order, then you can bet your last penny that the team is not an innovative team.

When it comes to innovation, the key is to find divergent words, as opposed to convergent words. Convergent words bring close order and tightness within a team and stamp out creativity and eventual innovation. On the other hand, divergent words project outwards, and therefore, by their very nature, are creative. Examples of convergent words are efficiency, functional, order, optimisation, equilibrium, certainty and so on. Divergent words are expressions such as fun, surprising, imagination, curious, holistic and so on. Once you have found a word that describes the team, everyone must come to know and understand the meaning of that word.

Values and a Team's Purpose

So, following on from this logic, if values set the meaning of a team, and govern that team's behaviour, a team's core values should also reflect what a team is attempting to achieve, what it is striving for and what the team's purpose and aims are. Clearly, in this case, a team's core values should reflect the needs of innovation. In fact, values development is as much a strategic management issue as it is a culture-building issue.

Take the Centre for Business Innovation (CBI) at Cap Gemini Ernst & Young. It has a clear value set that acutely reflects its operational goals: 'explore the new, recombine, ship quality, make a difference and enjoy the experience.' The CBI's values are designed to foster a culture of innovation, creating new services and businesses, providing new value for its clients, communicating to a broad audience around the world. It collaborates with a diverse network of leading thinkers, synthesising what it learns to catalyse change in the business world. The CBI's vision of an increasingly interconnected economy drives its research and consulting agenda. The CBI states:

> There's no doubt that connections and ways of connecting have proliferated wildly among firms, amongst people, amongst computers, and more. In a highly interconnected world, things don't simply happen faster. Different things happen. Industries behave in non-classical ways. Firms take on different structures. Different types of assets drive competitiveness. All this calls for new theories of management and new tools for management.

Innovation is the CBI's bread-and-butter work, applying breakthrough thinking and tools in the connected economy.

Values as a Management Control Mechanism

A team ethic is a more potent governing mechanism than any rule or policy. Individual and collective behaviour governed by a system of core values will outweigh any rule, such as 'clocking-in time is 7 a.m. sharp'. After all, rules and procedures, made up by some committee, are wholly artificial and often way out of context, given that innovation always gives up unique, sometimes truly unusual circumstances. Imagine telling a team to work to a set of governing rules and then expecting it to solve a problem under such capricious conditions. Impossible, I say.

Values shape behaviour beyond any rule while at the same time giving freedom to the individual to go about his or her job in a way that best suits the problem at hand and the individual or team involved. Try doing that with a set of top-down rules.

Conflicting Values and Teams

Again, what we select and see as important is strongly influenced by the values we hold most dear. In fact, in family relationships, the values held can be the single most important influence on how family members get along and, in the end, stay together. It is the same for innovative teams.

Take, for example, an individual who puts a higher price on efficiency and control, and then put him or her to work with someone who really relishes creativity and openness. What would be the consequence of such a marriage? Bedlam, I would expect. The values that drive efficiency and creativity are totally different, to the point where they simply clash with each other.

Far too many organisations are beset with conflicting, sometimes hostile values that all but destroy the very kind of organisation they are attempting to build. And since many management teams don't know what to do about instigating a set of innovative team values, there is little attempt to rectify the situation. But until executives do rectify this problem, a truly innovative team will not emerge.

In large systems innovation teams, a whole village of values can emerge. That is, a whole range of ideas and meanings can be exhibited that go to make up an entire culture. Again, this can give multiple conflicting views and perspectives.

The Seven Most Important Values an Innovation Team Holds

Innovative teams must have values that support both the unique nature of innovation (see Chapter 1) and the nurturing of innovation. And, as we have explored, innovation means uncertainty, risk and chance, which means that teams are going to trip up from time to time. And that means instigating and aligning values that promote creativity and the scope for risk taking. It also means instigating values that set a moral compass in times of uncertainty.

The values listed below are derived from my experience in working in or leading and building teams that design and create new products and services. They are not written in stone, neither are they a universal algorithm that will make the sun shine on your teams forever and a day. They are basic values that bring about the behaviours and outlook necessary for innovation.

1. *Integrity*: Is it possible to have an open, trusting relationship with someone or some group that lacks integrity? The odds are against it. How can anyone expect to connect and bond with people with little moral fibre, or if the culture is one of cynical character assassination, out-and-out personal sabotage? If the environment is hostile and fearful, what chance is there of teamwork or innovation? If information is hidden and kept back for self-gain, knowledge sharing is limited, ideas are sparse, and minds are closed, what chance is there of successful risk taking?

   Risk is part and parcel of innovation. Without risk taking, there is little chance that teams will be pushing the limits of what is possible. And all true innovation lies just beyond the boundaries of what was thought possible. However, without integrity, there can be no trust, and without trust, relationships will not bond. And if there are too few caring relationships present, there will be little support in failure. And believe me, failure within innovation teams is a marked trait, because, by definition, taking risks and pushing the envelope will mean that a failure of one degree or another will occur. Open, trusting, caring relationships are *the* key requisite to risk taking, and can only develop if integrity is instituted first and foremost above any other value.

   Integrity, however, is more than honesty, more than the capacity for the truth in difficult, politically uncertain times, even more than authenticity itself. When I listen to leaders from different walks of life, there is a common theme. They talk about integrity as an unbroken whole, of high ethical standing and principles that interlock and support each other. And it is from such high morality that all other virtues flow. Quite simply, trust and openness just cannot and will not flourish without such a virtue. And where there is no trust, there will be relatively little innovation.

2. *Trust*: Strictly speaking, trust begins with the expectations we have of each other. If we expect a person (a colleague, a friend, a relative) to behave in a positive (or negative) way, and they do, consistently, then trust will begin (or not begin) to emerge. So, following this logic, our expectations are reinforced by the predictability of that individual's behaviour. If one believes that a colleague will behave with integrity, then trust will indeed be strengthened. At its deepest, most trust comes about through the fight or flight response. If people feel secure around another person, because they feel they can predict such positive behaviours, then their expectations of a safe, reliable and secure behaviour will be embedded within the working relationship with that individual.

    And what is the most effective way to gain all this? Once again, it comes through true team collaboration. Collaborative teams are, after all, mutually supportive and reinforce the positive behaviours that the team needs to achieve its purpose and aims. Trust building is all practical, common-sense stuff.

3. *Forgiveness*: I am not talking about a theological doctrine here, but a common-sense, daily necessity within innovation. Again, you have to have a forgiving climate, otherwise people will stop pushing the envelope. Exoneration is a must, as a forgiving culture stimulates learning. It does not view basic market blunders or explosions in the laboratory as erroneous or incompetent acts. It views them as a learning experience.

    I vividly recall the media debating the *failure* of the Philips' experimental catamaran yacht – the world's largest ocean-racing catamaran, designed to set a new round-the-world speed record. Whilst on its first sea trials off the southwest of England, its port bow broke up. I remember the strain on the crew's and design team's faces as they read the story. But the media were, as so often, wrong. It was not a complete disaster, as the journalists reported. Philips' effort was an experiment, an extreme innovation that was pushing beyond the boundaries that anyone had gone before. For a start, the size of the vessel was unprecedented, 36.5 metres long, the size of a Wimbledon tennis court. The revolutionary structure was made of an untested carbon-fibre composite. So you could bet your shirt on it that something, somewhere was going to break or blow up. The point is that the negative exposure by the media did not help one bit. Of course, this can spur people on, but that misses the point. If innovative teams are to continue to push the envelope, there must be an air of compassion if their attempts fall short. If not, once again, teams will begin to limit

their risk taking and, in turn, amazing innovations such as the Philips'
catamaran would never make it beyond sea trials.

4. *Mutuality*: Mutuality is a deeply shared feeling of empathy towards
common interests and aims. At its most profound, it can lead to the
'great minds think alike' syndrome, where teams of people begin to see
and think in similar ways. Close friends sometimes experience it, loving
couples often have it. It is quite rare, but fortunately, not too rare. And
when it is present within a team, there seems to be a sixth sense and
collective knowledge of what is right and important for the collective.

   Mutuality brings with it a mutual respect too. I have even heard two
people talking about each other to a third person, saying that he/she
cannot believe that he/she is working with such a great guy. That is
mutualism at its best. Further, mutuality in times of crisis or when
things aren't going so well can mean the difference between breakthrough and triumph or breakdown and calamity.

   However, mutuality is not so easy to achieve. For example,
ingrained individualism is rife in western culture. Particularly in the
USA, the myth of the lone pioneer is what distinguishes latter-day
North American culture from many of the mutuality-based cultures
found in the Far East. This inherent individualism limits individuals,
with their solo acts, from investing their future in the collective – a
collective whose potential is far greater than the sum of the
parts – synergy again.

   Mutuality cannot be forced, it has to be grown and nurtured, developed over time through team learning experiences. The values of
integrity and trust are reinforced here. But mutuality grows as the team
grows towards a high performance team.

5. *Freedom*: At first, this value might appear to be in conflict with teamwork. But it is not only compatible, it is, I think, essential. It works on
two levels. Firstly, the freedom to do things in ways that the team and/or
individual thinks best at any given moment; and second, the freedom to
act as part of a team or as an individual, as and when required. The first
is about the capacity for creativity, the second is about the concept of
team autonomy (see Chapter 4).

   Freedom to do what is best is fundamental for innovation, because –
as we have seen – innovation is not a steady-state linear process. It is
always full of the capricious and surprising. Events rarely pan out
as expected, and such chaotic activity always requires high levels
of creativity to solve such complex problems. Many tasks and
outcomes will be the result of highly interactive, interdisciplinary work,

while many of the detailed tasks will be the result of highly focused, highly specialist, individual skills and actions. So freedom is a truly important value.

6. *Respect for the individual*: Such a value might seem to contradict the team ethic, but paradoxically it is important to respect individual views and beliefs, if teams are to perform at high levels. Respect begins, of course, with regard for individual needs and expectations, but it is much more than that. It means valuing what may seem like alien ideas and norms, as innovation is saturated with unusual and unique concepts and norms. After all, it would not be innovation if it did not contain such divergent ideas. Respect for the individual is not just about a human belief, it is about respect for the unique, the outstanding, the uncommon. Innovation requires such a disposition.

7. *Playfulness*: Sounds too frivolous for serious innovation? Well, the most productive, most innovative teams I know are playful teams (and I have known hundreds, across dozens of industries). The teams I am thinking of are full of eminent engineers, marketers and innovators, full of double-firsts in computer science, engineering, the arts and philosophy from Oxbridge, Stanford, Harvard and MIT.

My best example and memory of this is the time I worked with Open Computer Security Ltd. The team were out in the back car park practising for a pogo competition. Geoff Snowman was a 6ft 6in, 22 stone man with a double first from Cambridge in computer science and philosphy, Vince Gallo was the innovator of the personal identification number (PIN) for cashpoint machines. There were others present of equal status. I recall the maintenance manager appearing on the fire escape overlooking the car park. His face was a picture. We probably all looked like mad men on LSD. Well, this team produced a stream of products on the cutting edge of computer science. So how are pogo competitions, judo classes at lunchtime, bowling in the afternoon and in-house lectures on art, poetry and so on the stuff of effective innovation?

Centrally, play is an unstructured, stress-free way to test, practise and learn in new fields, without destroying old success patterns. It's about creating new ideas in neutral and interesting ways, where routine falls short. Tom Peters says that play causes unusual, wacky neurones in the brain to fire up, great for creativity and connecting unusual ideas across conceptual borders. At its most abstract, play is about tinkering with our minds, to open new ways of thinking and looking at the world. Play *is* creativity. When at play, we make space for our imagination to roam over notions we would not readily have time or room for. It is a chance to open up the unexplained, a chance to elucidate the arcane. Play can lead to extraordinarily original thoughts and ideas, if we actively value merriment as a normal part of work.

(NB: 'Understanding team values' is outlined in Exercise 27 in Appendix A.)

Developing and Reinforcing Innovative Team Values

I think the most successful teams are ones that identify, embrace and act with the core values of innovative teams. But the question remains, how do you embed such core values within an organisational culture? Here are five ways:

1. *Icons*: Anthropologists tell us that icons are the single most significant factor in values development. Think of a Hollywood superstar, such as Brad Pitt, and how he can, in an instant, start a new hairstyle craze. But more, such icons actually shape people's behaviour as well, what they strive for in life, what they see as important. And it is no different in the corporate or public world either. Leaders who behave in a particular way deeply influence their people's behaviour as well.

   The key here is to promote people who actually embody and act out the innovative team values discussed above. The more people there are at the top of an organisation who reflect such values, the more innovative and team oriented an organisation is going to be.

2. *Stories*: What makes icons such a powerful influence on organisational values development is the stories they convey. Watts Wacker and Jim Taylor, the innovative thought leaders, tell an interesting anecdote in their book *The Visionaries Handbook*, which succinctly describes the power of stories as a way of changing an organisational culture:

   > Lou Gerstner deserves credit for many things at IBM, not least of which is raising the company's share price eightfold, adjusted for splits, in his first six years as Big Blue's CEO. But maybe what Gerstner most deserves credit for is making the dour old mother ship of the computer age a fun place to work.
   >
   > The story got told around New York and elsewhere that shortly after Gerstner took over as IBM Chief in April 1993 he decided he wanted to meet as many employees as possible so that he could ask why everybody up and down the line was so pissed off. To that end, Gerstner had his people schedule a meeting with all the employees at IBM's data-acquisition and storage-device facility in San Jose, California. Shortly after the corporate jet

took off, headed for the San Jose get-together, Gerstner summoned the stewardess and asked for a martini.

'Oh, Mr. Gerstner,' she replied, 'we never serve alcohol on IBM aircraft!'

'Fine,' Gerstner is said to have replied, 'land the plane at the next available site and have me delivered a bottle of gin and another of dry vermouth.'

'But it's against the policy of the company,' the stewardess persisted. 'We don't do that.'

'Read my lips,' the new CEO told her: 'Land. Now. And. Have. Them. Deliver. Olives. Too.'

Was the story true? Watts and Jim have no idea, but say that the story, and all the values it entails, swept through IBM like a hurricane, and the behaviour change it instilled is thought to be key to IBM's new-found lust for innovation.

3. *Rituals*: Another way to reinforce the stories that icons bring is to embed them in rituals. Rituals connect people between daily events and something bigger, something more meaningful. Rituals come in many guises, from reward ceremonies to status symbols to competitions to company outings. Toyota, for example, holds competitions every year to work the imagination, one of them being 'The Idea Olympics', an exhibition of automobile designs ranging from the absurd to the downright crazy. The object is not to conceive feasible concepts, but to connect people to something bigger, more meaningful. The Idea Olympics is a ritual that brings Toyota people together from across the world, and connects them in a way that no other corporate retreat has ever achieved.

4. *Reward systems*: A very powerful way to reinforce innovative values is to honour the people who act them out. Anthropologists again tell us that whatever is held in high regard is often practised. Reward is simply a behaviour shaper. Reward for innovation, and that is the result you will probably obtain. However, I've found that most organisations build compensation systems entirely back to front in terms of building the values necessary for innovation (especially when it comes to complex innovation). Here, the understanding held by executives is that money and promotion are the keys to values development – a misinterpretation of the first order. In reality, people's behaviour and resultant actions are much more direct. People, we all know, are fickle creatures, and therefore not sustainably influenced by

longer term incentives, such as money. Yes, a pay increase will induce a new behaviour, but it won't last for long. What people need most is to be appreciated, given attention and feel involved in what they are doing. And they need to feel this now, without delay. The essentials are to: *appreciate* through immediate recognition via tangible rewards; *involve* with full ownership of outcomes; and give *attention* by simply listening to and supporting their wishes, concerns and accomplishments. Do this and you'll set up a powerful behaviour change system.

5. *Physical environment*: Image and layout of the physical working environment are just as important as function when it comes to values development. Working conditions give a clear message about the image the organisation is trying to achieve, and what is valued most. I have consulted in firms that have an exceptional environment for their executives and a bland, dead environment for the average worker. Again, values are acutely reflected in how you act, not just what you say. The physical environment reflects the key values you want to make happen.

For example, Francis Bouygues, the founder of Bouygues, one of the largest construction companies in the world, has built what he calls the 'challenger culture'. He believes that to win, organisations continually need to behave like a challenger. He is also adamant that people literally feed off the values of the company, it sets the stage for a particular behaviour. His remarkable head office in Versicles, France is not only designed as a functional office, but as a physical statement in support of the culture. The building is called 'Challenger' and looks nothing short of a palace fit for a king. When you walk into the building, you get a feeling of invincibility, and I can tell you the Bouygues' people feel that way too. Working for an organisation that gives an air of 'we are the best, most innovative, sexy, crazy, bold, dynamic (whatever's important)' tends to stimulate a sense of pride and confidence and in turn supports a level of risk taking. Does your physical environment evoke a challenging culture, not just to challenge the status quo, or the market ecology, but to constantly challenge your own mind-set? Can you constantly challenge and out-innovate yourself? Physical environment accounts for a lot here.

(NB: 'Innovative team values development' is outlined in Exercise 28 in Appendix A.)

A High Performance Innovation Culture

Why is it that in the world of classical music, it is acceptable for both the individual and the orchestra to strive to be the most superlative, the most accomplished they can be? Why is it in the world of athletics, individuals who break a world record are then celebrated as heroes? Why in the world of the arts do actors struggle to get to the top of their profession? Why, you may ask?

But why in the business world, if someone or some group strives to be the very best, are they all too often seen as some kind of upstart or troublemaker? Why is there so much mediocrity in the public sector? Why, if anyone comes up with an innovative idea, is it often sat on by the bureaucrat?

The answer, of course, is a cultural one. The value systems, particularly within governance and the corporation, are all too often set by indifference. Norms and protocols do not call for people to be the very best they can be. Of course, this is not always the case. There are businesses and public sector teams that have striven and have become the very best they can be. However, in the main, most teams are listless and about as bland as bean curd.

The point I am making is that if a team wants to become a high performance innovative team, then it has to endeavour to become the very finest it can be. Again, values are key here. What is important to an organization, and what its aims are, is underpinned by its values system. So, the question remains, what values need to be put into place to achieve the highest performance? What are the actions and stories that the icons must do and tell for a team to become the very best it can be? The answer is simple: put into place whatever you think is most appropriate to achieve that end. Values design and development is a creative process in itself.

However, alongside building the right kind of values system, is the setting of goals. Again, like values, the setting of high performance goals is integral to achieving high performance within innovation. This I will now address in the following chapter.

CHAPTER 8

The Need for High Performance Goals and Metrics

What gets measured gets done.
TOM PETERS

High performance teams and successful innovation are often the product of a virtuous circle. That is, successful innovation can be the result of high performance teamwork, and high performance teamwork can be the result of successful innovation. And one of the most significant contributions to achieving such a fortifying loop is in the design and measurement of high performance goals.

Before I begin to outline the design and measurement of high performance goals, I would like to briefly discuss the idea of performance as an issue in its own right.

The Idea of High Performance

Performance, in my experience, is rather misunderstood and all too often ignored within innovation. And that is unfortunate, because if one can grasp the basic concepts of performance, then it is quite possible to have a clear picture and acute control of any process or activity you care to mention, whether in the business world or the public domain at large.

Performance, in general terms, is about setting and meeting expectations and aspirations. High performance, in turn, is about setting out to define and achieve the very best one can accomplish under the given circumstances. Specifically, within the context of the business world, high performance is about competitive advantage. That is, setting out to define the most significant factors that give rise to advantages over and above the competition, and then, in turn, attempting to realise those factors.

On paper, this all sounds very crisp and clear. But actually attempting to define and accomplish such ends is not such an easy task. The secret to conquering this arduous task begins with setting the right performance goals and metrics.

The Need for SMART High Performance Goals

In the case of innovative teams, high performance is obtained by identifying a singular collective output (the innovation), which in turn is defined by a set of tangible targets, with directly associated performance metrics (see below). But tangibility is nearly always a contentious issue within goal design. Jon Katzenbach and Doug Smith, for example, in their book *The Wisdom of Teams*, say that many managers often set goals that are in fact intangible in terms of any meaningful outcome:

> As a result, people are unclear about how their work connects to the work of others and how it makes a difference to the whole enterprise. Unless and until people understand the performance goals that matter, organisations will fall short of meeting the aspirations of their leaders. This is critical for performance, which is largely dependent upon clear, compelling outcome-based goals – particularly when such goals distinguish between individual tasks and the collective work products that determine real team performance.

So, to begin with, high performance goals need to tangibly and objectively reflect the kind of performance required to achieve successful innovation.

But there is more to this than meets the eye. Not only do goals have to be tangible and objective, they also need to be meaningful, attainable, focused on end results and timely. In fact, there is a useful mnemonic that can be applied to goal design – SMART: Specific, Meaningful, Attainable, Results-oriented and Time-based:

■ *Specific*: The goal needs to be clear cut, pertaining to a specific outcome of an event or task.

■ *Meaningful*: It needs to be directly related to the overall aspiration of the project at hand.

- *Attainable*: Indeed, if the goal is unobtainable, then what is the point of setting that goal in the first place?

- *Results-oriented*: Outcome-oriented is key. If the goal does not focus on an end result – what you want to achieve at the end of the day – the goal will not be effective.

- *Time-based*: If an end date is not specified, then how will the team know when to complete the task?

Examples of such SMART goals could include: 'Technically qualify the new X-BOX platform to specification ISO:8000, by June 10, 2005', or 'All new customer orders received before 12 p.m. to be shipped the next day by 4 p.m.' Both of these goals express the SMART philosophy.

Attainable Stretch Goals

But what are the benchmarks to guide the limits to the setting of such goals? How far should one go in goal setting? Well, you know the proverb: put a 6ft tall man who cannot swim in a pool of water 7ft deep, and what happens? He probably drowns. Put a 6ft man who cannot swim in a pool of water 6ft 4ins deep, and what might happen? He somehow scrambles to the pool side. Of course, even if you do not know the maxim, you have no doubt worked out that the analogy holds in the setting of team performance goals as well. The lesson is that goals should always stretch a team's abilities, not pull them apart. As teams progress up the performance curve (see Chapter 11), more challenging goals may be set.

Integrated Systems Goals

Clearly, for a (Q4) systems innovation to be reliable and fully integrated, goals will not only have to be set in parallel, but as a project advances, these parallel goals will have to converge into integrated goals. That is, goals that integrate diverse, disciplined tasks and outcomes.

Firstly, in a durable product development project, such as a mobile phone or a digital TV, the various subsystems have to be brought together as a working whole. Therefore, objectives must reflect this integration, so cross-discipline goals need to be defined and quantified. Conflicts and compromise will arise here. Use the difference as inspiration and get different perspectives to resolve these. But more importantly, a synergy of goals that produces a meta-system of objectives is far superior to each stand-alone goal. An example here is mechatronic systems. Mechatronics is the technical discipline of intelligent integration of software, electronics and mechanical control systems (for example a robot arm) – the result of setting a goal that is complementary and synergetic to achieve a much better end product. Secondly, integrated goals enable teams to collaborate and learn together more effectively. The very action of setting integrated goals brings people together in all sorts of creative and productive ways.

Why Set Metrics?

On the surface it is about quantification. Obviously, metrics, in general, are needed to keep track of a programme's progress and eventual outcome. Quantifying performance opens up a window to a host of issues that you would perhaps be unaware of without such a view. Metrics can be used as a yardstick to tell how a programme is measuring up to expectations. They can also act as a weather vane for the direction of the project, that is, whether the project is actually making progress on schedule or otherwise.

At a more fundamental level, however, performance measurement has six main roles to play within the field of building high performance innovative teams:

1. *Objectivity*: First and foremost, metrics provide objectivity in terms of a desired performance. After all, if you know what exact performance you want, then you will have a concrete baseline on which to make joint decisions. And you know the old saying, don't you? You have to shoot the designer to get anything out on time. Well not if you have objective measures. Once a performance goal has been met, the designer can move on without having to put his life on the line.

2. *Behaviour shaper*: Metrics are yet another powerful behaviour shaper (see values development in Chapter 7). By attaching a metric to a performance goal, it informs of the kind of behaviour needed to achieve that goal. A metric that focuses on efficiency, for example, will signal for a specific kind of behaviour, such as a 'right first time' mind-set. Alternatively, a metric that focuses on creativity signals for a 'learn every time' mind-set (more on this below). However, and this is important, performance goals and metrics can turn out to be a double-edged sword. Metrics can bring about behaviours and changes that

result in unintended consequences. So the design of metrics must be thought about and then tested very carefully. See the principal characteristics of effective performance metrics below.

3. *Communication vehicle*: From an administration point of view, whether it be the executive board, or within the team itself, metrics provide an impartial communication vehicle and language on how a specific project is doing, particularly when new issues or problems arise. Performance measurements can be put up on a highly visible wall, or an intranet, for real-time monitoring.

4. *Feedback for self-correction*: Such objective measures provide a mechanism for self-organisation and correction of actions in the hubbub of daily activities. Remember, innovation of even the most simple kind is a complex operation. So turbulence will occur. And, as we have already begun to explore, self-organising teams are by far the best organisation for such chaos.

5. *Focus of attention*: They also signal for what is most important, the mission critical issues that must be fulfilled for the project to be completed on time, to budget and specification. Here, metrics help to prioritise, and indeed reprioritise, in real time. Likewise, metrics tell us what not to focus on, and that is significant as well.

6. *Motivation*: Metrics also motivate. Again they indicate how much effort is needed to meet a target. Little more gets people going than seeing objective evidence that a programme is behind schedule.

Principal Characteristics of Effective Performance Metrics

So what are the primary characteristics of suitable key performance metrics? What does the anatomy of an effective metric look like? The answer is not so easy, yet still attainable.

The key challenge, here, is to design metrics that actually achieve what is intended. That is, the result obtained from the metric is what was wanted in the first place.

Take a functional performance such as quality, for example. Now suppose that quality is the key performance goal, and you designed a set of metrics to monitor that goal. Obviously, it would focus attention on that goal, and the necessary behaviours, feedback, motivation and communication would also centre on that goal. Yet quality is only one of a number of elements that are necessary for innovation. There are other goals that must be met to achieve successful innovation. The point is that performance goals and associated metrics must be put into an overall context of total success, not merely an isolated functional performance. There must be a balance of focus on all the consequential factors that give rise to successful innovation.

But what are the key characteristics of metric design that give total success, so that behaviour, effort, motivation and so on are focused in just the right way? There are three distinguishing characteristics:

1. *Effectivity*: The metric gives objective data and facts that describe what is important to the outcome of a goal. At the end of the day, what is it that you want to achieve?

2. *Integrity*: Metrics must focus on the set of goals that give total success, not merely isolated and disparate factors (such as quality of service). Overlook one particular metric and the total outcome may be skewed away from success.

3. *Simplicity*: The best kind of metrics are simple in their design. They are highly condensed expressions of the fundamentals of a goal. This enables them to be easily understood, and also allows for efficient collection, collation and dissemination of the data.

Targeting: What to Measure

What successful innovation is and what makes it happen are two central issues that go a long way to define what goals and associated metrics are needed. Of course, what makes successful innovation happen is quite different from situation to situation. However, there are a handful of factors that underlie all successful innovation. These factors occur at three different levels: strategic precept performance, functional performance and behavioural/operational performance:

1. *Strategic precept performance*: At the highest level, a successful innovation needs to meet the three basic strategic precepts described in Chapter 1. First, an innovation must exceed the customer's unsatisfied, unarticulated and/or emerging needs and expectations, second, it must create a new market space, and third, it must provide a superior value return. The kind of metrics associated with such strategic precepts are all relative measures, and are the easiest to design (see below for the design of key performance indicators. Also see Appendix E for the Team Strategic Output Performance Questionnaire).

2. *Functional performance*: There are four main kinds of functional performance metrics within any corporate innovation project: *technical, market, financial* and *process*. The actual focus of each kind of functional performance is wholly project dependent. A typical technical functional goal might include a product reliability measure, such as mean time to failure. A market measure might include a customer satisfaction index. A financial measure might include total return on equity employed in a project. A process measure might include throughput over time. In the public sector, there are other functional issues to consider besides these: social acceptability, health and safety, environmental and so on.

3. *Behavioural and operational performance*: To realise such strategic and functional performance, the underlying behavioural and operational performance of an innovative team must be in place first. And this is where much of the metric design work must lie. Again, the seven Cs, first outlined in Chapter 2, are key here:

   1. *Collaborative*: Without learning collectively and pushing the boundary of knowledge and ideas, innovation will not occur.

   2. *Consolidated*: This is a team's combined outlook and expectations. This really all boils down to the values a team holds. Without such mutuality, individuals will not function as a team.

   3. *Committed*: The ability of teams to take the project in any direction at the drop of a hat is paramount to the success of an innovation project. Without commitment to one another, this cannot happen.

   4. *Competent*: Of course, without some level of competence related to intended outcomes, a team could not begin to produce and perform.

   5. *Complementary*: This is the capacity to bring together a wide variety of skills, know-how and talent that complement each other in the execution of tasks and the pursuit of goals.

   6. *Confident*: A high performance team has a positive can-do attitude. Furthermore, extraordinarily high performance teams have an untethered tenacity.

   7. *Camaraderie*: *Esprit de corps* is as important as all the other capacities. Without that sense of fraternity and empathy towards each other, mutual support and commitment will never arise, and, in turn, team performance will drop.

Without each of the seven Cs being in place first, none of the strategic precepts or functional performance goals will be realised.

The Basic Design of Key Performance Metrics

The basic design of key performance metrics has a central role to play here. By identifying what performance is required and appropriately focusing key performance metrics on either creativity or results, it is possible to regulate complex systems innovation teams to highly productive and high performance end results.

There are three general types of key performance metrics that can applied to each component level, namely:

1. *Attributes*: These are black and white, objective measurements. They apply to a condition being in only one of two possible states, either in or out, go or no go! For example, setting a date for the launch of a new product. A day late is a day late.

2. *Variable*: A band of limits is set, to which a variable can be in any one of a number of states within those limits. Variable measures can be applied in ambiguous situations. For instance, can the cleanliness of a restaurant be measured? On a scale of 1 to 10 (the variables), how clean was the last restaurant you went into? How comfortable was the last hotel you stayed at – excellent, good, average, poor or terrible? These are examples of variable scales being used in ambiguous situations. Carefully thought-out variable measures can be a very powerful way of quantifying subjective issues, such as cleanliness and comfort.

3. *Factors*: These are ratios, rates, indices and percentages of a unit of measure. For instance, the downtime as a percentage of total daily operating time for a particular machine, or the rate of customer throughput for a particular service in a given hour.

Where to Measure: Divergent Creativity or Convergent Results?

For innovation, there always has been and always will be a contest between the nature of creativity (the seeds of innovation) and the nature of results (the outcome of innovation). This is chiefly because, by its very nature, creativity is a divergent process, while on the other hand, achieving intended results is a highly convergent activity. But how does this work?

The very notion of creativity is the new and the unique. If a system shows creative properties, it is exploring novel innovation design-spaces, and therefore always unfolding and learning in unpredictable ways. On the other hand, the very premise of achieving a result means that a system has high levels of order and optimisation. It says that if a system is producing efficient outputs, the system has found the best possible way of doing things, but once it does this, the system is not doing anything new, it has stopped learning and begins to freeze.

Clearly, then, efficient results and open creativity are opposites (in fact, we can now see why it is so difficult to optimise for efficient results while adapting to new opportunities), but as these opposites play against each other, battling for dominance, you get innovation.

When to Focus Metrics on Creativity or Results?

Creativity is a divergent process and causes perturbations within a team, thereby making sure that the team is always exploring novel innovation spaces. In exact terms, if you want to build a creative culture, develop a novel strategy or form a highly adaptable organisation, you need to design and focus performance measures on creative issues. For example, focusing on issues such as learning creative-thinking techniques increases the gap between expectation and outcome.

Achieving a result is a convergent process and therefore focuses a team on key objectives. If the mandate is to have projects completed on time, to specification, to budget, performance metrics need to focus on end results. The end result is unconcerned with causality. By focusing on end results – a single variable – you regulate the whole team's efforts. Each team member adapts to the needs of the other members, in line with that single objective. By focusing on results, you will continuously calibrate the direction of the project team in real time. For example, by focusing on a single end date or customer expectation, the team works and adapts to that single end date or customer expectation.

The secret of innovative team performance measurement is in the dynamic balance of opposites. Focus on end results, and an organisation will eventually become a lean, mean, R&D machine; but won't be doing anything spectacularly innovative. Focus on upstream causes, and the organisation eventually becomes a maze of creativity; but won't be getting much to market on time, if at all. But focus on the right *balance* of cause and effect, the right balance of creativity and results, and a cascade of innovation may emerge.

(NB: The main points of designing high performance goals and metrics are outlined in Exercise 29 in Appendix A.)

CHAPTER 9

Organising Innovative Teams

*Dynamic complex order can spontaneously
emerge for free.*
S. KAUFFMAN

As we have already seen, complexity in innovation is up – way up. And this kind of complexity creates an ever-higher mountain for organisations – both commercial and public institutions – to climb in delivering ever-more sophisticated technologies, processes, policies and end products and services; and, in turn, those markets, industries and communities in which they are to be used and managed. This is known as the 'wall of complexity'.

Airbus and Intel, for example, are working with their noses flat against this wall in complexity. Airbus's A320 double-decker passenger airliner took them to the limits of current technological complexity. In the inner-space direction, Intel's X chip is again on the edge of complexity. The Japanese Council for Science and Technology has for some time now been deeply concerned about the level of technological and market complexity that corporations and research institutes now face. Molecular chemists and their retroviral pharmaceuticals, software hackers and the code length, telecom engineers and their connection models, corporate CEOs and their strategies all join this pack. As whole fields of technological and market life-cycles collapse, and complexity increases, the wall of complexity is going to destroy any chance of sustainable value creation. This is a monumental problem for businesses and society at large.

The point here? Creating and sustaining value through innovation means successfully managing this increasing complexity in terms of (a) new and diverse core technologies, new products and services; (b) competition and collaboration in increasingly turbulent social, economic and market systems; (c), in a wider context, innovating reliable and ethical organisational structures to facilitate such gargantuan demands. In short, all this requires a different approach when it comes to organising innovative teams.

Smarter, Simpler, More Agile Organisations

So what to do? Work harder? Increase effort? An all too common error when trying to heat up the pace of innovation in the face of increasing complexity is to use more agents, that is, more people, more managers, tighter rules, more policies, advanced technologies, fatter resources and often a bank load of capital in an attempt to increase effort and in turn raise output.

Innovation, and especially (Q4) complex innovation, however, is a highly uncertain and extremely interactive activity. Therefore, the more agents employed, the greater the number of possible interactions and communications there are, and in turn the system is overwhelmed. Consequently, the answer to managing complex, sometimes highly novel innovation at a faster pace is not to add yet more agents, but to innovate smarter, simpler, more agile organisations.

Organisational Structures and Content

All organisations are very alike, yet paradoxically very different. They are different in content. The nature of their aims and day-to-day activities are indeed particular. But look at any organisation at its highest level and you will find common processes, such as communications, distribution, training, accounting and innovation.

All that is described in this chapter is no more than an organisation that is smarter, simpler and more agile in order to compete in complex environments, and deliver increasingly diverse, complex and novel innovations. An organisation in which to fill your particular content and pursue your particular organisational context (that is, what your organisation does on a day-to-day basis). What is described below can be applied to any company or institution, of any size, in any environment, private and public.

Balancing the Top-down, Bottom-up Organisation

The traditional management paradigm is to organise top-down, that is, in steep, layered, pyramid structures with subordinates at the bottom and the boss at the top. Yet it is scientific fact, born of studies in the natural world, that this kind of top-down organisation gives rise to static, non-learning, non-flexible (management) systems – and all the burden that comes with it. This organisation, in truth, was designed for turn of the nineteenth-century, steady-state mass production, with relatively simple technologies. However, by definition, innovation is not about steady-state mass production, it is about doing something new and different. Managers and mainstay organisations are good at managing norms and conventional practice, and because of that, they are terrible at letting innovation happen.

The direct antithesis of the top-down pyramid organisation is the so-called interconnected organisation, which is a multidimensional, amorphous network of people linked to each other face to face or through collaborative technologies (see below).

However, a problem always arises when there are either too few or too many interconnections between people. Too few interconnections and the team begins to break down. In system dynamics speak, the organisation goes turbulent. Consequently, information and communication is lost and/or truncated. On the other hand, if there are too many interconnections – everybody needs to talk to everybody else – the network seizes up. For example, within a network of, say, 200 agents, the number of possible interconnections that network could have is just under 20,000. Clearly, this gives rise to wait-state situations. Agent 5 needs to talk with agent 106. But agent 106 is in a meeting with agents 83, 82, 91, 95, 136 and 147. Agent 147 has been waiting to see agent 5 all day, but is stuck in the meeting. Too great a number of interconnections overwhelms the whole system – the organisation moves beyond the dynamic state, and begins to freeze like the molecules in an ice cube.

The key here is to balance the extremes of the frigid top-down organisation with the fluid dynamics of a bottom-up network organisation. This is achieved via a team-based approach to innovation, and starts with defining the optimum size of a team.

Optimising the Size and Structure of Innovative Teams

Ideally a team should be no larger than 12 people, and 17 people seems to be the absolute limit for high performance innovative teams. In fact, we can see the effect of group size outside the fold of commercial and public systems innovation, in a wide variety of fields. It is well known that the native tribes of old America would hunt in packs of no more than a dozen warriors – any larger and the effectiveness of the hunting would begin to break down.

In the world of innovation, the lessons are carried over. Kim Clark and Takahiro Fujimoto explained this in their book *Product Development Performance*:

> The size of the team working on a development project has a profound influence on its performance. Too small a team and the work is likely to be burdensome, incomplete, and slow. Too large a team and the work is likely to be burdensome, incomplete and *confusing*, and slow. Experience in the auto industry suggests that engineering organizations are far more likely to be over-specialized than too broad in the focus of expertise, and that the drive for specialization has led firms to create development teams that are far too large. Integration is far easier and far more effective if teams are relatively small and team members' responsibilities are relatively broad. We have found car companies with much less specialization at the individual engineer level to be capable of putting high-quality, high-performance products into the market far faster and with much better productivity than the oversized specialists.

Large groups are prone to all kinds of contaminants that stop team performance in its tracks – logistical problems, communication problems, exhaustive political problems, turf-guarding issues, divergent approaches that conflict, incompatible world views and so on. The central reason for this is that large groups cannot learn or develop a common aim. Organisational entropy, that is, randomly generated interactions, soon becomes overwhelming. In fact, it is possible to witness this dynamic in rioting crowds. People lose their identity within large mobs, the sheer scale and intensity of random interactions takes away their sense of self, and once that goes, their values and beliefs go with it. People, quite sane people, become temporarily crazy. Moreover, you cannot reason with mad men, just as you cannot reason with a mob. In fact, they are the same entities. Mobs and mad men are beset by random chaotic thoughts. I am not saying that large organisations are totally insane, but that they do get a little chaotic and therefore crazy from time to time.

Even strong management teams and executives are not up to the job in these circumstances. I have worked for super-tough executives in the defence industry, who during their military career have killed in the battle-field (and I mean shot, strangled and bayoneted the enemy), and who scare the wits out of you. Yet, even they cannot control a large organisation. The system dynamics are far too complex, far too chaotic to control in a top-down, command and control manner.

The key here is in the design of top-down and bottom-up structures. For example, a team attempting to deliver a large-scale systems innovation

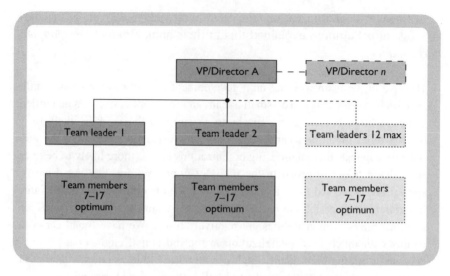

Figure 9.1   Team-based organisational structure

project – such as a radically new hydrogen-based automotive engine, or an industry-transforming healthcare system – can be organised into sub-teams of between 7 and 17 members, each with a team leader who reports to a vice president or director. This gives a structure of only three layers of hierarchy. Such a flat structure means that the communication up, down and across the organisation is very efficient (see Figure 9.1).

No matrix management is necessary. Each level up the hierarchy is totally responsible for both the functional and daily project issues for each team member. In fact, matrix management is yet another way to sandbag innovation, and only causes unnecessary political repercussions.

Furthermore, to keep innovative teams innovative, new teams must form out of old ones. But these new teams must form outside the fold of normal operations, with a new VP/director. And, yes, the VP/director might well be a 19-year-old or a 63-year-old. And that's the crunch. Most organisations shudder at such notions. But that's innovation.

Multidimensional Roles

In the traditional organisation, jobs were defined by breaking down big functional tasks into smaller functional tasks, where, once completed, the baton was handed to the next specialist – so-called division of labour.

Of course, innovative teams do need experts and specialists. Particularly within technically advanced projects or innovative marketing projects, it is common to find highly specialised roles, where one, or maybe a few, expert owns and tackles a specific task.

However, innovative teams really do need a kind of multiplication of labour, where most people have a comprehensive role that homes in on end-to-end processes. This is because, as more unusual and curious problems arise, there is a greater need for teams to be equipped with multi-dimensional people who can combine a variety of knowledge bases and skills from narrow subjects and disciplines into synthesised arenas and cross-related tasks. In real-world innovation projects today, more and different problems need a network-knowledge approach.

Such broad roles also enhance creativity and flexibility within the team. If new or unforeseen problems emerge, the team can swarm around the problem at the drop of hat. Furthermore, ownership of outcome is known to be a very effective motivation for high performance (even beyond interest and reward incentives). And this is one of the most striking advantages of multidimensional roles; they can own the whole project from start to finish. Such resultant ownership enables teams to address and overcome difficult challenges without tardy top-down command and control.

The goal, then, is for team members to become multiskilled, multi-knowledged. Yet, expanding towards the multidimensional, in terms of knowledge and skill, should not give rise to so-called stress burnout. What causes stress is lack of management support, learning productivity tools and continuous training.

Where Possible Collocate the Team

A collocated innovative team concurrently brings all the skills necessary to converge and resolve all the issues throughout a project life-cycle, in one space and at one time.

Sometimes, systems innovation is hard to define or put into words; collocation provides a means for tacit working practices and alliances, so that inexact or uncertain issues may be effectively dealt with. Collocated teams also remove a high ratio of wasteful activities, like walking long distances between offices or writing memos, as communication doesn't rely on paperwork and email. Data flow is made easy, making it conceivable for the whole team to have a single project plan, not just individual schedules. Quicker lead times are obtained as there is higher reliability in the tasks carried out. It also makes the definition of relationships between customer and supplier, and between the team and the wider alliance, easier to design and operate.

Innovative Team Project Rooms

Walk through the offices and corridors of the average insurance broker, solicitor or architect, and you'll notice something quite peculiar. What you will find strange is that there is not much difference between each of the physical working environments. In my opinion, most corporate, and especially public office, working environments are bland, mundane spaces, which prevent collaborative learning. This is yet another component of organisational learning disability.

First and foremost, in order that facilities produce fast results, the environment must be designed for collaborative learning. That means designing, experimenting, prototyping, testing and completing should be carried out right in the centre of the work environment. Very, very few do this. The exceptions are 3M, Nike and Canon but few others. The number of businesses I visit, whether service or manufacturing, that lack any such facility is still much too high. But even so, the few that do, still have these facilities dispersed around the organisation. This does not and cannot deliver what is necessary for even a reasonable amount of innovation, let alone complex systems innovation.

For an innovative team to be successful, a facility will require downstream prototyping upstream. That is, service infrastructure or component assembly machinery being mocked up at the same time as early initial sketch experiments. This also facilitates collocated cross-functional experiments that are the bedrock of complex systems innovations. This may turn out to be a very large, chaotic area that is very different from the typical work environment. It will be a hybrid of workshop-cum-laboratory-cum-office-cum-learning environment-cum-meeting area-cum-whatever you need to get the job done. This innovation team learning laboratory should look more like a stock exchange/carnival/zoo/gladiator arena of ideas and experiments being prototyped and tested; not row upon row of segregated people, with lists of things waiting to be done.

One common objection to this is the 'noise and dirt', that is, rapid prototype machinery churning away, lubricants and swarf piling up everywhere, prototype bits and creeping wires flying all over, or service infrastructure mock-ups like shop fronts or hotel reception areas being erected or torn down. But this is real-world innovation. Nice, neat, tidy computer-assisted design terminals, with people in shirts and ties sitting in rows is far from innovation. Innovation is about real tangible issues; anything less is bureaucracy. Innovation is like a day out to Disney World, not a draft into the military. Go to Canon's design centre, where you can eat your lunch off the floor. But Canon is a whirlwind of real-world experiments – real things being made and tested. With a little imagination and thought, you can design a noise-damping, dirt-reducing environment. The point is, do not let narrow objections get in the way of speedy learning experiments and other kinds of innovative teamwork.

Distributed Teams and Collaborative Technologies

It is not always possible, of course, to collocate every team member, or indeed any member of a team. Reasons range from international strategic alliances, where multiple organisations are working together on an innovation; or a team might need to work out in the field at a client or vendor site; or simply that an expertise is so specialist that the maestro finds that he or she is working on many different projects simultaneously. Indeed, the work of an innovative team is highly dynamic and, as a consequence, the form of any team's work environment might change at any moment. The environment might take the form of a coffee shop, a hotel lounge or an airport. And that is the challenge here.

Clearly, teams working in the field need to have access to information in real time. They also need to be in close contact with team members dispersed elsewhere. Any delays here will result in a significant drop in productivity, timeliness and even a dip in the overall performance of the team itself. Nevertheless, such dislocation should not and, indeed, does not stop high performance teamwork. And route number one to maintain such teamwork is through collaborative technology.

The goal of collaborative technology is to enable anywhere, anytime teamwork. Such collaborative technologies tie dispersed and remote work groups into close-knit crews, by enabling peer-to-peer access to information and design tools, which facilitates real-time sharing of data and ideas. There are many tools and technologies that apply here: simple mobile hand-held gadgets such as personal data assistants and computer tables; portable video-conferencing systems; intranet systems; collaborative software products; and old-fashioned mobile phones and pagers. The goal is to arm your team to the teeth with such collaborative technologies.

A Virtual Trip into the Future of Distributed Teams

As collaborative technologies develop, it will be even easier to bring far-flung people together in an instant, at ever lower cost, with ever higher bandwidth. But the tools and technologies outlined above are only the beginning. However, to give you an insight into what this all might look like in the near future, here is a possible scenario that might be commonplace by 2015.

---

2 a.m. It's cold. It's wet. It's dark outside, and there's nowhere to go. I just cannot sleep. The new model for the memetic algorithm has plagued my mind all day. The breakthrough is going to come, yet the code is as sticky as a lizard's tongue. Unexpectedly, Zen, my virtual guide, appears on my VT screen:

'Can't sleep either,' she tells me. 'Your pulse is racing, Chris.'

'I know … ' I sigh. 'This concept just won't go critical, and I'm way stressed.'

'Chris, the Thunderbolt Team are in Uplink, why don't you join them?'

'They can't sleep either? Okay.'

'See ya on the other si…!' Zen fades out.

I sprint over to my personal immersive dome: a tactile sensing booth of geodesic structure, with a trillion nanotransducers swarming across the inside surface, bathing my five physical senses in a bath of polymorphologic illusion. The inside surface slithers like a liquid, as it autojacks into my TURBO-central automation provider, hyperlinked to ULTRABAND-SKYNET. I reach for my gold plasma eye drops, drip two drops in each eye and insert two custom-made laser-optical contact lenses. Squeeze my eyes and a soft-peach ambient background light washes over my field of vision. Blink my eyelids and a list of highly detailed 3D-icons appear. I focus on a single icon, which looks like some kind of miniature detail scene from a cocktail bar. Another picture shows a moving sequence from a shopping mall, and another frames a sun-drenched beach, Brazil perhaps? A list of 3D-icons pours down like slot-machine cherries, until number 777 pops up.

I look with amazement at its intricacy. If I look close enough, I see a large gold and emerald-green pentagon-shaped room, with a chromium-steel circular platform at dead centre. Around the periphery of the central plinth, Egyptian hieroglyphics etched in red-ruby tell of secrets that I just can't make out. I stare into the 777 icon much harder … three, two, one, a snap of the fingers, and I'm there, instantly at the hypermachine; a purpose-designed hyperinnovation environment.

Yet I'm not. I'm safely at home. I'm in two worlds, the real world and an artificial world. The sharp hit of a fizzing cognitive enhancer hits my neural senses, while the hum of uniflowing information fills my inner-eye. The bright blue light of knowledge refracts through the prisms of my mind, almost blinded by incandescent poly-memes, as I immerse and drift off into a deeper world where new ideas are born.

Suddenly, the team – Kim, Annie, Chi, Jax, Gabriel, Baz and Clark – appear. Three of them live 5000 miles away, one of them lives next door. One of them can't speak a word of English, another has not yet left school, and another celebrates his 61st birthday soon. Baz is a design engineer. Annie and Chi are cryptographers, Gab is a creatologist, Jax is a zoologist. Ann looks like a wizard, Kim like Rubberman, Gab an archangel, Jax and Baz join as a dragon, and I dress in a yellow pinstripe. We greet with a Mexican wave, then focus in on this illusionary realm.

All at once, a thousand shining iridescent metallic balls begin to dance around our virtual crown, each one data-saturated from the web of far-flung minds, instantly cracking open like diamond-crazed crocodile eggs pouring out an endless list of tangled algorithmic digital code. Out spurts three days work on to an artifi-cial floor of gold and green chequered tiles. The beginning of the code is not defin-able, neither is the middle, nor its end. This code is as complex as any biology, if not more so. But then it has been designed using techniques that Lewis Carroll's white rabbit would have been proud of, via tricks that would have Merlin spell-bound.

Kim stretches one of his 20 arms, reaching for the other side of the pentagon, looking much like the Fantastic Four's Rubberman. He grasps a velvet cantilever with the glyphic 'boot-up' stamped on its top. Pulls back, and with one sharp jerk, the algorithm begins to boot-strap into play. A spiralling orange fractal begins to unravel. It expands out exponentially, each spiralling arm identical in form, yet each one different in detail.

'Wow,' Annie gasps, 'it's almost there!' No stopping us now. Each spiral repre-sents an ideaplex, a team dream. A concept for a new mediacar, or ultrasonic powerdrill that hums jazz, or synthetic smartmolecule. It might be a new kind of building fabrication or nanoreplicator engine or part of a chapter in *Building Innova-tive Teams*. But it is more likely to be what our clients now demand; a breakthrough multidimensional concept that no one has heard of or even imagined before, yet everyone will irresistibly crave for when it hits the marketplace. But it really doesn't matter, because with our virtual tools and processes, we are hyperinnov-ators. If we don't know the technology or the history or the theory or the hypo-thesis or the protocol, we can learn it, absorb the information at hugely accelerated rates, and with a recall and cross-referencing capacity matched by a supermind. We can prototype, build and test in this artificial world, in ways impossible in the real. We can escalate memetic symbiosis, self-organisation and build a wave of memes up to a crescendo of criticality, then in a cascade, the wall of memes comes crashing down, splaying a configuration that would take months, often years to realise in the cold, dark, wet, 2 a.m outside.

I lean forward. A translucent panel of faders, buttons and levels emerges from nowhere. Clark begins to manipulate the consol, effecting slight ultra-accurate adjustments to the fractal swarming high above. Every fourteenth, twenty-second and forty-eighth arm of the fractal suddenly move up and in towards the centre of the fractal mass, then multiverge at around 30 metres, meld and then morph into a rainbow of memes that rain down in a shower of memetic innovation. I retch, feeling sick with the perfuse injection of new concepts. As a team, we begin to see what I could not see before; we, us, whole, begin to figure and crack the code. The memetic algorithm of a billion lines of convoluted bits of string isn't such a monster after all. We had mastered the devil that had been riding on my back. We're kings of this illusionary world, where we can create technological empires and meme dynasties, a nirvana where we can intellectually play and create. This is our world, and all our future realities, where the physical ceases to restrain, where the limits of imagination know no bounds. Nothing will escape; all will eventually become artificial, all artificial will in time become very real – a memetic illusion, yet a concerto of memes as concrete as stone. And at this moment I now see that all is possible.

A little sci-fi to help the creative juices fly? Well no, all this kit and code and much more is being born in leading virtual reality (VR) laboratories and commercial systems innovation centres around the world today. To name just a few: MIT's media lab, NTT's Human Interface and Visual Media Lab and NASA's Aerospace Human Factors Research Division are smashing technological paradigms in this field. Companies such as Trimension, Sony, Industrial Light & Magic, Time Warner, Fujitsu, IBM and Nintendo collectively pour hundreds of billions of dollar capital, and multiple-million intellectual man-months on research and development. This is a multibillion-dollar business today, the tools are real, such advanced collaborative technologies are in use right now.

As a result of this fantastic-like R&D, there are three main areas of technology that are beginning to build such advanced teamwork environments:

1. *Team interface technologies*: These technologies not only replace the keyboard and mouse, they completely transform what it means to interact with technology and other team members. Technologies like portable virtual reality domes, where whole teams can be present in the same virtual space, are rapidly developing and dropping in cost. Haptic systems (technologies that integrate the sensations of motion to the human body in relation to the work environment), kinaesthetic systems (dynamic force feedback systems that give artificial tactile senses in real time), gesture recognition (systems that capture body language and gestures) and high-end visualisation technology (giant high-definition surround screens) are state of the art now.

2. *Seamless VR simulation tools*: These technologies allow a whole systems innovation to be simulated in the mind of a computer from preconception to end of market life-cycle. Everything from finite element analysis, to molecular design systems, to genetic algorithms that capture nature's design rules all come into the fold here. This area is burgeoning faster than I can write.

3. *Intelligent webs*: Through artificial intelligence software, these systems begin to build a man–machine relationship beyond any man–man relationships yet devised. They help teams to search through vast data-bases of information, build new and innovative concepts and also make critical decisions in highly complex situations.

Such advanced collaborative learning technology is with us now, and can only continue to become a vital component of facilitating high perform-ance within both collocated and vastly distributed innovative teams.

(NB: The main points of organising innovative teams are outlined in Exercise 30 in Appendix A.)

CHAPTER 10

Innovative Team Leadership

As for the best leaders, the people do not notice their existence. The next best, the people honour and praise. The next, the people fear; and the next, the people hate. When the best leader's work is done, the people say, 'we did it ourselves'. SUN TZU, 600 BC

The goal of any innovative team leader is to achieve something quite different – obviously. But it means more than that; it means not only doing things differently, but also leading differently. After all, how can one expect a team to deliver rule-breaking, industry-transforming systems innovation if it is led in the same old way as a conventional organisation? How can a team deal with uncertainty, risk and chance, if the leader is merely worried about resources, time, budgets and specifications?

Clearly, there is a need for a quite different kind of leadership here. This last chapter in this second part now begins to outline the necessary codes and discipline of such a leader.

Innovative Open Team Leadership

Paradoxically, the latest and most effective leadership philosophy and methods comes from a very old source. About 600 BC, Sun Tzu, the great Chinese sage and warrior, wrote in his treatise *The Art of War*:

Intelligent control appears as uncontrol or freedom. And for that reason it is intelligent control. Unintelligent control appears as external domination. And for that reason it is really unintelligent control. Intelligent control exerts influence without appearing to do so. Unintelligent control tries to influence by making a show of force.

These ancient and wise words still hold today in all walks of life; from marital relationships to parenting to teaching to military command, but none more so than innovation.

True intelligent control does indeed seem like uncontrol or freedom, yet this kind of intelligent control may not seem like intelligent control at all, but unreliable or unconvincing control. In the organisation of old, strong top-down command and control was the watchword. Everybody worked to a highly detailed plan and process. Everybody was organised in legions with a metaphorical centurion at the apex. So clearly, any move away from this kind of tight control may indeed seem like an ambiguous charge.

Time after time, I meet executives who demand stacks of paper-based analysis and plans, connected to clear reporting lines, worried sick to the point of paranoia about losing control of the project. And the reason? No matter how hard and tightly one controls like this, the best-laid plans will always go askew at some stage. All tight control is, at the end of the day, a fallacy. Ask Tom Peters, and he will tell you that tight management control is an illusion of the first order. Ask any leading chaos theorist, and they will tell you that control is only mildly possible at the single variable level. Ask any well-seasoned programme manager and they will tell you the same story. Top-down control is and always was a fantasy.

Beyond the peculiarities and practicalities of control, innovation is a non-linear activity, where new issues often spring out of the blue, and where one new event can lead to a cascade of ever-more novel and unexpected events. And this is the stuff of innovation. Innovation means exploring and experimenting with fresh ways and means and, by definition, your people are going to trip up from time to time. So, it is imperative that teams have the freedom to approach unique problems in unique ways, and that demands a completely open style of leadership, where individuals and teams can jump on a problem as it arises. Try doing that with the command and control style of leadership. I can tell you it will stop dead any chance of timely innovation and, when the results do come, the solutions will be less than satisfactory. Without an open kind of leadership, unexpected issues will overwhelm the project.

So what to do? To see and conduct the whole team towards high performance goals, the innovative team leader must facilitate collaboration. If the leader breaks a project into bits to hand out to individual members, the team will never gel together and work collaboratively. The leader will only secure a coordinated system, which, like any top-down system, is jerky and awkward, full of stop-start situations. In short, coordination is anti-collaboration. It means that the manager owns the problem, not the team.

Essentially, the leader must refrain from interfering with detailed team activities. In case after case, I have witnessed the toughest manager attempt to control every variable within a project, but fail, and fail dismally. The tensions that arise from such top-down ultra-control have dreadful consequences for morale, not to mention the steady progress of a given project. Top-down control in the context of innovation always throws the project into confusion, as the momentum of the project is all too often tipped on its head.

The best innovative team leaders I have known make and give space for a team to grow and improve their judgement in decision making and action taking. So there is a need for a balance between open guidance and authoritative control. Here is a list of traits that depict the gaping difference between the old top-down style and an open style of leadership:

Top-down	Open
Takes control	Gives control
Takes ownership	Gives ownership
Takes authority	Gives authority
Takes space	Gives space
Takes credit	Gives credit
Takes opportunities	Gives opportunities
Takes knowledge	Gives knowledge

We are all well aware of the notion of give and take, but, in the context of innovative teams, it takes on a whole new meaning.

Characteristics of an Innovative Team Leader

So what are the defining characteristics of the kind of person who leads in an open and innovative style? I find there are many such qualities. Here are some of the most significant:

■ *Holistic*: Individuals in such teams will have local knowledge, specialist discipline, parochial language and, importantly, unique experience, which collectively add up to a spread of individual realities and single-minded models of the world. This is quite common in all walks of life, but is often amplified within innovation projects, particularly at the beginning. So, there's a succinct need for the leader to continuously communicate the global picture emerging from the collective of individual realities; without this, excessive tension and unnecessary conflicts will occur. The goal is to share the team's mental models of the global picture. This global view often comes with time, but must emerge during the earlier stages of a project. Team-building skills can also help here (see below).

The most evolved form of holism consists of highly developed sensibilities to the business or public world. Holistic leaders can conceive and integrate business theory and practice. Their knowledge and experience is broad and highly developed. They're clear about the nature of complexity in the world today. In particular, they recognise and regulate the internal and external uncertainties and discontinuities that now sit with such complex innovation, and are attuned to the kind of counterintuitive issues that can emerge. They have a holistic attitude towards the building of a total systems solution. Hence, the innovative leader is essential for building teams that work in complex systems innovation.

■ *Empathic*: Leaders must display an understanding of and sensitivity to the emotional needs and personal goals of individuals. Innovative teams often live on the edge of creative hubbub, in an atmosphere charged with emotion. Bewilderment, ambiguity and sheer frustration often lead to near-manic, quite neurotic behaviour. If the leader shows no empathy towards the kind of trauma a team can experience, the dynamics of risk taking, alliance building and commitment simply will not transpire. Further, as individuals, we all have personal aspirations in life – don't we? Many ambitions will diverge from the main aim and key objectives of a systems innovation project, and some will be in direct conflict. It is through empathy that the leader can harmonise and, in some cases, capitalise on a personal agenda. The best leaders I have worked for have a knack of integrating the personal with the general aim of a project. Again, understanding the needs of the individual and the team as whole is central here. Sometimes, team members fall off the rails, some crash, and whether they can be put back on track often comes down to an empathic kind of leadership.

- *Patient*: Patience is a big virtue for the team leader, as patience can paradoxically speed up and motivate a team. Building teams is a little like planting a garden. It takes time and a lot of care and attention to sow the seeds and nurture the plants. But, as any gardener knows, the results of such patience are unbelievably fruitful. In the real world, the innovative leader will strike a balance between demanding speedy results and letting people and tasks take their natural course. Often, leaders with the best of intentions let their own impatience and sense of urgency fire up a team, but actually produce a situation where the end results are under specification, and in the end way over schedule. Again, patience is a real virtue for the innovative team leader.

- *Supportive*: The term 'steward' as leadership as been bandied about for years now, and still holds true, especially within an innovative team. Specifically, leaders need to have a supportive nature, that is, they have to be able to back up their people in times of uncertainty. Again, people will trip up and go down the wrong path; people and, indeed, whole teams will sometimes fail. So, standing by the team is essential. Believe me, if a leader stands by her/his team member over some contentious issue, then that individual will have great respect for and loyalty to that leader. If the team leader does not support his fellows during times of crisis, believe me, team members will never forget it, years and even decades later.

- *Virtuous*: Ethical management has never been so important. In a world of increasing interconnection, and in an environment where more people come together for shorter periods to deliver mission-critical projects, it is essential that the team leader is a trustworthy character. An unscrupulous leader will never win the hearts and minds of his/her team. In fact, the unscrupulous leader is the single most important reason for low performance innovation teams. People will simply not go the extra mile, they go into a defensive mode and eventually switch off. However, with a good guy leading the team, you will find team members bending over backwards for the team leader. Integrity is so important here.

- *Considerate*: If the team leader does not care about his or her team members, then the show is over. To care about the well-being of people, and actively show kindness – simple acts like if someone really likes sitting near a window, then that person should sit near a window. Consideration is not a big thing, it is a million little things.

- *Dogged*: Innovative leaders are not afraid of dealing with the inertia that can slow down the progress of an innovation project. They will prevail on the team's sense of self-preservation to get the job done. And that means the leader must be relentless (as well as patient) in the pursuit of goals. Innovation is the most complex activity that an organisation can take on, so it takes a dogged character to motivate people in order to achieve those breakthroughs.

Key Roles of an Innovative Team Leader

You may recall from Chapter 8 that high performance is the result of a self-reinforcing virtuous circle: that is, successful innovation is the result of high performance teamwork, and high performance teamwork is the result of successful innovation. Here, the innovative leader is pivotal in the realisation of such a virtuous circle. The leader must facilitate both the team-building issues and the actual project facilitation. Again, both of these go hand in hand. Here are the key issues that need to be addressed to achieve a virtuous circle of high performance innovation:

- *Build commitment*: This begins with a sense of destiny, a sense of purpose. A sense of destiny across the team is the number one route to building commitment. In my experience, the most effective way to develop that sense of destiny is to think in the longer term and that takes foresight. Foresight is not the product of hindsight, that is, looking back over history, extrapolating facts and figures, then constructing a projection from the past. In fact, that can limit ambition, imagination and, in turn, foresight. Foresight is the ability to look ahead and imagine what a particular future might be, whether it be a corporate-wide vision, or indeed a specific innovation project's aim. Hamel and Prahalad say that leaders do not need a crystal ball to see the future, rather, a set of wide-angled lenses with a strong set of headlights. And these kind of lenses and headlights come in the form of methods and tools (see my book *Hyperinnovation* for an outline of such tools). Leaders, then, must have a skill set that can build a sense of destiny. The other important aspect of building commitment is to secure team-wide accountability. One of the most effective ways to achieve this is to give constant feedback.

■ *Constant feedback*: Along with building commitment, feedback also gives the opportunity to learn and correct as the team progresses towards an outcome. It is simple to do:

1. Devise a weekly feedback monitor, on a single chart, to keep track.

2. Narrow down the points to key performance indicators (see Chapter 8).

3. Point out those results that are positive and performing well, as this motivates and builds commitment.

4. Above all, the feedback should be team based, that is, how well individuals collaborate within the team, and how the team works as a whole.

■ *Build confidence*: Early wins are the most effective way to build confidence for the individual and the team as whole. Likewise, motivation is another basic way to build confidence. Of course, there are many motivation theories, but just put them to one side for a moment and ask yourself this question. What is the common thread that's present when you excel, at anything? I wager it is the interest factor. Your finest subjects at school, your hobbies and your best work have all stemmed from the fact that you were keenly interested. And this is a secret of building confidence. People become interested in a project at hand if they can relate to the outcome, so ownership is key here. Ownership of end results and outcomes feeds self-esteem (I did that!).

■ *Facilitate functional skills building*: The role of open leader means a transformation from custodian and purveyor of knowledge and skills towards motivator, knowledge guide and skills co-learner. The leader must coach how to search, build and manipulate skills and knowledge; nurture and support an atmosphere and culture of learning; and equally, show how to be selective in focus and relevance of skills and knowledge, at a time when information comes in from all directions in massive volume and speed. This is vitally important in high performance innovative team building.

■ *Set high expectations*: The expectations of the leader are central to team performance. What leaders anticipate and foresee, the boundaries and limits they draw, directly and forcefully impinge upon team behaviour and outlook. If the leader's expectations are less than ordinary, then expect the less than ordinary outcome. If our leader's want to reinvent the world, create from where there's nothing, bring forth new venture and industry, then we can only anticipate that the best and different is yet to come.

- *Focus on high performance goals and metrics*: The team leader must act as a constant signal towards intended high performance goals – what is wanted in the hand at the end of the day. Only by focusing on goals, set by specific dates, will results come through. But who is in the best position to set such high performance project objectives? The manager? The project leader? After all, surely these people have a better overall grasp of the situation. Psychologists have observed that 75 per cent of people put themselves in the top quartile for personal ability, and that most like to live up to this. If the project host sets a target in isolation, the chance of meeting that target is remote. But, set a target in conjunction with the project team, and the odds for success improve dramatically. Ask your people to set their own target, and two things will happen: the goal will be of a higher standard, and people will bend over backwards to achieve the goal. Why? It's as I've said, we all think we are mountain movers and we have a built-in need to live up to that expectation. We can just about bear falling short of other people's expectations, but we flip if we fall short of our own. The power of this is grossly underestimated, yet it has proved itself time and time again. The project leader must facilitate goal setting, but encourage teams to set project goals. The other key role here is to measure the project team's performance against the project objectives. A description of performance goals and metric development is outlined in Chapter 8.

- *Facilitating team building*: The project leader has an extremely tough role to play here, as this role will take at least 50 per cent of his time. The team-building strategies and tools outlined in this book help, but again this is more of a commitment to building a high performance team which can produce successful innovation. The team leader must focus on both project issues and team-building issues as a kind of self-reinforcing virtuous circle. It is a dynamic process, where one issue can take precedence over another in an instant. The key is to lead by your calendar, and if, by the end of the week, little or no team building has taken place (even with the advent of a formal programme – see Part III), then time must be given up here, otherwise the team performance will start to diminish.

Building and Selecting Team Leaders

All great performers – individuals, teams, corporations, indeed whole nation-states – have or have had someone in their world who has had an animating and edifying influence upon them. Of course, these people appear in a range of guises from friends, colleagues, managers to parents and siblings. Clearly, leaders come from anywhere. And that is the point here, there is no one route to or from leadership. The short answer is that many kinds of people, with all kinds of personalities, can be team leaders.

Finding new team leaders with all these qualities and role skills from scratch will be an arduous task for any management team. Recruiting from the outside is the short-term answer, of course. But as teams grow within the wider organisation, it is important to develop and promote from within. This gives another layer for motivating staff in general, but specifically people's knowledge and skill will grow if they are given the scope to do so, and that means being given the chance and the support to lead teams. Opportunity is one thing, but support is an entirely different matter. Absence of support and development here can lead to wholesale failure. I've seen many a good candidate for team leader left out in the cold through lack of training, support and/or coaching, and as a result falling way short of the original intention and expectations.

There are few born leaders, in fact most leaders develop over time. As I will outline in Part III, when a team starts out in life, it most certainly will not be a high performance team. It will have to grow through various stages of development, and it is the same for a new team leader. The key here is to look for a potential match against the above characteristics and roles. Of course training helps, but it is only when a team leader is put to work with a real team with real innovation projects that he or she will start to grow.

The question always arises whether a team leader should come from a technical, marketing or operations background, or indeed any other kind of discipline. Indeed, if it is an advanced technology project, the leader must have a high degree of technical skill and knowledge, likewise, if it is a high-end marketing or operations project, again, the relevant skills must be held by the leader. However, the real issue is the environment that the project exists within; whether in a public sector environment or a commercial environment, the best leaders have a highly developed business acumen. Dealing with people outside the company, such as customers, regulatory bodies, suppliers, government officials, requires astute political abilities, good financial understanding and an ability to handle the many day-to-day corporate issues, such as unions, litigation and negotiation issues and so on. Again these qualities need to be developed, and the only way that potential leaders are going to develop sound judgement in all these areas is to get on and actually lead and build innovative teams.

(NB: The main points of leading innovative teams are outlined in Exercise 31 in Appendix A.)

PART III

Innovative Team-building Performance

You may be fortunate and employ the most friendly, broad-minded, agreeable group of people. But put them in highly collaborative teams, with challenging performance targets for extended periods, and that pleasant group will sprout horns and a tail, not turn up for work on Mondays, and be on the point of a nervous breakdown at the end of a relentless systems project, when you really need them to start afresh.

The point here is that not only does a high performance team bring about innovation, but that performance sets off another virtuous circle, where the most extraordinarily high performance teams are robust, highly durable work crews that can take on the toughest of challenges, and go on time and time again to produce extraordinary results.

In my experience, the most extraordinarily high performance innovative teams emerge from structured, well-tailored team-building programmes that are in themselves high performance. That is, the actual programmes are of an extremely high standard to begin with.

Part III outlines the methods for developing and instigating such high standard programmes.

Chapter 11 – Designing and Executing a Team-building Programme: This penultimate chapter provides the framework for the effective design and implementation of such team-building programmes.

Chapter 12 – Profiling and Selecting Team Members: This final chapter covers the methodologies for the profiling of competency and personality, and final selection of members that make up a high performance innovative team.

CHAPTER 11

Designing and Executing a Team-building Programme

Teams are always either improving or declining in effectiveness. Therefore the work of teambuilding is never done. JOHN ADAIR

A team is not a *real* high performance innovative team until and unless it can produce a constant and reliable stream of innovation. And this is perhaps the most challenging endeavour of all today. As Machiavelli recognised almost 500 years ago, there is no more exhausting challenge than to bring about a new order of things. Innovation is the most difficult and complex issue that any organisation can take on. As a consequence, the faster a team can rise towards a high performance position, the more value-creating and sustainable that organisation is going to be.

The Need for Accelerating Team Performance

Precisely because innovation has become the linchpin of competitive strategy, more and more people are finding themselves working in teams. Often these days complete strangers are put (and sometimes thrown) together and expected to produce high performance results at an ever-quickening pace. The reasons for this are many:

■ There are more start-up businesses and entrepreneurial units today than at any other time in the history of commerce. This means that there are more rapid growth scenarios. Rapid growth in high uncertainty environments can lead to high levels of stress, inducing people to behave in quite irrational ways. In the extreme, it can bring out the worst in people.

■ A more diverse range of people come together in teams these days. Again, complexity in innovation is up, so a greater number of different expertises, skills, knowledge and ideas is required.

■ There are shorter life-cycles; whether in projects, core technologies, products and services in the market or indeed whole industries, life-cycles are shrinking dramatically. Everything from competition to increasing consumer expectations crush the life of any given innovation. And so, the need for continuous innovation.

■ As the knowledge economy bites harder, so mobility increases. In the past, assets were physical objects and mostly fixed. Today assets are cerebral and can be transferred to any location in the world. This will only increase as technologies such as virtual reality and telepresence advance, and the price of long-haul travel shrinks.

■ Teams must become robust teams. That is, they must be capable of ongoing and challenging project work. Without such durability, the mental and emotional fatigue that innovation can bring will leave people's heads reeling when you really need then to start afresh. In fact, without team building, the desired high performance innovative teamwork is not sustainable over the long haul.

These factors themselves present an enormous challenge for building innovative teams. For all the reasons outlined in Part II, when people come together in large groups, common thoughts, reflexes and emotions are going through their minds, which all too often stop collaborative interaction and learning. This is mainly because, at the initiation stage of an innovation project, people are a group of disparate individuals, not an innovative *team*. An innovative team is something quite different. In fact, the most innovative teams I have known are *not* those that fuse in some mysterious, positive chemistry – as often purported – but are those built on the dynamics and psychology of innovation.

The Team-building Programme Template

Beyond innovation itself, collaborative learning also provides the most effective way to build teams. Teams that learn together bond and develop together. The shared experience, the mutual piece of knowledge, the consolidated competence and the joint experiment are the raw building materials of any team. The greater and more rapid the feedback from such shared work, the faster a team will head towards high performance.

More often than not, team learning happens within normal day-to-day, on-task experiences (and this is where most of the team-building work happens). However, where on-task learning can fall short is in break-throughs. That is, innovation always requires new insights, new methods, new skills and of course new knowledge and ideas. Consequently, there is a definite need to experiment with new knowledge and ideas, outside live project work. Obviously, this reduces risk, but also offers a neutral environment for pushing through established boundaries. So there is a need to complement on-task learning with a fully developed programme of team learning and development. This gives the opportunity to look at currently unrelated areas, providing a legitimate space and neutral environment for development when needed.

However, as much research has shown, the best results in team learning and development happen when it is directly related to the real work content. Learning on task, in real projects, with real issues to solve, turns out to be a major part of team learning, as one true insight in the real world is worth a week in the classroom.

The key, then, is a combination of in-class learning and real work learning and review. To achieve this, there is a need to draw up a formal team-building programme that rolls out over the life-cycle of each innovation project. Such programmes need to be tailored to each specific project requirement. For example, an experienced team that has achieved high performance results will need much less team-building effort and time than a novice team that is just starting out. Intermediate teams, teams that have obtained some level of performance, but not high performance, will require somewhat more building than a true high performance team.

The design and monitoring of such programmes need to follow a process template, a pattern of tried and trusted ideas that shape the content and roll-out of each team-building programme. There are many well-known and tested process templates that can be applied to the design and execution of team building. I now outline some key concepts for putting together such a template.

The Classic Sigmoid Curve and Team Performance

All teams, of all kinds, follow a specific pattern as they grow as a team, and develop towards high performance. In fact, the pattern can be tracked via a well-known scientific phenomenon called the 'sigmoid curve'. The sigmoid curve is a classic template that indicates the typical pattern of growth within organic systems. Such a pattern is typically depicted by a flat 'S'-shaped curve (Figure 11.1). The 'S' pattern of the sigmoid curve can be observed in many different walks of life from biology to political systems to product and corporate life-cycles.

Basically, all organic systems seem to follow such a curve. Take a flower: it is born, then it grows, blossoms, fruits, seeds and finally withers to make way for its offspring. The reason for such a growth pattern can be found, once again, in the discipline of system dynamics and feedback. As a system starts and begins to grow, positive feedback is at work. Technically speaking, positive feedback amplifies the gap between the present situation and the actual outcome. It ramps up small changes in the system, thus forcing the system to open up and fly in the opposite direction from the centre, average or intent.

Then, after a certain critical point, negative feedback comes into play. Negative feedback has a tendency to shrink the gap between what is expected and the system's actual outcome. It ramps down small changes in the system, thus closing the system towards the centre, average or intent. At this point, diminishing returns begin to occur. The system at large has

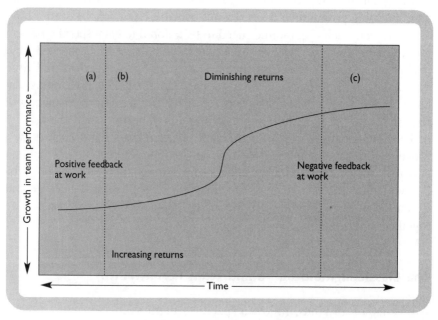

Figure 11.1 The classic sigmoid curve

reached a point where it cannot cope with rapid growth, and so begins to slow the growth rate down.

Many team-building experts apply the sigmoid model with its inherent positive and negative feedback dynamic to give a structure for developing a particular team-building programme. Specifically, the sigmoid curve can be applied to building innovative teams, illustrating the typical progress life-cycle that a team advances through towards high performance.

The archetypal pattern of team performance development starts with a slow flat line, indicating little or no performance improvement. Then, over time, team performance, with the right set of team-building strategies and tools, begins to enter a phase of rapid improvement (positive feedback kicks in), then, after a time, performance improvement begins to level out (negative feedback kicks in) and finally enters the endgame of equalisation (look at the flow sequence of the curve in Figure 11.1).

Here, the sigmoid model infers that people in groups must advance through the early life-cycle stages to become a high performance team.

In line with this model, the psychologist B. W. Tuckman observed that whenever a small group of people are initially put together (especially people from a diverse range of backgrounds) and then work together throughout a project life-cycle, the group as a whole seems to go through a common sequence of working relations development, on both human and task levels. Tuckman narrowed these sequences into four phases (my interpretation):

1. *Forming*: On a task level, people establish objectives and begin to fathom out how and what they need to meet those objectives. On a people level, they try to understand what is suitable behaviour (key values) and look towards the stronger or more senior people in the group for guidance.

2. *Storming*: On both task and people level, this is a very emotional time, as people are trying to exert their own experiences and individuality.

3. *Norming*: Cohesion, group spirit, standards, key values and roles begin to be accepted.

4. *Performing*: Words like flexibility and collaboration spring to mind. People have found their space and now most of the emotional energy can be focused on the project.

Again, the pattern of the sigmoid curve can be seen. The forming and storming stages are obviously highly chaotic stages, with little or no performance improvement. The norming stage is the period when teams are climbing up the sigmoid curve and are experiencing a time of expeditious progress. Lastly, the team hits the top part of the curve and begins to enter high achievement, but then quickly reaches the point of diminishing returns.

And perhaps now it can be seen that confusion, conflict, inflexibility and so on may just be a result of the earlier forming and storming stages of development.

A key, then, must be to find ways to accelerate team building through the early stages, make best use of the norming stage, then advance to the performing stage.

Putting Together the Team-building Programme

To advance effectively and rapidly along the team performance curve, there is a need for an action plan; a step-by-step real-world programme of activities and instructions that give rise to high performance innovative teams. I now list the six key stages of such a programme:

1. **Set up the management infrastructure**: Management systems are the powerhouse that drive all of this. Without the right governance infrastructure in place, it will not happen. Here are five critical things to do here:

    (i)   *Strategic top team*: Set up a small strategic top team, made up of relevant senior people from across the organisation(s), and give them executive authority for strategic and policy issues regarding the team-building programme. The very act of team-building programmes must have problem owners. It is also important to include professional team-building expertise on such a team to give advice and fill in the blanks where necessary.

    (ii) *Employ a part-time programme manager/facilitator*: A single member of staff must be employed to oversee the team-building initiatives on a daily basis. This individual will oversee both the development of the team-building programmes and facilitate the actual team-building activities across the organisation. It is best that this individual is a senior member of staff, reporting to the top team.

    (iii) *Obtain training budgets*: Clearly, there is both a financial and opportunity cost to team building. The cost of a facilitator, consulting if needed, materials and physical environment will need to be accounted and paid for. However, I would add that much of the team-building effort is self-directed, and the cost of not doing anything is often much more than execution.

(iv) *Announce strategic intent*: It is important to let the organisation know what is coming. That is, that high performance innovative teams are the core organisational structure for delivering complex systems innovation, and that a structured team-building programme will be implemented within the relevant areas of the organisation.

(v) *Set up communications*: Formal organisation-wide communication channels must be set up to inform how the team-building programmes are progressing. This can be included in conventional top-down communication reports, company newsletters and formal meetings. Also, it is important to provide a means for bottom-up feedback, so that people at the coalface can air their views, concerns and suggestions for improvement.

2. **Set up the team-building activity action plan**: Next, define and develop the key team-building strategies and activities. There are a number of things to consider here:

■ *Outline key strategies*: Each of the key strategies for building high performance teams can be taken from the chapters in Part II. For clarity, I list them once more:

   – The brain, learnt behaviours, and human interaction
   – Creativity and innovative teams
   – Developing an innovative team's whole mind
   – Collaborative learning beyond knowledge
   – Innovative team values
   – The need for high performance goals and metrics
   – Organising innovative teams
   – Innovative team leadership

■ *Develop the action plan*: From the above list of strategies, the relevant tools (that is, games, exercises, quizzes and so on) may be identified, and the team-building activities developed in a structured way. Once this is achieved, each activity can be put together in an overall programme, in terms of time, length of activity, equipment needed, who needs to be involved and so on. Appendix A lists such activities in 31 easy to apply action plan templates. Each template gives all the information in one place, so that a definitive programme can be developed.

- *Bespoke action plans*: A balanced, customised programme may be developed for each new project team. As, noted above, different teams have distinct performance development requirements, depending on their life-cycle stage. Again, the templates in Appendix A may be used as a gauge and point of reference.

- *Programme documents*: Each team-building activity and the overall programme need to be set in formal documents. These are step-by-step guides that show how each activity is carried out. This can then be used in situ and kept as a reference for each team member's progress. Once again, the team-building activity templates in Appendix A can be used here.

3. **Set up the key strategies for accelerating team performance**: In addition to the team-building activities, there are further strategies that can be applied to help accelerate team performance development. These are high impact initiatives and actions that can be applied on a day-to-day basis:

  - *Set a compelling agenda*: Whether it be a particular innovation project or team-building programme (remember, both reinforce each other), the content must be an exciting, fulfilling, enjoyable experience. Few other strategies motivate like a compelling agenda.

  - *Set a demanding pace*: Tempo is set by the pace of the team leader's actions, the intensity with which s/he carries out tasks, holding impromptu dialogue sessions, and dramatising all this.

  - *Short-term wins through immediate results*: Psychologically speaking, it is about immediacy, instant gratification. A small win shows the team that it is actually accomplishing something. Without a small win, the large-scale complex systems innovation project overwhelms a team, and the short-term need for gratification is negated. So small is not only beautiful, but small wins encourage bigger wins.

  - *Ownership*: When we think we own something, we will go the extra mile to make it just right. In innovative team-building terms, the team must do the lion's share of the team-building work. That is organising and executing the team-building programmes.

  - *Constant feedback*: Once again feedback is important. Communicate quickly and directly what is going well and what needs to be improved – this builds commitment, informs how well the programme of performance development is going and also motivates.

- *Team reward for results*: Again, rewarding what you want to happen in short bursts is another feedback mechanism to stimulate motivation.

4. **Monitor performance development**: In conjunction with designing the team-building programme, there is a need to measure and monitor team performance development along the 'S' curve. There are five such monitors here:

   (i) *Team-building knowledge performance*: First, each team member must understand the building blocks of high performance teams, those elemental strategies of knowledge that give insight into how high performance teams come about. The questionnaire in Appendix B lists such knowledge in a way that each team member can monitor his or her progress in performance along such lines.

   (ii) *Team behavioural performance development*: Second, a team must express specific behavioural patterns in line with the above strategies to achieve high performance. The questionnaire in Appendix C lists and measures the key behavioural issues here.

   (iii) *Team operational performance development*: Third, a team must meet specific operational performance parameters to become a high performance team. Appendix D sets out such operational performance parameters and metrics in a further questionnaire.

   (iv) *Team strategic output performance development*: This is to do with the end product the team produces, what the team actually achieves in terms of real innovations. Appendix E outlines the key performance metrics here in the form of a questionnaire.

   (v) *Aggregate performance development equation:* Finally, Appendix G integrates the results of Appendices B, C, D and E in a single equation. The result of the equation indicates the overall performance effectivity of a given innovative team.

5. **Benchmark the team performance at the beginning**: Effective performance development always starts with benchmarking the current performance situation. That is, how well a team is performing when they first come together. Without such information at the beginning, a team will lack any idea of how they are progressing over time. Again the above-mentioned performance monitoring questionnaires can be used here.

6. **Design and set up the team-building laboratory**: Groups will need spaces to help them become teams, not merely on a day-to-day work basis, but places designed expressly for the purpose of building innovative teams. This kind of environment looks a little like an overgrown playground-cum-classroom-cum-lecture theatre, full of tools and toys for the development of collaborative learning and experimentation. The central idea behind such team-building laboratories is that they are immersive environments, which shift the mind-set of groups by totally surrounding them with the conception of teamwork. The best team-building laboratories have a rich environment of diverse learning tools, as the more alien and convoluted these tools, the greater the potential for innovation. We can learn from the likes of Consignia Research Group's Innovation Lab, Rugby UK. It has developed a multifunctional environment that integrates an experience zone, a creativity domain, a home of the future, a play area (for adults) and a tranquil relaxation zone. Here is a short list of the key elements of such a team-building laboratory:

■ *Interpersonal review areas (IRAs)*: Group self-analysis that enables individuals to review and understand their role and behaviour as a greater whole is core to building innovative teams. To hold effective interpersonal reviews, a designated area that provides both a neutral space and the appropriate tools is absolutely necessary. If a facilitator is to hold the context of the dialogue, he/she must be given the space to do so, with the appropriate tools to collect hard facts and data to keep it objective and maintain focus.

■ *Diverse learning tools*: There are many kinds of team learning tools available on the internet. Search them out and experiment. It is no use any team-building expert telling you exactly what learning tools to use at this stage. The whole idea is for the teams themselves to search for, play and experiment with such tools, so that they begin collaborative learning development from the start.

■ *Game spaces*: These are often large, open-plan areas for team problem solving, with no partitioning or fabricated offices, as physical openness helps to promote cultural openness.

■ *Visibility*: Planning and analysis areas are specifically designed in conjunction with the game spaces and IRAs. Problem-solving methodology charts are mounted on the surrounding walls. Information about customers, competition, technology and especially team performance is displayed in an open manner, on every available space – the idea being real-time, highly visible, cross-discipline information.

Executing the Team-building Programme

Next the actual team-building programme is brought to life and applied in a real setting. Again, in order to achieve a smooth operation, executing each exercise in such a programme needs to follow a basic set of application principles:

1. **Assemble the team for an initial programme overview**: An initial get-together in the team-building laboratory to overview the programme is a must. Such an initial meeting might include the following issues for review:

   - *Outline basic objectives*: The team must be aware from the outset what kind of performance improvement is required in terms of end results and the kind of teamwork necessary. Issues such as the level and complexity of innovation need to be outlined, what kind of team interaction and collaboration is required, how rapidly performance might grow and the natural limitations to such growth and so on.

   - *Overview of programme*: A basic, outline run-through of the programme is a good idea. This gives the team an awareness of what to expect. Issues like how much time and effort might be spent, what kind of strategies and techniques might be used, how the programme might develop over time and so on.

   - *Communicate leader's commitment*: It is important for the would-be team to understand that the leader (team and executive) is committed to the building of high performance innovative teams. This reinforces commitment from all sides.

   - *Set level of expectations*: The would-be team needs to have a realistic level of expectation of what a high performance team means, and what a team may look and behave like. The team leader can ask each member what they might expect and what limitations they envisage to building a high performance team. This kind of feedback helps the team to set their expectations, and also helps the leader to identify initial doubts or concerns in team development.

2. **Prepare for the programme**: There are a number of issues that should be set in place first before a real team-building programme begins in earnest:

   ■ *Team-building file*: Give each team member their own file with the relevant formal documentation (above) to follow and monitor both their own and the whole team's growth in performance. The file will also include customised team-building strategies and tools for each member's own reference. Again, Appendix A gives useful templates for such information.

   ■ *Outline of time and venue*: Communicating where and when the actual programme will roll out is important for building commitment and a sense of formality in the initiative. In time the programme will begin to take on an air of normal working practice. Also, each team member will have a hectic schedule of his/her own to meet, so session dates need to be defined and communicated as early as possible. This also gives forewarning of any travel and expenses that may be required.

   ■ *Outline of who is to attend*: Wherever possible, declare who is to attend each programme initiative. Again this gives an air of certainty. However, there are a number of reasons why it is not always possible to define exactly who is to attend a given programme. New people may be coming in all the time. Changes in the project may require a refocus of attention or redeployment of staff. People may leave, and people may simply not be able to make it on that day. After all, innovation is a dynamic, uncertain activity.

   ■ *Familiarise with strategies*: Ask team members to further orient themselves with the basic strategies in their programme file before they attend the first sessions.

3. **Put the programme into action**: Finally, the actualisation of the programme itself. Again, a step-by-step approach is essential:

   ■ *Conduct each exercise in a consistent approach*: Each exercise needs to follow a logical sequence from start to finish. The templates in Appendix A give such a step-by-step methodology. This helps both the continuity of the programme and the intake of the information and lessons learned. An inconsistent programme with inconsistent organisation will only lead to confusion.

- *Review each exercise with the group before execution*: Each member of the group must be familiar with each exercise before it begins. This gives a much better chance for the group to think ahead and understand the purpose of the exercise. Issues to consider here are:

  - The purpose and aims of the exercise
  - Run through step-by-step process
  - Who does what and when
  - Set time allotted
  - Describe and demonstrate any special materials needed
  - Have fun.

- *Ask for questions*: This allows each group to gain information pertinent to their particular situation, and of course further improves understanding.

- *Start the exercise promptly and get to the point quickly*: Again this helps comprehension and simplifies the process.

- *Do not interfere with the group once the exercise has started*: Stopping or intervening is another source of confusion. However, if the group gets stuck or cannot follow the process, *do* stop and intervene, and go back to the 'review each exercise' stage. Then start the exercise from the beginning.

- *Concluding each exercise*: Each exercise must be brought to a definitive close at the end of the allotted time. This makes the whole process crisp and clean.

- *Debriefing each exercise session*: This again clarifies and reinforces information intake and the lessons learned. Here are some questions that you may like to ask each group during the debriefing:

  - How did you feel about the exercise?
  - What did you learn?
  - Did the exercise meet your expectations?
  - What did you not like about the exercise?
  - What did you like about the exercise?
  - What would you like to have done differently?
  - Did all the questions get answered properly?

4. **Some further points**: Here are some further overarching issues that will make the whole programme more effective and run that much smoother:

- *Focus of implementation*: As team members progress up the performance curve, they may develop at a different pace, and have different degrees of proficiency with each team skill. Consequently, some of the exercises may need to be run through in more depth until the concepts and resultant behaviour emerge as required.

- *Monitoring against the 'S' curve*: Because different people progress at different rates, it is important for individuals to *self-monitor* their progress up the 'S' curve. Once this is the case, catch-up programmes can be instituted as required.

- *Endgame*: Without an endgame, or a next-game strategy, a team-building programme may lose sight of its aims and objectives and, in the extreme, result in unnecessary political repercussions. In simple terms, state the criteria for the end of a team-building programme in objective terms (that is, the team is now operating at a high performance level).

Escaping the Diminishing Returns Performance Trap

As noted above, inevitably there will eventually be a diminishing return on performance. However, it is possible (although not easy) to boost performance further by jumping onto a new 'S' curve. To do that, the team has to find superior ways and means to build and organise teams over and above what has already been practised. And there is no reason why this should not happen. There are many kinds of team-building philosophies on the market, all with something to contribute to building innovative teams. The world of business management research is, after all, an ever-growing field.

A typical pattern is that once a team and its members reach a high level of performance and innovation, they usually become quite expert in the subject of team building themselves, and, in turn, often go out and look for a better mousetrap. The key is to give individuals the scope to pursue new ideas here. Give them space and they will do the rest.

Embedding Team Building into the Organisational Culture

It is not easy to build an innovation team. Pursuing and developing that *whole* team philosophy is a serious and continuous activity, driven by highly developed methodologies, borrowing concepts from social psychology and behavioural science. The long-term aim is to make the team-building strategies and tools part and parcel of everyday work practice.

To embed the ideas of shared mental models and dialogue development into the culture of the company takes time, practice and effort. In fact, if you are not spending a significant portion of time on building teams during any project life-cycle, then you will not achieve the breakthroughs in dialogue or mental model sharing necessary for such innovation. The metaphor of the antibiotic applies here. If you only take seven out of eight of the antibiotics from a prescribed treatment, not only will the treatment not work effectively, the next time you catch the contagion, the antibiotic will not work at all. The message is that if you do not see the programme through to completion, the situation can end up worse than before. In short, this is not a 'tick the box and we're finished here' issue, it is a never-ending journey of development.

CHAPTER 12

Profiling and Selecting Team Members

The challenge for any potential team lies in striking a balance between selection and development as the means for building the full set of complementary skills needed to fulfill the team's purpose over time.

J.R. KATZENBACH AND D.K. SMITH

This final chapter closes the loop for building innovative teams. It describes the types of individual needed within a team to bring a systems innovation to market, or indeed into the public sector.

There are three main issues to consider here. First, the types of competencies needed in the form of skills, knowledge, experience and aptitudes to conceive, realise and introduce a systems innovation. Second, the types of personality within a team determine how individual members might actually go about solving real problems and making decisions, and in turn how they are likely to interact with other team members. Finally, and most importantly, the actual profiling and selection methods of individuals appropriate for a systems innovation team.

Identifying Core Competencies for Systems Innovation

To take an innovation from preconception right through to the end of market life-cycle, a mixed group of skills, knowledge, experience and aptitudes has to form and develop within one team. Each particular project will of course require particular skills and so on and appropriate manning can be planned for each case. However, beyond the individual, it is important to develop a fully rounded team of individuals who have a balance of characteristics that complement and fill in each task area so that there is little or no gap in the ability to conceive, develop and introduce a systems innovation.

The goal of identifying competency is to determine the deeper intellectual essence that makes a systems innovation possible. Here, the metaphor of the building block can be applied to the construction and in turn identification of a particular competency. Think about your own particular competencies for a moment. They are made up of blocks ranging from explicit and tacit knowledge, skills and tools, to experience, processes and focus of content itself. Not unlike the different types of brick one would use to build a house, one can configure different skills, knowledge and so on to build a particular competency set. Here is a description of five such building blocks:

1. *Explicit knowledge base*: The most basic type of block is your explicit knowledge base. There are four issues here:

    (i) Fundamental principles of current and emerging technology, such as engineering science, direction of evolution (chance and intended) and application and market potential.

    (ii) Explicit knowledge of market dynamics such as segmentation, regulations, standards, trends and, most importantly, how and what will influence discontinuities within a market ecology.

    (iii) Explicit knowledge of the competition, such as their particular competencies, end product and services, strengths, weaknesses, opportunities that the competition have not yet addressed and the threats they represent.

    (iv) Explicit knowledge of customer demands such as latent wishes or needs, probable future demands and preferences, who the current customer base is now and how the future customer base is likely to change.

2. *Skills*: One popular definition of skill is knowledge plus experience in application. One can learn conceptual structures to improve problem solving. Skills can also be physical. Learned physical techniques in application is a skill. So a skill can be defined as the application of mental and physical knowledge, experience and learned conceptual processes that give rise to a potential outcome. When we say highly skilled, we mean that these processes have been honed to the point of effectiveness.

3. *Tools*: This block is made up of direct application and conceptual technological resources that assist and amplify innovation. These

range from communication infrastructure such as machine tool centres, to design aids, to specialist test equipment, to the very buildings one works within. Tools are fundamental to competence building.

4. *Processes*: This forth block builds relevant cross-discipline processes that take a technological research programme from inception to application, or take a seed from inception to commercialisation. Processes also include functional issues such as management and project accounting, information systems, operations, distribution, management of strategic alliances and supplier development and even the process of managing competency development.

5. *Focus*: The heart of the core competency: when all is said and done it is the essential essence of a proficiency. Examples range from, say, SONY and their micro-miniaturisation talents; the focus of difference between, say, an electronic engineer and mechanical engineer; and even the whole locus of a business context like steel or communications.

Competency Chart

One effective and visible way to identify competency is to generate a competency chart. The chart lists the desired building blocks that need to be assembled to yield a specific core competency. Table 12.1 lists the necessary knowledge base, skills, tools, processes and focus to make thermal insulation materials.

Take tools for instance; it is possible to list the desired applied tools one by one. These can be physical tools such as machine tools or specialist

Table 12.1 Core competency chart

CORE COMPETENCY: Thermal dynamics	Explicit knowledge base	Skills	Tools	Processes	Focus
	Heat mass transfer analysis and calculation	Materials science	CAD solid modelling	Statistical design of experiments	Efficient thermal insulation materials
	Material heat energy conduction	Mechanical engineering	Finite element analysis Design engineering methodology	Work flow mapping	

equipment, even warehousing facilities. Tools can be software programmes like manufacturing planning systems or CAD packages. Equally, tools can be intellectual tools such as methodologies. Once the entire competence set has been defined using the above chart, it is then possible to identify particular people with particular skills for a given project. This is quite simple to do, once again, if information is defined in such a structured and methodological way.

Understanding Personality and Behaviour Profiles for Innovation

Individual personalities are yet another key to team performance. The range and types of personality define the scope of world view and outlook, and the resultant behavioural traits go some way to define how problems will be solved and decisions will be made, and in turn how individuals might interact with each other.

Of course, there are as many different kinds of personality as there are people. However, there are general personality types which are good for innovative teamwork, or not. The goal is to recruit a balanced set of personalities, because, without a balance, critical points of effort and capacities may be lacking at different phases within a project.

Here are a handful of the important kinds of personality desirable for a rounded innovative team:

- *The chairperson*: These people help to balance an innovative team. They are calm and self-assured, and often very controlled. They stop to think and weigh up the situation, they differentiate between reliable and unreliable information, and do not (often) jump to conclusions; conclusions that may lead down blind allies or compound risk. They have a strong sense of objective, so they are good at getting the team focused, and in the end delivering results. They are great in political situations, because they are so often unbiased. They can take each issue on its own merit and do not often discriminate against new or different ideas. They can make good team leaders or principal staff within a team. However, their creative abilities often leave a lot to be desired.

- *The multidimensionalist*: They are holistic in their thinking with a keen ability to combine skill, knowledge and ideas from disparate disciplines to build highly original concepts and solutions. This personality trait is key, as innovations become more complex, teams need multidimensional thinkers who can provide such lateral answers. As process and outcome become more interrelated with other processes and outcomes, we need people who can break down the borders of knowledge into broad interconnected wholes. Although the days of the true polymath are gone, we do need a few people who are more holistic, who say: How does this all knit together? What are the ramifications for tax, health and so on when we do this?

■ *The expert*: All innovation projects need specialists who have expert, even arcane knowledge in particular fields. These people are often single-minded, and have a narrow focus and outlook. They are great at defining and solving highly specialised, technically challenging tasks. They can resolve extremely forbidding problems. However, they do not like to do too many different tasks at once – multitasking is not for them.

■ *The innovator*: These people are independent thinkers and noncon-formists. They can be deceptively clever and creative. They have broad and sometimes deep knowledge within their field, and often go on to develop aspects of their given discipline. They are impor-tant to an innovation team as they often come up with original ideas for techniques, methods and processes for solving equally unique problems. However, you often find them with their heads in the clouds. They sometimes disregard important details and tend to neglect conventions.

■ *The adventurer*: These types take calculated risks and can handle high levels of ambiguity and uncertainty. They are often ready to venture into the unknown, and sometimes offer leadership qualities when things are not so clear, or not going as expected. They are often worldly, well-travelled, well-read, leathery, battle-hardened, scarred, storytellers, yet with their feet on the ground and the track record to prove it.

■ *The inquisitor*: These types are often extrovert, enthusiastic about what they do and very curious. In fact, curiosity is without doubt the most important personality trait for creating something new, as all that is creative and ultimately innovative is derived from curiosity. Inquisi-tive people have an acute learning disposition, a never-ending urge to acquire new knowledge and practise new things, an infinite desire to pull things apart and analyse them and an irresistible addiction to exploration. These types are never satisfied, they will always find new and better ways, because they are always searching, looking, wondering.

■ *The resourcer*: These people are good at tracking down new information or people and very good at finding resources to solve, create or make things. They like a challenge. However, they are inclined to lose interest after the initial stages of a project.

■ *The judge*: These people are quite sober, fairly unemotional and very prudent. They are often hard-nosed and tend to stop people in their tracks. As a result, they have excellent judgement. However, they often lack inspiration and the ability to motivate others. Some people perceive this type as quite boring, particularly when working with inquisitive and innovator types.

■ *The teamer*: These people have acute social sensibilities. They are empathic to others' feelings. They are quite sociable and often mild mannered. They have the ability to promote team spirit and often have a great sense of humour. Humour is important for so many reasons. Studies have shown that when people are humorous, they are in passive mode, that is, they are open to other people's views and ideas. Just as important, humour is the sign of a creative mind. Spontaneous wit is the product of a very agile, creative mind.

■ *The jester*: This breed often have different perspectives and ideas. They are future oriented, and frequently have the ability to imagine what the future could be like. They are intuitive and can feel when something is wrong or, indeed, right. They are playful, like to toy with ideas, and the best of them are generally people-people because they interact and communicate well.

■ *The doer*: They are obviously hard working. If the project is worth doing, they'll see it through to the end, come criticism, hell or high water. The doer overcomes uncertainty too, finding a way through to certainty via persistent learning and problem adaptation. Because of this, these people are essential to an innovative team – they get the work done. However, they are often overcautious and do not like to take risks.

■ *The finisher*: These people are highly convergent thinkers. They have the knack of reducing issues and problems down to their fundamentals. Like the doer, they are painstaking and very conscientious. They like to be methodical and systematic in their approach to work. Because of this, they follow through. However, they are often reluctant to let go of a problem, they view the work as their own and as part of them. But, paradoxically, that is why they are so good at finishing.

Of course any one of these personalities are ideals. You can find bits of each personality present in everyone from time to time. We are all different people at different times, after all. However, if you attempt to optimise your team with a balance of these general personalities, you will be more likely to achieve higher performance.

People Power: The Tom Peters' Quiz

Before we go on to the process of actually selecting team members, let us play a final game. I call it the Tom Peters' Quiz; a game inspired by the big man himself. The idea of the game is that it begins to highlight the fact that such personalities can be found everywhere, but more, it also reveals the amazing potential of people and, at the same time, how people are grossly underestimated, ordinary people from every walk of life.

Questions: What sort of people surround you? What types of people have you employed in the past? What characters have been thrust upon you? Do you think you have amongst you the expert, the inquisitor, the multidimensionalist, the adventurer type and so on? Do not speculate here, prove it, collect the facts.

Go now and collect ten people at random, from different functional areas, suppliers, service people, people in roles that you do not know much about. Now do roughly what I did on a consulting project in an 800-strong, innovatively lagging telecommunications business.

I gathered ten people, five mostly in jobs below the status of line manager, and five in staff positions such as engineer and buyer. I put them in a room together and asked them about what they did when they were not working for the company. The initial reaction was one of suspicion, but after a while a rapport began to develop. Each one had several chances to reveal what they did. This is what I found.

Tracy Hillner is a 37-year-old housewife who says that she works only for the money. She sits at a bench 40-plus hours a week, soldering circuit boards. She said:

> I haven't got much time to myself, it's the kids you know, and I've to get my husband's dinner and the other things a mum has to do ... I suppose when

I've put the kids to bed I get a bit of time to myself and I read a bit on quilt making or do a bit more on the patchwork quilt I'm making.

I asked her to tell me more.

Well, some of my quilts have won competitions, you know. I was runner-up in a competition they had on the television. They invited me and the kids up to the programme and I had to explain some of the things I do in my quilt making ... It was really funny seeing myself on the telly, but I must admit I enjoyed it. After that, a lady from *Woman's Own* asked me to write about quilt making. You know, I didn't know I could write so well.

I asked her to describe some of the techniques she uses. I found myself listening to the expert, the innovator and the inquisitor at one and the same time!

Tim James is a 53-year-old widower employed as a warehouseman. He said:

I've got a lot of time to myself now my wife's passed on; so I spend a lot of time over at the Blue Bell railway, renovating old steam locos. It's filthy work, but I love it.

I asked him to tell me about one of the locomotives he'd worked on. He immediately pulled out two photographs. The first was of an old wrecked locomotive.

When we got this one in, we had our doubts whether we could do anything with it, but we did and this is the result of five years' work.

He showed me the second photograph. It was of a beautiful red locomotive with smoke pouring out of the stack. I couldn't believe my eyes. I asked him to tell me more about the loco. He went on to describe the principles of the locomotive engine. I found myself listening to the doer, the multidimensionalist and the finisher all in one!

Sidney Stuart amazed me the most. Now 63 years old, he had been in the British Merchant Navy, and was now a cleaner in this company. He said:

Well I'm different. I don't do anything. I just watch the television a lot and read the papers.

I asked which newspaper.

> All of 'em. I like the *Telegraph* best. Some of the other newspapers are too centred on British news. They don't give a wide enough view.

I asked him to give me his view on the possible federalisation of Europe. His face went as red as a cherry. 'Well, look at it this way,' he said, and went on to describe how the concept and benefits of European integration would only enhance different cultures. I thought I was listening to a political scientist. I asked if he'd ever thought about going into politics.

> Well, since you ask, I was in politics in a way. I belonged to the Merchants Guild, the Merchant Navy trade union. Those were great days.

I asked why he had left the job.

> I was laid off. Our Merchant Navy started to lose contracts, so the time eventually came when I was made redundant. But after I left I became seriously ill, and had to go through lots of operations. After that I just didn't get back into anything special ... I did join Mensa though. I enjoy the brain-teasers, especially the logic ones. My IQ is in the top five per cent!

Just a cleaner? Come on. No way. I was listening to the judge and the chairperson.

Then came Derrick Porter, an electronic development engineer who has been with the company for 16 years. He runs projects worth millions, yet he doesn't have the authority to sign for petty cash. I asked him what he did in his spare time.

> I enjoy writing. I've written two books,

he said proudly,

> both on mountaineering. In my younger days I'd go off on treks to places like the Alps and the Pyrenees. As well as some other climbs you wouldn't have heard of. I used to climb glaciers thousands of feet high, that were smooth as glass ... I lost two of my best friends and nearly my own life in an accident. It took me a long time to get over that. That's why I wrote one of my books,

about the story of what happened. But after a time that compulsion to climb came back. My other book is about famous or classic climbs.

He lent over and pulled a book out of his briefcase. It was a hardback book with a picture of K2 on the cover.

I nearly made it up that one. It's the toughest climb in the world. In 1972 I went on an expedition. The only thing that stopped us was the weather. We would have made it.

He then flipped through the book, showing me breathtaking panoramic photographs taken from the top of some of the highest peaks. He showed one of a view that made me feel dizzy just looking at it. 'I wouldn't have liked to have been in his shoes,' I said, laughing. 'What do you mean? I took it!' came Derrick's reply.

Who was I listening to? The adventurer, the doer again and the … well, who do you think?

We are all surrounded by such people, in their abundance, I might add. The other six so-called average people, with little scope within their role, had equally diverse personality traits and were just as productive and effective – except for the eight hours they worked for the company! So now go out and look for such types. Ask them what they are doing when they are not working for you.

In Pursuit of Optimising an Innovative Team Mix

What does it mean to have an optimised and balanced innovative team? And what do you have to do to optimise the mix of people in a team to obtain high performance results?

First, there is no such thing as a truly optimised team. Perfection does not exist within any innovation or within any innovative team. The reason is that innovation is about novelty, newness. And if it is new, you are not going to understand it that well. And if you do not understand it, you are not going to be able to optimise it. Nonetheless, the philosophy and goal of team optimisation is indeed a just and important aim.

The key issue to understand here is that different personalities (and indeed skills) are needed at different stages within any given project. One useful template for defining the key stages of an innovation project and, in turn, the necessary personalities is outlined in Figure 12.1.

Genesis is the creation of a seed idea. This first stage represents a highly dynamic phase. Genesis is not by any stretch of the imagination rational or

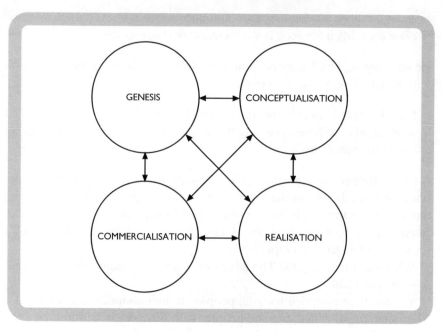

Figure 12.1 Key stages of innovation

obvious, this is primarily a creative thinking, playing, toying process. Some of the issues and the matching personalities might include:

Stage task	*Ideal personalities needed*
Synthesise the idea	The multidimensionalist
	The jester
	The innovator
	The inquisitor
	The adventurer
	The chairperson
Gather relevant market/ customer information	The doer
	The resourcer
Analyse relevant market/ customer information	The inquisitor
	The judge
Find the best competitors for benchmarking	The doer
	The resourcer
	The judge

Build a financial model	The judge
Estimate the technological feasibility	The judge The multidimensionalist
Approximate project scaling	The judge The multidimensionalist

Conceptualisation is the objective definition of the innovation's features and characteristics in the form of robust concept outlines and models (whether physical or virtual). This is a *what if* stage. It is a chance to experiment with options and ideas. The concept must define the 'what' but not the 'how'. This opens up creativity. Some of the issues and the matching personalities might include:

Outline experimental design or service concept	The finisher The innovator The multidimensionalist The teamer The chairperson
Generate prototype models	The expert The finisher
Core technology acquisition or development	The expert The adventurer The resourcer The chairperson
Project capital acquisition	The judge The chairperson
Deeper project scaling	The judge
Risks and uncertainty analysis	The judge
Resource planning	The resourcer The chairperson

Realisation is the development of a manufacturable, reliable, marketable and profitable product or service. Some of the tasks and the matching personalities might include:

The design of experiments	The expert The doer The finisher

	The multidimensionalist
	The innovator
Prototype trials in the market	The expert
	The finisher
	The multidimensionalist
Develop and test systems functionality	The expert
	The multidimensionalist
	The doer
	The finisher
	The teamer
Manufacturing or service systems development	The expert
	The doer
	The finisher
	The multidimensionalist
	The teamer
Specifications and documentation	The expert
	The doer
	The finisher
	The teamer
Qualification and certification	The expert
	The doer
	The finisher
	The teamer
Quality systems development	The expert
	The doer
	The finisher
	The teamer
Production process development	The expert
	The doer
	The finisher
	The teamer
Preproduction/service trials and feedback	The expert
	The doer
	The finisher
	The teamer

Commercialisation is the market penetration and commercial marketing of the invention. Some of the issues and the matching personalities might include:

Identify specific markets	The expert
	The judge
	The chairperson
Develop a commercial marketing strategy	The adventurer
	The innovator
	The expert
	The judge
	The chairperson
Define and select the point/s of sale	The innovator
	The expert
	The judge
	The chairperson
Find relevant distributors and retailers	The resourcer
Find commercial sales partners	The resourcer
Define financial accounting systems	The expert
	The judge
	The chairperson

As previously noted, innovation is a non-linear activity. Each stage will at some point interact with each other stage. Product prototypes will evolve as learning through experiments and testing evolves. Marketing strategy will change in line with the information coming in from conceptualisation prototypes. Quality systems will change as manufacturing systems prototypes develop. All of this is a highly dynamic, ambiguous den of activities. So the need for a particular personality type is a dynamic process in itself.

Team Profiling and Personnel Selection

Finally and most importantly, there is the actual profiling and selection of individuals appropriate for a systems innovation team. Appendix F is a personality indicator questionnaire, which each potential member needs to complete. Once each potential candidate has completed the questionnaire, the management team can assess and build an overall team profile using the charts provided at the end of Appendix F. This will assist in the optimising and balancing of the team.

Here are some further questions you may like to consider when selecting team members once the questionnaire in Appendix F has been filled in:

- Does the candidate have the necessary competencies to fulfil the project specification and bring it to a successful conclusion?

- Does the candidate have a rounded set of personality traits that match his or her skills and talent?

- Does the potential candidate have the rounded set of personality traits needed by the project tasks he or she might be involved with?

- Does the group of candidates have the overall technical/commercial/ operational competency to bring the project to successful fruition?

- Does the group of candidates have a fully rounded set of personality traits to meet the overall needs of the project?

Overall Team-building Strategy

There are no perfect teams, only a continuous and often discontinuous journey of discovery and development. There are no perfect team-building programmes either, only a road of learning and evolution. However, the gains achieved by such a programme of team selection and building are orders-of-magnitude better than what is often gained if a group of people are thrown together and left to their own devises. In a high pressure, relentless innovation project environment, people will sprout horns and a tail from time to time – this is not only human nature, it is clinical psychology.

Innovative team building, then, turns out to be an essential part of organisational life if there is a need for complex (Q4) systems innovation. Without it, I very much doubt that organisations will ever break from the all too common failure statistic outlined in the Introduction to this book. Today, innovative team building is not merely a nice-to-do, it is a must-do strategic issue, if sustainable, higher value-creating innovation is going to become the norm.

PART IV

Appendices

Appendix A – Team-building Exercise Templates
Appendix B – Team-building Knowledge Performance Development Questionnaire
Appendix C – Team Behavioural Performance Development Questionnaire
Appendix D – Team Operational Performance Development Questionnaire
Appendix E – Team Strategic Output Performance Questionnaire
Appendix F – Personality Profiling Questionnaire and Charts
Appendix G – Aggregate Performance Development Equation

Team-building Exercises

On the following pages there are 31 self-contained, step-by-step exercises that describe various hands-on tools and techniques that go towards building innovative teams. Each exercise can be carried out in its own right, or as part of a full-blown team-building programme described in Chapter 11.

Exercise 1   Understanding the unique nature of innovation

Notes: This exercise is designed for all members within a team. Seventeen members maximum, in groups of 3 to 4. A facilitator must coach the process and hold the context. See Chapter 6 for roles of a facilitator.

Purpose and aim	Process	What to do	Materials	Time
To understand why innovation is so different from any other human activity To understand the characteristics and principles of the unique nature of innovation	Each member to study Chapter 1 Group discussion to compare notes and main points	Each member to write a short, 1000-word essay on Chapter 1's main points *Discuss:* 1. The leading definitions of innovation 2. What innovation is 3. What innovation is not 4. What innovation can be 5. The connection between failed invention and deep uncertainty 6. The key features and content of the innovation uncertainty matrix and its significance in determining uncertainty for a given innovation 7. The relationship between successful innovation and accelerated learning 8. The key elements within innovation that drive out uncertainty	Copy of *Building Innovative Teams* for each team member Pad of writing paper and pen for each team member Drymarker board and pen Meeting tables big enough for each subgroup A chair for each member Quiet, light, airy room	Three hours
	Feedback:	*Review:* 9. What was learnt most 10. What new insights came out most 11. How lesson learnt will affect future work 12. Any other points		

Exercise 2	Understanding the unique nature of innovative teams

Notes: This exercise is designed for all members within a team. Seventeen members maximum, in groups of 3 to 4. A facilitator must coach the process and hold the context. See Chapter 6 for roles of a facilitator.

Purpose and aim	Process	What to do	Materials	Time
To understand the unique nature of innovative teams To understand the characteristics and principles of such innovative teams	Each member to study Chapter 2 Group discussion to compare notes and main points	Each member to write a short, 1000-word essay on Chapter 2's main points *Discuss:* 1. The key differences between innovative and steady-state teams 2. The nature of multifaceted change and its impact on innovation 3. The characteristics of Q4 systems innovations 4. The three key difficulties with complex systems innovations 5. The characteristics of an innovative team, and why they are needed for complex systems innovations 6. The seven Cs of an innovative team: Collaborative Consolidated Committed Competent Complementary Confident Camaraderie	Copy of *Building Innovative Teams* for each team member Pad of writing paper and pen for each team member Drymarker board and pen Meeting tables big enough for each subgroup A chair for each member Quiet, light, airy room	Two hours
	Feedback:	*Review:* 7. What was learnt most 8. What new insights came out most 9. How it will affect future work 10. Any other points		

Exercise 3 Understanding the human brain, primitive emotions and the cortex

Notes: This exercise is designed for all members within a team. Seventeen members maximum, in groups of 3 to 4. A facilitator must coach the process and hold the context. See Chapter 6 for roles of a facilitator.

Purpose and aim	Process	What to do	Materials	Time
To understand the difference between hard-wired emotions and learnt intellectual responses and their impact on team collaboration	Each member to study Chapter 3 Group discussion to compare notes and main points	Each member to write a short, 1000-word essay on Chapter 3's main points *Discuss:* 1. The basic structure and physiology of the human brain 2. The difference between the primitive brain and the cortex 3. The difference between the ideas and habits we learn and the emotions and reflexes we are born with 4. The tests on pp. 38–40 5. The flight/fight response 6. Uncertainty and the flight/fight response 7. How to shape up the mind for teamwork 8. Control, the flight/fight response and teamwork	Copy of *Building Innovative Teams* for each team member Pad of writing paper and pen for each team member Drymarker board and pen Meeting tables big enough for each subgroup A chair for each member Quiet, light, airy room	Two hours
	Feedback:	*Review:* 9. What was learnt most 10. What new insights came out most 11. How it will affect future teamwork 12. Any other points		

Exercise 4 Basic communication stress scenarios (1)				
Notes: This exercise is designed for all members within a team. Seventeen members maximum, in groups of 3 to 4. A facilitator must coach the process and hold the context. See Chapter 6 for roles of a facilitator.				
Purpose and aim	**Process**	**What to do**	**Materials**	**Time**
To begin to understand the impact of stressful situations on team performance To begin to raise the tolerance to stress scenarios so that high performance teamwork begins to emerge	Pick any team-building exercise game *Feedback:*	See exercises 21 to 25 Carry out the game as process requires, but in a quarter of the allotted time Facilitator must push the exercise very hard *Review:* 1. The effect of time on performance 2. The effect of time on stress 3. What new insights came out most 4. How it will affect future teamwork 5. Any other points	As game requires *For after exercise:* Pad of writing paper and pen for each team member Drymarker board and pen Meeting tables big enough for each subgroup A chair for each member Quiet, light, airy room	Quarter of time allotted to selected game

Exercise 5 Stress scenarios outward bounding (2) limited information

Notes: This exercise is designed for all members within a team. Seventeen members maximum, in groups of 3 to 4. A facilitator must coach the process and hold the context. See Chapter 6 for roles of a facilitator.

Purpose and aim	Process	What to do	Materials	Time
To show that: (a) People holding narrowly specified roles is inherently restricting (b) Multidimensional roles are more suited to complex innovation (c) Effort to meet an objective depends on interactive communication and collaboration	Pick a number of group games that limit what the individual can contribute to the group, under time pressure Feedback:	See 23 for example For example, each member has a role to play and cannot do more Various games can be played to reinforce the learning points, such as no talking, blindfolding, one arm tied to another person's arm etc. Review: 1. What helped 2. What hindered 3. Who participated most 4. What was learnt most 5. What new insights came out most 6. How it will affect future teamwork 7. Any other points	As game requires For after exercise: Pad of writing paper and pen for each team member Drymarker board and pen Meeting tables big enough for each subgroup A chair for each member Quiet, light, airy room	Six hours maximum

Exercise 6 Stress scenarios (3) treasure hunt

Notes: This exercise is designed for all members within a team. Seven members maximum. A facilitator must coach the process and hold the context. See Chapter 6 for roles of a facilitator.

Purpose and aim	Process	What to do	Materials	Time
To highlight the benefits of whole team problem solving and the impact of a lack of information on team performance	The treasure hunt is spread over three or four square miles in unfamiliar territory	Each team member is randomly given a cryptic, one-paragraph clue on a piece of paper to keep The team set off together to find each piece of treasure within the allotted time No one is permitted to ask for anyone else's clue in any manner. Information can only be given voluntarily, which restricts commun-ication to a one-way street	Three items of hidden treasure Three different sets of cryptic clues in envelopes Each set of clues has the number of clues to match the number of team members	Six hours maximum
	Feedback:	*Discuss:* 1. What it was like not to be able to ask or have information that was available at a particular point in the treasure hunt (problem) 2. The effect of this lack of information on time 3. The effect of pressure and stress on performance 4. The effect of pressure and stress on anxiety	*For after exercise:* Pad of writing paper and pen for each team member Drymarker board and pen Meeting tables big enough for each subgroup A chair for each member Quiet, light, airy room	

Exercise 7	Stress scenarios (4) control-flight/fight-trust cycles

Notes: This exercise is designed for a six-member team. The step-by-step process needs to be developed by an experienced outward-bound and abseiling instructor based on the 'what to do' column. For after-exercise discussion, see Chapter 6 for roles of a facilitator. THIS TEMPLATE IS FOR THE FACILITATOR'S EYES ONLY.

Purpose and aim	Process	What to do	Materials	Time
This is a game of fear versus trust, in uncertainty To explore 'control-flight/fight-trust cycles' and their impact on teamwork	All of this must be done in complete safety with experts surrounding the activity	Each member thinks that they are going to abseil down a 200-metre cliff face, over a rapid river, in a pitch black pothole! Actually, the drop is only 9 metres, with no river at the bottom, just a CD player. But when they set out in groups of six and begin the descent, they don't know that the drop is only 9 metres A team member must act as anchor (safety person at the top)	Abseiling kit for each team member Pothole and a 9-metre (approx.) cliff face A CD player and CD with the sound of rushing river	As required
	Feedback:	Discuss: 1. The lessons of control flight/fight-trust cycles 2. How the development of ownership and control from within the team reduces fear and increases trust in uncertain environments 3. How such control starts a virtuous win–win cycle 4. How when individuals and teams lose ownership and control, fear builds and trust evaporates into the ether 5. The relationship between control, fear and trust 6. Why lack of trust and fear are symptoms, but lack of control is the core precipitant of anxieties	For after exercise: Pad of writing paper and pen for each team member Drymarker board and pen Meeting tables big enough for each subgroup A chair for each member Quiet, light, airy room	

Exercise 8 Understanding the creative individual and the team				
Notes: This exercise is designed for all members within a team. Seven members maximum. A facilitator must coach the process and hold the context. See Chapter 6 for roles of a facilitator.				
Purpose and aim	**Process**	**What to do**	**Materials**	**Time**
To be aware of the impact of the primitive brain on creativity, and the general nature of creative people	Each member to study Chapter 4 Group discussion to compare notes and main points *Feedback:*	Each member to write a short, 1000-word essay on Chapter 4's main points *Discuss:* 1. Creativity as a subject 2. The differences between left and right brain functions 3. The primitive brain and creativity 4. The general nature of creative people 5. Individual autonomy and teamwork 6. The general issues of surfacing conflict as a source of learning and innovation *Review:* 7. What was learnt most 8. What new insights came out most 9. How it will affect future teamwork 10. Any other points	Copy of *Building Innovative Teams* for each team member Pad of writing paper and pen for each team member Drymarker board and pen Meeting tables big enough for each subgroup A chair for each member Quiet, light, airy room	Two hours

Exercise 9 Standing in the other person's shoes (conflict resolution 1)

Notes: This exercise is designed for one-on-one or group-to-group settings. A facilitator must coach the process and hold the context. See Chapter 6 for roles of a facilitator.

Purpose and aim	Process	What to do	Materials	Time
To get each side (individual or group) to imagine what their rival(s) is experiencing	Get each side to ask the other side questions in the 'what to do' column Use the theatre of the mind technique (outlined in Exercise 10) to gain deeper insights here *Make a list of each side's:* 1. Emotions 2. Circumstances 3. Expectations 4. Agenda 5. Values 6. Constraints *Then look for:* 7. Areas of mutual overlap 8. What one side might gain if they gave up some ground	*Ask:* 1. In graphic detail, what are they actually feeling and thinking? 2. What are their own unique circumstances? 3. What are their expectations? 4. What is their agenda? 5. Can you gain an insight into their value systems? 6. What are their political constraints? *Ask and write down the answers to:* 7. Where do we not have areas of conflict? 8. What can I (we) give to get something back?	Pad of writing paper and pen for each team member Drymarker board and pen Meeting tables big enough for each subgroup A chair for each member Quiet, light, airy room	One hour

Exercise 10 Theatre of the mind (conflict resolution 2)

Notes: This exercise is designed for the individual.

Purpose and aim	Process	What to do	Materials	Time
To amplify the power of the imagination in competitive situations so that mutual compromise or synergistic solutions may come about	The theatre of the mind is constructed in the imagination, looking much like a real theatre, with a big projection screen and comfortable chairs	Relax in a chair and close your eyes Imagine a big white projector screen in front of you Now imagine your opponent's circumstances as vividly and as detailed as possible projected onto that screen Then stop the film when you are ready and actually jump into the opponent's shoes and become your opponent's character Let the subconscious take over and now run the film where it thinks it should go Now consciously think where a solution to the conflict can emerge	One chair A human brain and its imagination	Ten minutes

Exercise 11   Difference as inspiration (conflict resolution 3)

Notes: This exercise is designed for one-on-one or group-to-group settings. A facilitator must coach the process and hold the context. See Chapter 6 for roles of a facilitator.

Purpose and aim	Process	What to do	Materials	Time
To provide a way to mediate between two or more contrasting ideas and gain a solution that is acceptable to all parties	Ask the group to arrange their chairs in a circle, and to sit facing outwards Ask a representative from each group to outline their version of the conflict The mediator then asks each group to think about the points in the 'what to do' column Then write down the answers on a drymarker board	1. Pick out three good things about each conflicting idea and three issues that might be seen in a different way 2. Pick out three aspects of conflicting ideas that you have observed to work together elsewhere 3. Pick out three fundamental themes from each conflicting idea that should be incorporated into an innovation 4. Pick out three attributes of difference that affect internal people positively and directly 5. Pick out three attributes of difference that affect external people positively and directly 6. Pick out three measures of success that are germane to each of the conflicting ideas	Pad of writing paper and pen for each team member Drymarker board and pen Meeting tables big enough for each subgroup A chair for each member Quiet, light, airy room	One hour

Exercise 12 Understanding the development of whole team minds

Notes: This exercise is designed for all members within a team. Seven members maximum. A facilitator must coach the process and hold the context. See Chapter 6 for roles of a facilitator.

Purpose and aim	Process	What to do	Materials	Time
To be aware of the power of the collective team mind and the practical skills of mental model development	Each member to study Chapter 5	Each member to write a short, 1000-word essay on Chapter 5's main points *Discuss:* 1. The concept of the mental model 2. The influence of dominant mental models 3. The reasons for transforming mental models 4. The reasons for sharing mental modles	Copy of *Building Innovative Teams* for each team member Pad of writing paper and pen for each team member Drymarker board and pen Meeting tables big enough for each subgroup A chair for each member Quiet, light, airy room	Two hours
	Feedback:	*Review:* 5. What was learnt most 6. Which new insights came out most 7. How it will affect future teamwork 8. Any other points		

Exercise 13 Transforming mental models

Notes: This exercise is designed for all members within a team. Seven members maximum. A facilitator must coach the process and hold the context. See Chapter 6 for roles of a facilitator. This is a discontinuous exercise. See 'Time' below for various examples.

Purpose and aim	Process	What to do	Materials and special needs	Time
To construct new mental models aligned with dynamic market changes To construct new mental models that ultimately create the new competitive space	Define existing mental models: Start the transformational process Seek the underground fringe:	*Ask:* 1. What are the limits of each member's constructed reality? 2. What are the key ingredients and precepts that define each member's mental models? 3. How are they defined? *Think about:* 4. The emerging political, economic, social and technological (PEST) climate 5. Customer needs 6. Technology 7. Competitors 8. Distribution channels 9. Product/service concepts *Ask:* 10. Who can I employ or ally with to get a view beyond my existing world view? 11. How can I get on the edge of my boundaries to see over the horizon? *Do:* 12. Visit new far-off places, cities, exhibitions, cultures 13. Build relationships with innovative practices, strange alliances, quite different people and institutions	For in-class analysis: Drymarker board and pen Chair for each participant Large round table Quiet room Budgets for travel, courses, new reading materials and so on	One hour a week ongoing in-class At least one far off and unusual place to visit every six months Constant innovative relationships building Six-month sabbatical every five years

Exercise 13 continued				
Purpose and aim	**Process**	**What to do**	**Materials and special needs**	**Time**
		14. Read a book/attend a lecture/speak to an expert on a subject that has nothing to do with anything you are doing		
		15. Take sabbaticals		
		16. Hire multidimensionalists		
		17. Play games, have toys in and around your work environment, flood your time with creativity-enhancing activities and devices		
	Look beyond the boundaries of your mental models:	*Ask what's new and around the corner:*		
		18. Politically, economically, socially, technologically (PEST)		
		19. Managerially		
		20. Competitors		
		21. Distribution channels		
		22. Product/service concepts		
	Innovatively interconnect with adjacent mental models:	*Ask:*		
		23. What new insights, near and far, can I interconnect to each member's current mental model outline, that would begin to create a new mental model definition?		
		24. What unarticulated and unsatisfied customer demands or challenging issues could each member fulfil by expanding their mental models with ideas outside the current fold?		
		25. What emerging ideas in other industries could I interconnect with to reinvent each member's world view?		

Exercise 14   Open exploration (sharing mental models 1)

Notes: This exercise is designed for all members within a team. Seven members maximum. A facilitator must coach the process and hold the context. See Chapter 6 for roles of a facilitator.

Purpose and aim	Process	What to do	Materials	Time
To gain the capacity to collectively explore what is on the mind of each individual within a team	Make a legitimate space:	Switch off your mobile phones and lock the door if you can. Quiet is important, and a tranquil setting will stimulate the deepest explorations	Pad of writing paper and pen for each team member	One hour
	Multiway reflection:	There are seven steps to begin to develop the ability of multiway reflection within a team:	Drymarker board and pen	
			Meeting tables big enough for each subgroup	
		1. Practise pausing before member's answer a question or even think of a retort. Count to three (1, 2, 3) then reply	A chair for each member	
		2. Ask peer(s) to elaborate (e.g., 'I'd like to understand more...) on their view or idea	Quiet, light, airy room	
		3. Pause once again (1, 2, 3) before replying. Let the subconscious, and indeed conscious, cogs turn in the mind		
		4. Ask peer(s) to consider what they feel, think (I'd like to give my views/experiences/ issues relevant to this if that's OK with you...)		
		5. Be constructive		
		6. Stop and listen to the response.		
		7. Repeat 1 to 6		
	Stop the show/start the show phrases:	There are thousands of words and phrases that stop the exploration and sharing of mental models		
	Stop the show:	We've tried that before It costs too much Put it in writing It's impossible That just stupid You can't do that here		

Exercise 14 continued				
Purpose and aim	**Process**	**What to do**	**Materials**	**Time**
		Our team's too small That would take too long If it ain't broke, don't fix it		
	Start the show:	That's a good question Let me see it That might be fun if ... How could we do it? What other ideas do you have? I like that, please elaborate How could we improve? Let me ask you this ... If it ain't broke, improve it		
	Reiteration:	Collectively go over and over the same ground Condense information within subject boundaries and write it down		

Exercise 15 Get a new perspective by asking original questions (sharing mental models 2)

Notes: This exercise is designed for all members within a team. Seven members maximum. A facilitator must coach the process and hold the context. See Chapter 6 for roles of a facilitator.

Purpose and aim	Process	What to do	Materials	Time
To get a new perspective by asking original questions	Ask 'what if' questions:	*Ask:* 1. What if it was inverted, upside down, back to front, a different shape, and so on? 2. What if we looked at it from our competitor's/customer's perspective? 3. What if we stopped altogether? 4. What if ... ?	Pad of writing paper and pen for each team member Drymarker board and pen Meeting tables big enough for each subgroup A chair for each member Quiet, light, airy room	One hour
	Don't ask 'why', but 'how' questions:	5. How does it work? 6. How did it come about? 7. How did we get here? 8. How is it that ... ? 9. How are we going to do that?		
	Out-of-the-box questions:	10. Think of a metaphor that interconnects ideas 11. Think of a lateral question that cuts across boundaries		

Exercise 16 Understanding the wheel of reinforcement (sharing mental models 3)

Notes: This exercise is designed for all members within a team. Seven members maximum. A facilitator must coach the process and hold the context. See Chapter 6 for roles of a facilitator.

Purpose and aim	Process	What to do	Materials	Time
To expand and understand that most of our beliefs are based on assumptions To illustrate the basic thought processes that lead to the misunderstanding and/or rejection of an idea	The wheel's seven steps: 1. Assert idea:	State basic idea (for example new concept, detailed solution, unformed opinion, or pure gossip, and so on)	Pad of writing paper and pen for each team member Drymarker board and pen Meeting tables big enough for each subgroup A chair for each member Quiet, light, airy room	Twenty minutes
	2. Apply to context:	A particular challenge within an innovation project, or a formal management meeting, or even an informal social gathering		
	3. Recall exper-ience of context:	The unique and particular circumstances		
	4. Make assump-tion about idea:	Make a supposition about the idea within context, through tacit represen-tations, assumptions and ideologies (mental models)		
	5. Judge idea:	Draw unconscious conclusion or judgement about idea in context		
	6. Go with, hold or reject idea:	Reject, hold as a may be, or take on board as fact		
	7. Idea rein-forcement:	Reinforce the view of the idea as good, bad or indifferent by going around the wheel		

Exercise 17 Stopping and opening the wheel
of reinforcement (sharing mental models 4)

Notes: This exercise is designed for all members within a team. Seven members maximum. A facilitator must coach the process and hold the context. See Chapter 6 for roles of a facilitator.

Purpose and aim	Process	What to do	Materials	Time
To make the teams' thought processes more visible	Opening the wheel: 1. Recall original idea:	Paraphrase the idea or notion, so that all parties are clear about its content	Pad of writing paper and pen for each team member	Twenty minutes
To see how conflict between tacit assumptions can be overcome	2. Reapply idea to context: 3. Recall experience (if any) of context and question:	This helps to clarify *Ask:* 1. What mental models are present that may distort actuality? 2. Are there any experiences (good, bad, indifferent) colouring thinking? 3. What loyalties are present? 4. What legacies have the team inherited?	Drymarker board and pen Meeting tables big enough for each subgroup A chair for each member Quiet, light, airy room	
	4. Outline objective information:	*Ask:* 5. What information is a hunch, guesswork or political work? 6. Which facts are real, which are mere fiction? 7. What quantitative studies have been carried out to verify data?		
	5. Reflect on idea via open exploration and getting a different perspective (above):	Reflect on the idea in a more objective context and reduce earlier assumptions via inquiry and comparison with real data		
	6. Make a 'more' objective judgement based on reflection and comparison:	Make a new, more impartial conclusion about idea		
	7. Go with or reject idea:	Reject or take idea on board		

Exercise 18 Perception orientation

Notes: A facilitator must coach the process and hold the context. See Chapter 6 for roles of a facilitator.

Purpose and aim	Process	What to do	Materials	Time
To align perceptions so that individuals begin to see the world from a similar standpoint	Bring about parity through learning together	Develop a team-building programme by practising all the 31 exercises	As required	As required
	Set expectations	State the objectives and performance metrics of the project at the start		
	Control from within the team	Put control into the heart of the team		

Exercise 19	Understanding collaborative learning beyond knowledge				

Notes: This exercise is designed for all members within a team. Seven members maximum. A facilitator must coach the process and hold the context. See Chapter 6 for roles of a facilitator.

Purpose and aim	Process	What to do	Materials	Time
To be aware of: (a) The power of dialogue within teams (b) How dialogue enhances collaborative learning within teams (c) The practice skills of dialogue development	Each member to study Chapter 6 Group discussion to compare notes and main points Feedback:	Each member to write a short 1000-word essay on Chapter 6's main points *Discuss:* 1. The limits of innovation possibilities and information theory 2. Collaborative learning 3. The concept of dialogue and its impact on team learning 4. The concept of supercool dialogue *Review:* 5. What was learnt most 6. What new insights came out most 7. How it will affect future work 8. Any other points	Copy of *Building Innovative Teams* for each team member Pad of writing paper and pen for each team member Drymarker board and pen Meeting tables big enough for each subgroup A chair for each member Quiet, light, airy room	Two hours

Exercise 20 Team dialogue development

Notes: This exercise is designed for all members within a team. Seventeen members maximum. A facilitator must coach the process and hold the context. See Chapter 6 for roles of a facilitator.

Purpose and aim	Process	What to do	Materials	Time
To build an open dialogue where ideas, views and opinions emerge from the collective intelligence of a group To impart the art and skills of dialogue development	Overcoming initial resistance and alienation:	1. A continuous programme must be put into place so that the stages and tools become an embedded part of the work practice and culture 2. Acknowledgement that there will be initial difficulties. Outline the need for explicit willingness to explore the tacit structure of thought as a collective whole	Pad of writing paper and pen for each team member Drymarker board and pen Meeting tables big enough for each subgroup A chair for each member Quiet, light, airy room	Two hours
	Comfortable settings:	3. Comfortable chairs and a clean, bright room are essential. No distractions or interruptions must occur during the session 4. Sit in a circle facing each other, with no table to block out body gestures		
	Starting the session:	5. Ask open-ended questions (for example 'What's the definition of a high performance team?' 'I was thinking about such and such, what do you think?')		
	Suspend assumptions:	6. Don't ask 'Does anybody have anything on their mind?' This will lead down divisive paths 7. Present ideas, feelings and opinions for reflection and inquiry, in such a way that the whole team observes the deeper, more subtle meanings 8. Observe intensely, without any preconceptions		

Exercise 20 continued				
Purpose and aim	**Process**	**What to do**	**Materials**	**Time**
		9. Let concepts, questions and ideas flow, to go down inventive and unusual thought paths towards original insights and conceptions		
		10. Continued application and practice of suspending assumptions is important		
	Treat each other as peers:	11. Boss/subordinate roles must be suspended to develop an open, friendly atmosphere		
	A facilitator should hold context:	12. The facilitator must bring in different points of view, encourage open thinking and generally monitor the suspension of assumptions		
		13. The facilitator should think: – How can I improve my collective listening skills? – Who is emotionally fragile, who's tough?		
		14. The facilitator must: – Observe non-verbal language – Not criticise or make judgements – Above all, stop talking, start listening and facilitating		
	Ending the session:	15. Remind the team about the time as the close draws near		

Exercise 21 Team narrative building (collaborative learning 1)

Notes: This exercise is designed for all members within a team. Seven members maximum. A facilitator must coach the process and hold the context. See Chapter 6 for roles of a facilitator.

Purpose and aim	Process	What to do	Materials	Time
Assist in the building of a team mind-set To reveal how collectives can build complex, highly creative, in-depth narratives, in shorter cycles	The group must write a meaningful story (a tragedy, comedy, whatever) which must be spelt and punctuated accurately, printed and finished in a binder within twenty-four hours *Feedback:*	The story must be original Each member must write a single chapter, at least one page in length The team must integrate each chapter into the whole *Review the experience:* 1. What difficulties arose? 2. What limited progress? 3. What limited teamwork? 4. How did you feel? 5. What did you learn most?	A4 binder Dictionary Pad of writing paper and pen for each team member Drymarker board and pen Meeting tables big enough for each subgroup A chair for each member Quiet, light, airy room	Twenty-four hours

Exercise 22 Role redeployment (collaborative learning 2)

Notes: This exercise is designed for all members within a team. Seven members maximum.
A facilitator must coach the process and hold the context. See Chapter 6 for roles
of a facilitator.

Purpose and aim	Process	What to do	Materials	Time
To accelerate team learning experiences in unfamiliar territory at the beginning of a real project	Each member must swap their role with another team member for one day (for example games publisher with software author) *Feedback:*	Complete a complex task within a specific time frame (for example develop a technical or marketing specification for a new product) *Review the experience:* 1. How did it feel to be working in a new world? 2. What communication issues arose? 3. What did you learn most?	Pad of writing paper and pen for each team member Drymarker board and pen Meeting tables big enough for each subgroup A chair for each member Quiet, light, airy room	One working day

Exercise 23 Whole team problem solving (collaborative learning 3)

Notes: This exercise is designed for all members within a team. Seven members maximum. A facilitator must coach the process and hold the context. See Chapter 6 for roles of a facilitator.

Purpose and aim	Process	What to do	Materials	Time
To understand that one-way communication hinders team performance To understand that keeping back information can jeopardise the solving of complex problem To understand that to meet an objective depends on interactive communication and collaboration	Present each member of the team with three pieces of the puzzle that fit together	Do not show any member the completed puzzle Break the puzzle up and give three pieces of the puzzle to each member No one can ask for information No one can look at any other members pieces of the puzzle No one is allowed to describe what the picture of the puzzle is as it is forming Ask the team to assemble the puzzle	One complete picture puzzle Pad of writing paper and pen for each team member Drymarker board and pen Meeting tables big enough for each subgroup A chair for each member Quiet, light, airy room	Twenty minutes
	Feedback:	*Review:* 1. What helped 2. What hindered 3. Who participated most 4. What was learnt most 5. What new insights came out most 6. How it will affect future teamwork 7. Any other points		

Exercise 24 The synergy game (collaborative learning 4)

Notes: This exercise is designed for all members within a team. Seven members maximum. A facilitator must coach the process and hold the context. See Chapter 6 for roles of a facilitator.

Purpose and aim	Process	What to do	Materials	Time
To show how mental models inform and guide what we see and pick out in any given situation To show how different people see and prioritise quite distinct issues and facts from the same situation To show that many individual views can be a source of holistic creativity	Part I – individual perspective:	Take a poster picture, with detailed content (say a panoramic city view) and put it on a wall in front of the group Give each member an identical piece of card Ask each of them to write down a 'creative' description of the picture (on the card) in their own words Give them five minutes to do so Gather up the cards and randomly shuffle the stack Read aloud each description in turn	Large picture poster Cards for notes Large piece of paper Pad of writing paper and pen for each team member Drymarker board and pen Meeting tables big enough for each subgroup A chair for each member Quiet, light, airy room	One hour
	Part II – holistic description:	On a single large piece of paper, ask the whole team to consider each member's thoughts and expressions about the picture Ask them to reserve judgement and listen to each comment and view Ask them to interconnect each individual idea so that a team description of the picture emerges		
	Feedback:	Review results and have a dialogue on: 1. Why did each individual see their own version of the picture? 2. How did each mental model of the picture change when confronted with other mental models? 3. Why was the collective narration more descriptive? 4. How was the collective narration more creative?		

Exercise 25 Context perspective (collaborative learning 5)

Notes: This exercise is designed for all members within a team. Large groups can be accommodated by splitting into groups of three or four. A facilitator must coach the process and hold the context. See Chapter 6 for roles of a facilitator.

Purpose and aim	Process	What to do	Materials	Time
To show that even though we may have shared mental models when we read from the same hymn sheet, different context perspectives lead us to see and prioritise things differently	This game is designed for groups that have spent some time together Split the group into a set of smaller groups Give each subgroup a copy of the text, then ask each sub-group to think of an individual theme (e.g. computer programming, market learning, organisational theory, whatever's appropriate)	Copy a one-page piece of text from a book (preferably text with some abstruse insights) Ask each sub-group to read the text from the point of their theme, and write down what they learn What usually happens, is that each subgroup picks out quite unique insights and ifeas from the very same sentences Brainstorm to gel these disparate insights together	Pad of writing paper and pen for each team member Drymarker board and pen Meeting tables big enough for each subgroup A chair for each member Quiet, light, airy room	Thirty minutes

Exercise 26 The egg game (collaborative learning 6)				

Notes: This exercise is designed for all members within a team. Seven members maximum. A facilitator must coach the process and hold the context. See Chapter 6 for roles of a facilitator.

Purpose and aim	Process	What to do	Materials	Time
To assess team initiative building and evaluation Design and make a protective packaging for one egg, which will withstand a drop from 3-metres onto a hard floor	Present the team with a standard box of eggs Evaluate team's effort:	The team must use their initiative and collaborate to build impact-proof egg packaging After the allotted time is up, the team submit their idea and test the design *Look for strengths and weaknesses in:* 1. Performance of design 2. Quality and quantity of suggestions 3. Range of thinking 4. Focus on results 5. Budgetary management 6. Team traits (such as mutuality, trust and so on) Review overall team performance against evaluation data	Box of farm eggs Modest budget Whatever the team uses in the building of the impact packaging Pad of writing paper and pen for each team member Drymarker board and pen Meeting tables big enough for each subgroup A chair for each member Quiet, light, airy room	Three hours for exercise 30 minutes for test and evaluation 30 minutes for feedback Total four hours
	Feedback:	Ask: 7. Each member to think about how they could improve the team performance 8. What would they do differently next time?		

Exercise 27	Understanding innovative team values

Notes: This exercise is designed for all members within a team. Seven members maximum. A facilitator must coach the process and hold the context. See Chapter 6 for roles of a facilitator.

Purpose and aim	Process	What to do	Materials	Time
To be aware of the significance of innovative team values, and how they are reinforced within the team	Each member to study Chapter 7 Group discussion to compare notes and main points	Each member to write a short, 1000-word essay on Chapter 7's main points *Discuss:* 1. The idea of a set of core values 2. Values and a team's meaning 3. Values and a team's purpose 4. The consequences of conflicting values 5. The seven most important values an innovative team can hold 6. Developing and reinforcing innovative team values	Copy of *Building Innovative Teams* for each team member Pad of writing paper and pen for each team member Drymarker board and pen Meeting tables big enough for each subgroup A chair for each member Quiet, light, airy room	Two hours
	Feedback:	*Review:* 7. What was learnt most 8. What new insights came out most 9. How it will affect future teamwork 10. Any other points		

Exercise 28 Innovative team values development

Notes: This exercise is designed for all members within a team. Seven members maximum. A facilitator must coach the process and hold the context. See Chapter 6 for roles of a facilitator.

Purpose and aim	Process	What to do	Materials	Time
To begin to embed and reinforce the core values of innovative teams	Group dialogue on values development Sit the team in a circle facing each other	Get each team member to think and talk about their own particular behaviour and beliefs and how their own values drive that behaviour and build their belief system *Discuss:* Which values are important for innovative teams? The meaning of the values: 1. Integrity 2. Trust 3. Forgiveness 4. Mutuality 5. Freedom 6. Respect for the individual 7. Playfulness	Pad of writing paper and pen for each team member Drymarker board and pen Meeting tables big enough for each subgroup A chair for each member Quiet, light, airy room	Two hours
	Feedback:	*Review:* 1. How each value interacts and reinforces the others in a holistic way 2. How they affect team performance 3. The impact they have on the meaning and purpose of the team 4. How such values become embedded within the team culture		

Exercise 29 Understanding the design of high performance metrics and goals

Notes: This exercise is designed for all members within a team. Seven members maximum. A facilitator must coach the process and hold the context. See Chapter 6 for roles of a facilitator.

Purpose and aim	Process	What to do	Materials	Time
To be aware of the significance of high performance goals and their associated metrics To learn how to design and apply high performance goals and metrics	Each member to study Chapter 8 Group discussion to compare notes and main points Feedback:	Each member to write a short, 1000-word essay about Chapter 8's main points Ask: 1. Why are high performance goals and metrics important for innovative teams? 2. What are the principal characteristics of effective goals and metrics? 3. What does high performance mean in terms of innovation? 4. What is meant by SMART high performance goals? 5. Why are attainable and integrated goals important for systems innovation? 6. Why is there a need to design performance metrics? 7. What should be measured? 8. How are performance metrics designed? 9. What is the significance of focusing metrics on divergent or convergent goals? Review: 10. What was learnt most 11. What new insights came out most 12. How it will affect future work 13. Any other points	Copy of *Building Innovative Teams* for each team member Pad of writing paper and pen for each team member Drymarker board and pen Meeting tables big enough for each subgroup A chair for each member Quiet, light, airy room	Three hours

Exercise 30 Understanding organising innovative teams

Notes: This exercise is designed for all members within a team. Seven members maximum. A facilitator must coach the process and hold the context. See Chapter 6 for roles of a facilitator.

Purpose and aim	Process	What to do	Materials	Time
To understand the significance of team organisational design for complex systems innovation Understand how to organise for innovative teams	Each member to study Chapter 9 Group discussion to compare notes and main points	Each member to write a short, 1000-word essay on Chapter 9's main points *Ask:* 1. Why and how is the complexity of innovation increasing? 2. What are the characteristics of a smarter, simpler, more agile organisation? 3. Why and what is the optimum size and reporting structure for innovative teams? 4. Why are end-to-end multidimensional roles necessary for systems innovation? 5. Why is collocation important? 6. What is the significance of team project rooms? 7. What are the key collaborative technologies now available for distributed teams?	Copy of *Building Innovative Teams* for each team member Pad of writing paper and pen for each team member Drymarker board and marker pen Meeting tables big enough for each subgroup A chair for each member Quiet, light, airy room	Two hours
	Feedback:	*Review:* 8. What was learnt most 9. What new insights came out most 10. How it will affect future work 11. Any other points		

Exercise 31 Understanding innovative team leadership				

Notes: This exercise is designed for all members within a team. Seven members maximum. A facilitator must coach the process and hold the context. See Chapter 6 for roles of a facilitator.

Purpose and aim	Process	What to do	Materials	Time
To understand the significance of the style and roles of an innovative team leader	Each member to study Chapter 10 Group discussion to compare notes and main points Feedback:	Each member to write a short, 1000-word essay on Chapter 10's main points Ask: 1. What is meant by an innovative open leadership style? 2. What are the characteristics of an innovative team leader? 3. What are the key roles of an innovative team leader? 4. What makes for a good innovative team leader? Review: 5. What was learnt most 6. What new insights came out most 7. How it will affect future work 8. Any other points	Copy of *Building Innovative Teams* for each team member Pad of writing paper and pen for each team member Drymarker board and pen Meeting tables big enough for each subgroup A chair for each member Quiet, light, airy room	Two hours

Team-building Knowledge Performance Development Questionnaire

This questionnaire lists the key strategies and tools that each team member needs to grasp in order to be an effective and innovative team player. Each strategy and tool has been taken from each chapter in Part II and the team-building exercise templates in Appendix A. It is a self-assessment questionnaire that each member needs to complete as part of team performance monitoring described in Chapter 11.

Each statement has a range of five potential responses, with five abbreviations and associated scores to indicate the team member's rating:

Strongly agree	=	SA
Agree	=	A
Not demonstrated consistently	=	N
Disagree	=	D
Strongly disagree	=	SD

There is no time limit.

1. You are aware of the leading definitions of innovation.

SA	A	N	D	SD
(10)	(8)	(6)	(4)	(2)

2. You know what innovation is.

SA	A	N	D	SD
(10)	(8)	(6)	(4)	(2)

3. You know what innovation is not.

SA	A	N	D	SD
(10)	(8)	(6)	(4)	(2)

4. You know what successful innovation can be.

SA	A	N	D	SD
(10)	(8)	(6)	(4)	(2)

5. You understand the relationship between failed invention and deep uncertainty.

SA	A	N	D	SD
(10)	(8)	(6)	(4)	(2)

6. You are aware of the innovation uncertainty matrix.

SA	A	N	D	SD
(10)	(8)	(6)	(4)	(2)

7. You understand the relationship between successful innovation and accelerated learning.

SA	A	N	D	SD
(10)	(8)	(6)	(4)	(2)

8. You are aware of the difference between innovative teams and steady-state teams.

SA	A	N	D	SD
(10)	(8)	(6)	(4)	(2)

9. You understand the impact of multifaceted change on innovation.

SA	A	N	D	SD
(10)	(8)	(6)	(4)	(2)

10. You understand the need for complex (Q4) systems innovation.

SA	A	N	D	SD
(10)	(8)	(6)	(4)	(2)

11. You are aware of the 'seven Cs' of innovative teams.

SA	A	N	D	SD
(10)	(8)	(6)	(4)	(2)

12. You thoroughly understand the difference between hard-wired emotional responses and learnt intellectual responses, and their different effects on team collaboration and performance.

SA	A	N	D	SD
(10)	(8)	(6)	(4)	(2)

13. You understand the relationship between the flight or fight response and uncertainty.

SA	A	N	D	SD
(10)	(8)	(6)	(4)	(2)

14. You know how to get your brain into shape for teamwork.

SA	A	N	D	SD
(10)	(8)	(6)	(4)	(2)

15. You understand the significance of local and autonomous control and a team's performance.

SA	A	N	D	SD
(10)	(8)	(6)	(4)	(2)

16. You understand the techniques of tolerance building and communication stress scenarios.

SA	A	N	D	SD
(10)	(8)	(6)	(4)	(2)

17. You are aware of the impact of the primitive brain on creativity.

SA	A	N	D	SD
(10)	(8)	(6)	(4)	(2)

18. You are aware of the general nature of creative people.

SA	A	N	D	SD
(10)	(8)	(6)	(4)	(2)

19. You are aware that creative types need latitude and autonomy within the team.

SA	A	N	D	SD
(10)	(8)	(6)	(4)	(2)

20. You comprehend the value of difference within a team.

SA	A	N	D	SD
(10)	(8)	(6)	(4)	(2)

21. You are aware that conflict can be a source of learning and innovation.

SA	A	N	D	SD
(10)	(8)	(6)	(4)	(2)

22. You understand the need to move towards a win–win team position.

SA	A	N	D	SD
(10)	(8)	(6)	(4)	(2)

23. You understand the technique of standing in the other person's shoes.

SA	A	N	D	SD
(10)	(8)	(6)	(4)	(2)

24. You can see difference as source of inspiration for new ideas and solutions.

SA	A	N	D	SD
(10)	(8)	(6)	(4)	(2)

25. You are aware of the significance of mental models and their impact on teamwork.

SA	A	N	D	SD
(10)	(8)	(6)	(4)	(2)

26. You are aware of the significance of dominant mental models and their impact on teamwork.

SA	A	N	D	SD
(10)	(8)	(6)	(4)	(2)

27. You are aware of the need to constantly transform team mental models.

SA	A	N	D	SD
(10)	(8)	(6)	(4)	(2)

28. You understand the need for sharing mental models within a team.

SA	A	N	D	SD
(10)	(8)	(6)	(4)	(2)

29. You understand the technique of open exploration for sharing mental models.

SA	A	N	D	SD
(10)	(8)	(6)	(4)	(2)

30. You understand the technique of getting a new perspective by asking original questions.

SA	A	N	D	SD
(10)	(8)	(6)	(4)	(2)

31. You are aware of the impact of the wheel of reinforcement.

SA	A	N	D	SD
(10)	(8)	(6)	(4)	(2)

32. You understand the technique of stopping and opening the wheel of reinforcement.

SA	A	N	D	SD
(10)	(8)	(6)	(4)	(2)

33. You understand the effects of an individual's perception orientation on team performance.

SA	A	N	D	SD
(10)	(8)	(6)	(4)	(2)

34. You understand the concept of synergy.

SA	A	N	D	SD
(10)	(8)	(6)	(4)	(2)

35. You understand the nature of collaborative learning.

SA	A	N	D	SD
(10)	(8)	(6)	(4)	(2)

36. You understand how learning reduces risk and uncertainty.

SA	A	N	D	SD
(10)	(8)	(6)	(4)	(2)

37. You understand dialogue development techniques.

SA	A	N	D	SD
(10)	(8)	(6)	(4)	(2)

38. You thoroughly understand the practice games for collaborative learning.

SA	A	N	D	SD
(10)	(8)	(6)	(4)	(2)

39. You are aware of the concepts and impact of core values on a team's performance.

SA	A	N	D	SD
(10)	(8)	(6)	(4)	(2)

40. You are aware of the concepts and impact of values on a team's meaning.

SA	A	N	D	SD
(10)	(8)	(6)	(4)	(2)

41. You are aware of the concepts and impact of values on a team's purpose.

SA	A	N	D	SD
(10)	(8)	(6)	(4)	(2)

42. You are aware of the impact of values as a control mechanism.

SA	A	N	D	SD
(10)	(8)	(6)	(4)	(2)

43. You understand why differing values can cause conflict within teams.

SA	A	N	D	SD
(10)	(8)	(6)	(4)	(2)

44. You are aware of the seven most important values an innovative team holds.

SA	A	N	D	SD
(10)	(8)	(6)	(4)	(2)

45. You are aware of the issues that develop and reinforce innovative team values.

SA	A	N	D	SD
(10)	(8)	(6)	(4)	(2)

46. You understand the concepts of high performance.

SA	A	N	D	SD
(10)	(8)	(6)	(4)	(2)

47. You understand the concept of SMART high performance goals.

SA	A	N	D	SD
(10)	(8)	(6)	(4)	(2)

48. You are aware of the need for attainable stretch goals.

SA	A	N	D	SD
(10)	(8)	(6)	(4)	(2)

49. You are aware of the need for integrated systems goals.

SA	A	N	D	SD
(10)	(8)	(6)	(4)	(2)

50. You understand the need for performance metrics.

SA	A	N	D	SD
(10)	(8)	(6)	(4)	(2)

51. You understand the principal characteristics of effective performance metrics.

SA	A	N	D	SD
(10)	(8)	(6)	(4)	(2)

52. You understand the three key innovative team performance metrics.

SA	A	N	D	SD
(10)	(8)	(6)	(4)	(2)

53. You know the basic design rules for key performance metrics.

SA	A	N	D	SD
(10)	(8)	(6)	(4)	(2)

54. You understand the difference between divergent creativity and convergent results.

SA	A	N	D	SD
(10)	(8)	(6)	(4)	(2)

55. You know when to focus metrics on creativity.

SA	A	N	D	SD
(10)	(8)	(6)	(4)	(2)

56. You know when to focus metrics on results.

SA	A	N	D	SD
(10)	(8)	(6)	(4)	(2)

57. You are aware of the difference between top-down and bottom-up organisations.

SA	A	N	D	SD
(10)	(8)	(6)	(4)	(2)

58. You know how to optimise the size and structure of teams.

SA	A	N	D	SD
(10)	(8)	(6)	(4)	(2)

59. You understand the significance of multidimensional roles and their impact on innovation.

SA	A	N	D	SD
(10)	(8)	(6)	(4)	(2)

60. You know how to design multidimensional roles.

SA	A	N	D	SD
(10)	(8)	(6)	(4)	(2)

61. You understand the significance of team collocation.

SA	A	N	D	SD
(10)	(8)	(6)	(4)	(2)

62. You know how to construct innovative team project rooms.

SA	A	N	D	SD
(10)	(8)	(6)	(4)	(2)

63. You are aware of the need for distributed teams.

SA	A	N	D	SD
(10)	(8)	(6)	(4)	(2)

64. You understand the basics of collaborative technologies.

SA	A	N	D	SD
(10)	(8)	(6)	(4)	(2)

65. You understand the concept of innovative open team leadership.

SA	A	N	D	SD
(10)	(8)	(6)	(4)	(2)

66. You are aware of the key characteristics of an innovative team leader.

SA	A	N	D	SD
(10)	(8)	(6)	(4)	(2)

67. You understand the key roles of an innovative team leader.

SA	A	N	D	SD
(10)	(8)	(6)	(4)	(2)

68. You know how to select a team leader.

SA	A	N	D	SD
(10)	(8)	(6)	(4)	(2)

From a total number of 68 statements, there is a maximum possible score of 680 points. By dividing the actual *total score* by the *total possible score* (680) and then multiplying the *result* by 100, the knowledge performance rating is expressed as a percentage. For example, an actual score of 340 will give you a team-building knowledge development rating of 50 per cent. Clearly, the nearer the score moves to 100 per cent, the more expert the team member is going to be in the strategies and tools for building innovative teams.

Team Behavioural Performance Development Questionnaire

This questionnaire lists the key behavioural issues – based on the seven Cs in Chapter 2 – that a team must exhibit to achieve high performance. The questionnaire is best completed on both an individual and team basis. First, the individual rating will orientate the individual on their own performance against the team's performance. Second, the team performance rating can be set against each individual's rating. This gives a balanced insight into where to improve on both an individual and team level.

There is also a third benefit. As the group of individuals develop towards a high performance team, they will find that the process of team-based performance rating improves dramatically as well. In fact, the first time a team carries out a team-based scoring approach, it gives a great benchmark and telling insight into how much a team actually needs to improve in the area of team behaviour.

Each statement has a range of five potential responses, with five abbreviations and associated scores to indicate individual and team ratings:

Strongly agree	=	SA
Agree	=	A
Not demonstrated consistently	=	N
Disagree	=	D
Strongly disagree	=	SD

There is no time limit.

1. There is a high level of mental model sharing and ongoing mental model transformation.

SA	A	N	D	SD
(10)	(8)	(6)	(4)	(2)

2. There is a high degree of knowledge and information sharing within the team.

SA	A	N	D	SD
(10)	(8)	(6)	(4)	(2)

3. There is a high level of dialogue within the team.

SA	A	N	D	SD
(10)	(8)	(6)	(4)	(2)

4. There is a high level of collaborative learning (concepts, experiments, tests and so on) within the team.

SA	A	N	D	SD
(10)	(8)	(6)	(4)	(2)

5. The team often pushes the boundaries of knowledge and ideas.

SA	A	N	D	SD
(10)	(8)	(6)	(4)	(2)

6. Conflict within the team is often used as a spur for creativity.

SA	A	N	D	SD
(10)	(8)	(6)	(4)	(2)

7. When necessary, there is a high degree of individual autonomy within the team.

SA	A	N	D	SD
(10)	(8)	(6)	(4)	(2)

8. The team often pushes the boundaries of what is thought possible.

SA	A	N	D	SD
(10)	(8)	(6)	(4)	(2)

9. In its actions, the team expresses the values necessary for the meaning.

SA	A	N	D	SD
(10)	(8)	(6)	(4)	(2)

10. In its actions, the team expresses the values necessary for the purpose.

SA	A	N	D	SD
(10)	(8)	(6)	(4)	(2)

11. The team as a whole has a high degree of integrity.

SA	A	N	D	SD
(10)	(8)	(6)	(4)	(2)

12. There is a strong sense of trust within the team.

SA	A	N	D	SD
(10)	(8)	(6)	(4)	(2)

13. There is a strong sense of mutuality within the team.

SA	A	N	D	SD
(10)	(8)	(6)	(4)	(2)

14. Individual members have a sense of freedom to do what they think best for each new situation.

SA	A	N	D	SD
(10)	(8)	(6)	(4)	(2)

15. There is a real sense of playfulness within the team.

SA	A	N	D	SD
(10)	(8)	(6)	(4)	(2)

16. In his/her daily actions, the team leader reflects what the team is aiming for.

SA	A	N	D	SD
(10)	(8)	(6)	(4)	(2)

17. There is a strong sense of purpose within the team.

SA	A	N	D	SD
(10)	(8)	(6)	(4)	(2)

18. The leader is building a sense of destiny for the team.

SA	A	N	D	SD
(10)	(8)	(6)	(4)	(2)

19. The leader has a sense of foresight.

| SA (10) | A (8) | N (6) | D (4) | SD (2) |

20. There is team-wide accountability.

| SA (10) | A (8) | N (6) | D (4) | SD (2) |

21. The team leader gives constant direct feedback.

| SA (10) | A (8) | N (6) | D (4) | SD (2) |

22. There is a high degree of commitment to one another.

| SA (10) | A (8) | N (6) | D (4) | SD (2) |

23. There is a sense of collective ownership and responsibility.

| SA (10) | A (8) | N (6) | D (4) | SD (2) |

24. Team members see what they are doing through to the end result on a consistent basis.

| SA (10) | A (8) | N (6) | D (4) | SD (2) |

25. The team has the overall skill set and knowledge pool to do the job effectively.

| SA (10) | A (8) | N (6) | D (4) | SD (2) |

26. There are ongoing team-building programmes for each project.

| SA (10) | A (8) | N (6) | D (4) | SD (2) |

27. There are individual-based skills development programmes.

| SA (10) | A (8) | N (6) | D (4) | SD (2) |

28. There is sufficient focus on team skills.

| SA (10) | A (8) | N (6) | D (4) | SD (2) |

29. There is ongoing training for multiskilling.

| SA (10) | A (8) | N (6) | D (4) | SD (2) |

30. The right tools are available to get the job done.

| SA (10) | A (8) | N (6) | D (4) | SD (2) |

31. There is in-class learning as well as on-task learning.

| SA (10) | A (8) | N (6) | D (4) | SD (2) |

32. There is a sufficient level of experience of the nature and nurture of innovation within the team.

| SA (10) | A (8) | N (6) | D (4) | SD (2) |

33. There is a balanced set of personalities within the team to get the job done.

| SA (10) | A (8) | N (6) | D (4) | SD (2) |

34. There are the appropriate personalities within the team at each stage of the innovation activity.

| SA (10) | A (8) | N (6) | D (4) | SD (2) |

35. People are given open 'end-to-end' roles so they can work across functions and disciplines.

| SA (10) | A (8) | N (6) | D (4) | SD (2) |

36. The leadership style is open and innovative.

| SA (10) | A (8) | N (6) | D (4) | SD (2) |

37. Individual skill sets are multidisciplinary.

SA (10)	A (8)	N (6)	D (4)	SD (2)

38. There is a sense of give and take.

SA (10)	A (8)	N (6)	D (4)	SD (2)

39. Each team member is clear about what
he/she is meant to achieve and by when.

SA (10)	A (8)	N (6)	D (4)	SD (2)

40. There is a sense of concurrent work
going on in the team.

SA (10)	A (8)	N (6)	D (4)	SD (2)

41. The team leader builds individual confidence.

SA (10)	A (8)	N (6)	D (4)	SD (2)

42. The team leader builds the team's confidence.

SA (10)	A (8)	N (6)	D (4)	SD (2)

43. There is a strong sense of tenacity within the team.

SA (10)	A (8)	N (6)	D (4)	SD (2)

44. The team is producing short-term wins.

SA (10)	A (8)	N (6)	D (4)	SD (2)

45. There is an atmosphere where individuals feel they
can carry out a high risk experiment without
fear of reproach if the test fails.

SA (10)	A (8)	N (6)	D (4)	SD (2)

46. There is a high level of support amongst team members.

SA (10)	A (8)	N (6)	D (4)	SD (2)

47. Individuals speak their mind without fear
of recrimination.

SA (10)	A (8)	N (6)	D (4)	SD (2)

48. There is a high level of ownership and
control within the team.

SA (10)	A (8)	N (6)	D (4)	SD (2)

49. There is an informal atmosphere within the team.

SA (10)	A (8)	N (6)	D (4)	SD (2)

50. There is an overall sense of fun and play.

SA (10)	A (8)	N (6)	D (4)	SD (2)

51. There is a high degree of empathy within the team.

SA (10)	A (8)	N (6)	D (4)	SD (2)

52. There is a sense of fraternity within the team.

SA (10)	A (8)	N (6)	D (4)	SD (2)

53. Bureaucratic and social graces are minimised.

SA (10)	A (8)	N (6)	D (4)	SD (2)

54. The team leader organises competitions, games,
trips out and so on on a regular basis.

SA (10)	A (8)	N (6)	D (4)	SD (2)

55. New ideas are gained or pursued through play.

SA (10)	A (8)	N (6)	D (4)	SD (2)

56. A reasonable cross-section of the team
participate in playful experiments.

SA (10)	A (8)	N (6)	D (4)	SD (2)

Seven Cs behavioural performance chart

Once the questionnaire has been completed, each score should be entered in the appropriate box in the seven Cs performance chart below. The total score for each type of behavioural performance category (collaboration, commitment, competences and so on) should then be added up within the box under each category.

To find the average score for each performance category, divide each category score by 8, then enter it into the relevant 'average performance' box under each total score box. When completed by each team member, the chart will give an impartial indication of the behavioural performance development, which, in turn, will indicate where performance needs to be improved.

Lastly, by adding up each average score to give an average performance total, a bottom-line number can be determined for behavioural performance development. For example, the total possible score for overall performance is 560. By dividing the actual average score by the total possible score then multiplying by 100 you derive a percentage performance indicator.

Seven Cs behavioural performance chart

	Collaboration		Consolidation		Committed		Competent
1		9		17		25	
2		10		18		26	
3		11		19		27	
4		12		20		28	
5		13		21		29	
6		14		22		30	
7		15		23		31	
8		16		24		32	
Total							
Ave							

	Complementary		Confidence		Camaraderie
33		41		49	
34		42		50	
35		43		51	
36		44		52	
37		45		53	
38		46		54	
39		47		55	
40		48		56	
Total					
Ave					

Team Operational Performance Development Questionnaire

This questionnaire lists the key operational factors that a team must accomplish in order to be a high performance innovative team. Each operational parameter has been taken from the chapters in Part II.

The questionnaire is best completed on both an individual and team basis. First, the individual rating will orientate the individual on their own performance against the team's performance. Second, the team performance rating can be set against each individual's rating. This gives a balanced insight into where to improve on both an individual and team level.

Each statement has a range of five potential responses, with five abbreviations and associated scores to indicate the team member's rating:

Strongly agree	=	SA
Agree	=	A
Not demonstrated consistently	=	N
Disagree	=	D
Strongly disagree	=	SD

There is no time limit.

1. You know what successful innovation is and apply the key factors that make it come about.

   | SA (10) | A (8) | N (6) | D (4) | SD (2) |

2. You apply rapid collaborative learning to make innovation happen.

   | SA (10) | A (8) | N (6) | D (4) | SD (2) |

3. You apply the innovation uncertainty matrix as a gauge for measuring complexity and novelty within a given innovation.

   | SA (10) | A (8) | N (6) | D (4) | SD (2) |

4. You apply the techniques for getting your brain into shape for teamwork.

   | SA (10) | A (8) | N (6) | D (4) | SD (2) |

5. You have local and autonomous team-based control.

   | SA (10) | A (8) | N (6) | D (4) | SD (2) |

6. You apply the techniques of tolerance building and communication stress scenarios.

   | SA (10) | A (8) | N (6) | D (4) | SD (2) |

7. You give creative types latitude and autonomy within the team.

   | SA (10) | A (8) | N (6) | D (4) | SD (2) |

8. You value difference within a team.

   | SA (10) | A (8) | N (6) | D (4) | SD (2) |

9. You use conflict as a source for learning and innovation.

   | SA (10) | A (8) | N (6) | D (4) | SD (2) |

10. You always move towards a win–win team position.

    | SA (10) | A (8) | N (6) | D (4) | SD (2) |

11. You apply the techniques of standing in the other person's shoes.

    | SA (10) | A (8) | N (6) | D (4) | SD (2) |

12. You apply difference as source of inspiration for new ideas and solutions.

    | SA (10) | A (8) | N (6) | D (4) | SD (2) |

13. You constantly expand and transform your mental models.

    | SA (10) | A (8) | N (6) | D (4) | SD (2) |

14. You share your mental models within a team.

    | SA (10) | A (8) | N (6) | D (4) | SD (2) |

15. You apply the technique of open exploration for sharing mental models.

    | SA (10) | A (8) | N (6) | D (4) | SD (2) |

16. You apply the technique of getting a new perspective by asking original questions.

    | SA (10) | A (8) | N (6) | D (4) | SD (2) |

17. You apply the technique of stopping and opening the wheel of reinforcement.

SA (10)	A (8)	N (6)	D (4)	SD (2)

18. You apply the techniques for perception alignment.

SA (10)	A (8)	N (6)	D (4)	SD (2)

19. You always move towards a synergy within the team.

SA (10)	A (8)	N (6)	D (4)	SD (2)

20. You apply dialogue development techniques.

SA (10)	A (8)	N (6)	D (4)	SD (2)

21. You practise games to improve collaborative learning.

SA (10)	A (8)	N (6)	D (4)	SD (2)

22. You apply the concepts of building core values to improve a team's performance.

SA (10)	A (8)	N (6)	D (4)	SD (2)

23. You apply values as a team coherency mechanism.

SA (10)	A (8)	N (6)	D (4)	SD (2)

24. You harmonise values to reduce conflict within teams.

SA (10)	A (8)	N (6)	D (4)	SD (2)

25. You constantly develop the seven most important values an innovative team holds.

SA (10)	A (8)	N (6)	D (4)	SD (2)

26. You apply the factors that develop and reinforce innovative team values.

SA (10)	A (8)	N (6)	D (4)	SD (2)

27. You apply concepts of high performance.

SA (10)	A (8)	N (6)	D (4)	SD (2)

28. You apply the concept of SMART high performance goals.

SA (10)	A (8)	N (6)	D (4)	SD (2)

29. You determine attainable stretch goals.

SA (10)	A (8)	N (6)	D (4)	SD (2)

30. You determine attainable integrated systems goals.

SA (10)	A (8)	N (6)	D (4)	SD (2)

31. You apply the principal characteristics of effective performance metrics.

SA (10)	A (8)	N (6)	D (4)	SD (2)

32. You apply key innovative team performance metrics.

SA (10)	A (8)	N (6)	D (4)	SD (2)

33. You apply basic design rules for key performance metrics.

SA (10)	A (8)	N (6)	D (4)	SD (2)

34. You appropriately focus metrics on creativity.

SA (10)	A (8)	N (6)	D (4)	SD (2)

35. You appropriately focus metrics on results.

SA (10)	A (8)	N (6)	D (4)	SD (2)

36. You appropriately apply top-down and bottom-up organisation.

SA (10)	A (8)	N (6)	D (4)	SD (2)

37. You optimise the size and structure of teams.	SA (10)	A (8)	N (6)	D (4)	SD (2)
38. You design and apply multidimensional roles.	SA (10)	A (8)	N (6)	D (4)	SD (2)
39. You construct innovative team project rooms.	SA (10)	A (8)	N (6)	D (4)	SD (2)
40. You apply collaborative technologies in distributed teams.	SA (10)	A (8)	N (6)	D (4)	SD (2)
41. You practise open team leadership.	SA (10)	A (8)	N (6)	D (4)	SD (2)
42. You practise the key roles of the innovative team leader.	SA (10)	A (8)	N (6)	D (4)	SD (2)

From a total of 42 statements, there is a maximum possible score of 420 points. By dividing the actual score total by the total possible score (420), and then multiplying the result by 100, an operational performance rating is expressed as a percentage.

For example, an actual score of 210 will give you an operational performance rating of 50 per cent. Clearly, the nearer the score moves to 100 per cent, the higher the team operational performance is going to be, also indicating where and what areas of operational performance need to be improved.

Team Strategic Output Performance Questionnaire

This questionnaire lists the key factors a team must meet to achieve high performance strategic outputs in terms of actual innovation. It should be filled out by all members of the team on a regular basis, as this will continually recalibrate and focus effort.

Each statement has a range of five potential responses, with five abbreviations and associated scores to indicate the respondents answer:

Strongly agree	=	SA
Agree	=	A
Not demonstrated consistently	=	N
Disagree	=	D
Strongly disagree	=	SD

There is no time limit.

1. In current markets, the innovation exceeds the target customer's unsatisfied needs and expectations.		SA (10) / A (8) / N (5) / D (0) / SD (-5)
2. In new markets, the innovation exceeds the target customer's unarticulated needs and expectations.		SA (20) / A (15) / N (5) / D (0) / SD (-5)
3. In nascent markets, the innovation exceeds the target customer's emerging needs and expectations.		SA (30) / A (20) / N (5) / D (0) / SD (-5)
4. The innovation reinvents or creates a new category of competition.		SA (20) / A (15) / N (5) / D (0) / SD (-5)
5. The innovation is disruptive in the competitive context.		SA (10) / A (8) / N (5) / D (0) / SD (-5)
6. The innovation is an improvement on past models, and improves the position in current markets.		SA (10) / A (8) / N (6) / D (0) / SD (0)
7. The innovation creates new segments outside traditional markets.		SA (20) / A (15) / N (5) / D (0) / SD (-5)
8. The innovation is a radical, category-breaking innovation that creates a completely new market.		SA (10) / A (8) / N (5) / D (0) / SD (-5)
9. The innovation provides superior value return on total investment.		SA (10) / A (8) / N (5) / D (0) / SD (-5)
10. The value expectations of the customer are being upheld.		SA (10) / A (8) / N (5) / D (0) / SD (-5)
11. The value return is superior relative to the industry at large.		SA (10) / A (8) / N (5) / D (0) / SD (-5)
12. Best value in the market is being achieved.		SA (10) / A (8) / N (5) / D (0) / SD (-5)

Once complete, the questionnaire will indicate whether the team is producing a real strategic innovation that has a higher probability of success in the market over the longer term, or otherwise.

The lowest possible score is −55. The highest possible score is 170. The higher the total score, the more strategic the innovation is. The lower the score, the more tactical the innovation is. If the score turns out to be a negative score, then no strategic innovation is being achieved.

Personality Profiling Questionnaire and Charts

This questionnaire and its associated charts are designed to indicate the type of personality profile a potential team member exhibits and serve as an aid when selecting members for a specific project team.

Each applicant should take no longer than 30 minutes to fill in the initial questionnaire, and the results should be scored and presented as directed below.

Each statement has a range of five potential responses, with five abbreviations and associated scores to indicate the applicant's answer:

Strongly agree	=	SA
Agree	=	A
Not demonstrated consistently	=	N
Disagree	=	D
Strongly disagree	=	SD

1. You are mostly calm and self-assured in almost all situations.

SA	A	N	D	SD
(10)	(8)	(6)	(4)	(2)

2. You have a holistic approach to your work.

SA	A	N	D	SD
(10)	(8)	(6)	(4)	(2)

3. You are single minded about your work.

SA	A	N	D	SD
(10)	(8)	(6)	(4)	(2)

4. You like to challenge the norm from time to time.

SA	A	N	D	SD
(10)	(8)	(6)	(4)	(2)

5. You like to take risks.

SA	A	N	D	SD
(10)	(8)	(6)	(4)	(2)

6. You like radically new ideas, means and ways.

SA	A	N	D	SD
(10)	(8)	(6)	(4)	(2)

7. You are good at getting hold of new or specialist information.

SA	A	N	D	SD
(10)	(8)	(6)	(4)	(2)

8. You are quite a sober character.

SA	A	N	D	SD
(10)	(8)	(6)	(4)	(2)

9. You like to be around people for most of the time.

SA	A	N	D	SD
(10)	(8)	(6)	(4)	(2)

10. You can be quite provocative at times.

SA	A	N	D	SD
(10)	(8)	(6)	(4)	(2)

11. You are hard working much of the time.

SA	A	N	D	SD
(10)	(8)	(6)	(4)	(2)

12. You can easily reduce a problem to it fundamental constituents.

SA	A	N	D	SD
(10)	(8)	(6)	(4)	(2)

13. You like to think things through quite thoroughly before you act.

SA	A	N	D	SD
(10)	(8)	(6)	(4)	(2)

14. You can quite easily fuse disparate pieces of information and knowledge to create new ideas or solve unique problems.

SA	A	N	D	SD
(10)	(8)	(6)	(4)	(2)

15. Your work is highly focused.

SA	A	N	D	SD
(10)	(8)	(6)	(4)	(2)

16. You do not much like conventions and standards.

SA	A	N	D	SD
(10)	(8)	(6)	(4)	(2)

17. You do not mind ambiguous situations.

SA	A	N	D	SD
(10)	(8)	(6)	(4)	(2)

18. You are outgoing.

SA	A	N	D	SD
(10)	(8)	(6)	(4)	(2)

19. You know how things work and where to source and get them made.

SA	A	N	D	SD
(10)	(8)	(6)	(4)	(2)

20. You are an equable character.

SA	A	N	D	SD
(10)	(8)	(6)	(4)	(2)

21. You are quite sociable and genial.

SA	A	N	D	SD
(10)	(8)	(6)	(4)	(2)

22. You can read a situation and make good decisions using your intuition.

SA	A	N	D	SD
(10)	(8)	(6)	(4)	(2)

23. You like to take extreme care with your work.

SA	A	N	D	SD
(10)	(8)	(6)	(4)	(2)

24. You are time conscious.

SA	A	N	D	SD
(10)	(8)	(6)	(4)	(2)

25. You would rather wait and see what happens in a given situation as opposed to acting first.

SA	A	N	D	SD
(10)	(8)	(6)	(4)	(2)

26. You can often see the downstream and secondary effects of new ways and means in new situations.

SA	A	N	D	SD
(10)	(8)	(6)	(4)	(2)

27. You can easily define complex problems in objective and simple ways.

SA	A	N	D	SD
(10)	(8)	(6)	(4)	(2)

28. You do not fuss over detail.

SA	A	N	D	SD
(10)	(8)	(6)	(4)	(2)

29. Uncertainty does not faze you.

SA	A	N	D	SD
(10)	(8)	(6)	(4)	(2)

30. You relentlessly learn and explore new things.

SA	A	N	D	SD
(10)	(8)	(6)	(4)	(2)

31. You like extremely tough challenges.

SA	A	N	D	SD
(10)	(8)	(6)	(4)	(2)

32. You are a prudent individual.

SA	A	N	D	SD
(10)	(8)	(6)	(4)	(2)

33. You always listen to other people's ideas and views before you act.

SA	A	N	D	SD
(10)	(8)	(6)	(4)	(2)

34. You are a people person.

SA	A	N	D	SD
(10)	(8)	(6)	(4)	(2)

35. You can factor a criticism into your work.

SA	A	N	D	SD
(10)	(8)	(6)	(4)	(2)

36. You are clinically methodical in your work.

SA	A	N	D	SD
(10)	(8)	(6)	(4)	(2)

37. You are extremely good at distinguishing between reliable and unreliable information.

SA	A	N	D	SD
(10)	(8)	(6)	(4)	(2)

38. You can often see interconnections between seemingly separate issues.

SA	A	N	D	SD
(10)	(8)	(6)	(4)	(2)

39. You like highly specialist work.

SA	A	N	D	SD
(10)	(8)	(6)	(4)	(2)

40. You are skilfully creative in your work.

SA	A	N	D	SD
(10)	(8)	(6)	(4)	(2)

41. You do not like routine.

SA	A	N	D	SD
(10)	(8)	(6)	(4)	(2)

42. You have a real passion for your chosen work field.

SA	A	N	D	SD
(10)	(8)	(6)	(4)	(2)

43. You have many contacts with people who can solve specialist problems.

SA	A	N	D	SD
(10)	(8)	(6)	(4)	(2)

44. You are often fairly unemotional about the decisions you make.

SA	A	N	D	SD
(10)	(8)	(6)	(4)	(2)

45. You have a highly developed sense of humour.

SA	A	N	D	SD
(10)	(8)	(6)	(4)	(2)

46. You interact well with a wide range of people.

SA	A	N	D	SD
(10)	(8)	(6)	(4)	(2)

47. You often overcome difficult problems through persistence.

SA	A	N	D	SD
(10)	(8)	(6)	(4)	(2)

48. You are very conscientious in your work.

SA	A	N	D	SD
(10)	(8)	(6)	(4)	(2)

49. You do not often jump to conclusions.

SA	A	N	D	SD
(10)	(8)	(6)	(4)	(2)

50. You do not like to attack a problem in bits and pieces.

SA	A	N	D	SD
(10)	(8)	(6)	(4)	(2)

51. You like a highly focused role within a project.

SA	A	N	D	SD
(10)	(8)	(6)	(4)	(2)

52. Your friends often call you clever.

SA	A	N	D	SD
(10)	(8)	(6)	(4)	(2)

53. You like a new challenge.

SA	A	N	D	SD
(10)	(8)	(6)	(4)	(2)

54. You cannot help pulling things apart to study them.

SA	A	N	D	SD
(10)	(8)	(6)	(4)	(2)

55. You prefer the initial stages of a project, rather than the end.

SA	A	N	D	SD
(10)	(8)	(6)	(4)	(2)

56. You usually have excellent judgement.

SA	A	N	D	SD
(10)	(8)	(6)	(4)	(2)

57. You like making people laugh at work.

SA	A	N	D	SD
(10)	(8)	(6)	(4)	(2)

58. You are a good influencer.

SA	A	N	D	SD
(10)	(8)	(6)	(4)	(2)

59. You are systematic in the organisation of your work.
`SA (10) | A (8) | N (6) | D (4) | SD (2)`

60. You do not let obstacles stand in the way of
completing your task.
`SA (10) | A (8) | N (6) | D (4) | SD (2)`

61. You are wholly objective in your decision making.
`SA (10) | A (8) | N (6) | D (4) | SD (2)`

62. You can often see the bigger picture.
`SA (10) | A (8) | N (6) | D (4) | SD (2)`

63. You like to get on with the job on your own initiative.
`SA (10) | A (8) | N (6) | D (4) | SD (2)`

64. You have developed aspects of knowledge within
your field of expertise.
`SA (10) | A (8) | N (6) | D (4) | SD (2)`

65. You have often ventured into the unknown
with some success.
`SA (10) | A (8) | N (6) | D (4) | SD (2)`

66. You spend a lot of time wondering about new things.
`SA (10) | A (8) | N (6) | D (4) | SD (2)`

67. You can get hold of a rare piece of knowledge quickly.
`SA (10) | A (8) | N (6) | D (4) | SD (2)`

68. You sometimes lack inspiration.
`SA (10) | A (8) | N (6) | D (4) | SD (2)`

69. You do not like working on your own.
`SA (10) | A (8) | N (6) | D (4) | SD (2)`

70. You often have quite contrasting views and perspectives
to your peers.
`SA (10) | A (8) | N (6) | D (4) | SD (2)`

71. You can easily adapt a situation or piece of information
to solve a tough problem.
`SA (10) | A (8) | N (6) | D (4) | SD (2)`

72. You can easily bring a task to conclusion.
`SA (10) | A (8) | N (6) | D (4) | SD (2)`

73. You often deliver intended results on time.
`SA (10) | A (8) | N (6) | D (4) | SD (2)`

74. You can often see the knock-on effects of upsteam issues.
`SA (10) | A (8) | N (6) | D (4) | SD (2)`

75. You do not like working on a wide spread of different
tasks or projects at the same time.
`SA (10) | A (8) | N (6) | D (4) | SD (2)`

76. You can easily come up with highly original, but
practical solutions to new problems.
`SA (10) | A (8) | N (6) | D (4) | SD (2)`

77. You have travelled to far-off lands under
your own initiative.
`SA (10) | A (8) | N (6) | D (4) | SD (2)`

78. You always think there is a better way.

SA	A	N	D	SD
(10)	(8)	(6)	(4)	(2)

79. You do not like to be kept waiting.

SA	A	N	D	SD
(10)	(8)	(6)	(4)	(2)

80. You are considered to be a strong character.

SA	A	N	D	SD
(10)	(8)	(6)	(4)	(2)

81. You can calm a tense atmosphere.

SA	A	N	D	SD
(10)	(8)	(6)	(4)	(2)

82. You like to have the ear of key executive staff.

SA	A	N	D	SD
(10)	(8)	(6)	(4)	(2)

83. You are often quite cautious in your approach to your work.

SA	A	N	D	SD
(10)	(8)	(6)	(4)	(2)

84. You do not like loose ends.

SA	A	N	D	SD
(10)	(8)	(6)	(4)	(2)

85. You are effective in political situations.

SA	A	N	D	SD
(10)	(8)	(6)	(4)	(2)

86. You enjoy fitting the pieces of the problem into the wider picture.

SA	A	N	D	SD
(10)	(8)	(6)	(4)	(2)

87. You enjoy technically challenging problems.

SA	A	N	D	SD
(10)	(8)	(6)	(4)	(2)

88. You like blue-sky ideas.

SA	A	N	D	SD
(10)	(8)	(6)	(4)	(2)

89. You have many life and work stories to tell.

SA	A	N	D	SD
(10)	(8)	(6)	(4)	(2)

90. You are always on the lookout for new ways and means.

SA	A	N	D	SD
(10)	(8)	(6)	(4)	(2)

91. You can usually find people with the right experience for a project quickly.

SA	A	N	D	SD
(10)	(8)	(6)	(4)	(2)

92. You like to take on long, arduous tasks.

SA	A	N	D	SD
(10)	(8)	(6)	(4)	(2)

93. People generally like you.

SA	A	N	D	SD
(10)	(8)	(6)	(4)	(2)

94. You like extreme ideas.

SA	A	N	D	SD
(10)	(8)	(6)	(4)	(2)

95. You get a lot of work done in a short time.

SA	A	N	D	SD
(10)	(8)	(6)	(4)	(2)

96. You enjoy hard work.

SA	A	N	D	SD
(10)	(8)	(6)	(4)	(2)

97. You are mostly unbiased.

SA	A	N	D	SD
(10)	(8)	(6)	(4)	(2)

98. You do not like piecemeal solutions.

SA	A	N	D	SD
(10)	(8)	(6)	(4)	(2)

99. You do not enjoy highly diverse challenges.

SA	A	N	D	SD
(10)	(8)	(6)	(4)	(2)

100. You are an independent thinker.

SA	A	N	D	SD
(10)	(8)	(6)	(4)	(2)

101. You have your feet on the ground, but at the same time enjoy taking the occasional risk.

SA	A	N	D	SD
(10)	(8)	(6)	(4)	(2)

102. You watch/read a lot of technical/factual and/or future-oriented TV/journals.

SA	A	N	D	SD
(10)	(8)	(6)	(4)	(2)

103. You can sift through and understand dense stacks of information quickly.

SA	A	N	D	SD
(10)	(8)	(6)	(4)	(2)

104. You are not fazed that easily.

SA	A	N	D	SD
(10)	(8)	(6)	(4)	(2)

105. You have many friends from different walks of life.

SA	A	N	D	SD
(10)	(8)	(6)	(4)	(2)

106. You can imagine what the future might be like.

SA	A	N	D	SD
(10)	(8)	(6)	(4)	(2)

107. You like to solve new problems by persistent learning and adaptation.

SA	A	N	D	SD
(10)	(8)	(6)	(4)	(2)

108. You nearly always finish what you are doing at the cost of neglecting secondary issues in your work life.

SA	A	N	D	SD
(10)	(8)	(6)	(4)	(2)

109. You are more practical than creative.

SA	A	N	D	SD
(10)	(8)	(6)	(4)	(2)

110. You like integrating ideas.

SA	A	N	D	SD
(10)	(8)	(6)	(4)	(2)

111. You prefer to work on one issue at a time.

SA	A	N	D	SD
(10)	(8)	(6)	(4)	(2)

112. You like new challenges, but you also mostly see them through to fruition.

SA	A	N	D	SD
(10)	(8)	(6)	(4)	(2)

113. You often take the lead when things start to go wrong.

SA	A	N	D	SD
(10)	(8)	(6)	(4)	(2)

114. You have a lifetime learning disposition.

SA	A	N	D	SD
(10)	(8)	(6)	(4)	(2)

115. You have a great many professional contacts.

SA	A	N	D	SD
(10)	(8)	(6)	(4)	(2)

116. You are prepared to stop the show if you think it needs to go in another direction.

SA	A	N	D	SD
(10)	(8)	(6)	(4)	(2)

117. You are a member of a number of clubs and extracurricular activities.

SA	A	N	D	SD
(10)	(8)	(6)	(4)	(2)

118. Having lots of fun is important to you.

SA	A	N	D	SD
(10)	(8)	(6)	(4)	(2)

119. You like a heavy workload much of the time.

SA	A	N	D	SD
(10)	(8)	(6)	(4)	(2)

120. You prefer to introduce projects into the next stage, rather than begin them.

SA	A	N	D	SD
(5)	(4)	(3)	(2)	(1)

Personality indicator chart

Once the questionnaire has been completed, each score should be entered in the appropriate box in the personality indicator chart below. The total score for each type of personality (chairperson, expert, multidimensionalist and so on) should then be added up within the box under each personality type. To find the average score for each personality type, divide each personality type score by 10, then enter it into the relevant 'average personality' box under each total score box.

When completed by each applicant, the following chart will give an impartial indication of the type of personality profile the candidate holds. This information can then be entered into the team personality balancing chart.

Personality indicator chart

Personality	No	Chairperson	No	Multidimensionalist	No	Expert	No	Innovator	No	Adventurer	No	Inquisitor
	1		2		3		4		5		6	
	13		14		15		16		17		18	
	25		26		27		28		29		30	
	37		38		39		40		41		42	
	49		50		51		52		53		54	
	61		62		63		64		65		66	
	73		74		75		76		77		78	
	85		86		87		88		89		90	
	97		98		99		100		101		102	
	109		110		111		112		113		114	
Personality total												
Average score												

Personality	No	Resourcer	No	Judge	No	Teamer	No	Jester	No	Doer	No	Finisher
	7		8		9		10		11		12	
	19		20		21		22		23		24	
	31		32		33		34		35		36	
	43		44		45		46		47		48	
	55		56		57		58		59		60	
	67		68		69		70		71		72	
	79		80		81		82		83		84	
	91		92		93		94		95		96	
	103		104		105		106		107		108	
	115		116		117		118		119		120	
Personality total												
Average score												

Personality balancing chart

This chart is designed to assist in balancing the distribution of personalities within a given innovative team. It should be completed by the team's leader or an appropriate executive on the strategic top team (see Chapter 11).

The chart is completed by taking the top three highest scores to indicate the personality bias of each candidate. Then for each of the highest three scores, tick the personality trait box. For example, if a candidate has a personality profile bias of chairperson, judge and doer, then tick each appropriate box for each personality.

Personality balancing chart

Personality	Individual candidates																			
	1	2	3	4	5	6	7	8	9	10	11	12	13	14	15	16	17	18	19	20
Chairperson																				
Multidimensionalist																				
Expert																				
Innovator																				
Adventurer																				
Inquisitor																				
Judge																				
Resourcer																				
Teamer																				
Jester																				
Doer																				
Finisher																				

Once the personality balancing chart is complete with the available candidates' scores, it will show at a glance: (a) the range of personalities available, (b) which personalities are overrepresented, and (c) which specific personalities are missing.

The chart can also be used to indicate the balance of personalities of specific teams. Simply enter the personality bias of each team member (or candidate) in each appropriate box, and it will show the balance of personalities within that team, and indicate which specific personalities are lacking.

Aggregate Performance Development Equation

This last appendix integrates the results from the innovative team performance development questionnaires in Appendices B, C, D, and E into one simple equation that gives a bottom-line number for how well each innovative team is progressing through its development.

For clarity, this appendix will work through the process step-by-step with a real example.

The innovative performance development equation:

$$\frac{[\text{tkdp} + \text{tbdp} + \text{todp} + \text{tsodp}] \times 100}{\text{tps}} = \text{apd}$$

Where: tkdp = total knowledge development performance (Appendix B)
tbdp = total behavioural development performance (Appendix C)
todp = total operational development performance (Appendix D)
tsodp = total strategic output development
    performance   (Appendix E)
tps = total possible score (of all questionnaires)
apd = aggregate performance development

Worked example:

If   the actual tkdp   = 340
        the actual tbdp   = 280

the actual todp   = 210
the actual tsodp   = 60

And   the actual tps = 1660

Then $$\frac{[tkdp + tbdp + todp + tsodp] \times 100}{tps} = apd$$

Therefore: $$\frac{[340 + 280 + 210 + 60] \times 100}{1660} = apd$$

$$\frac{890 \times 100}{1660} = 53.6\%$$

BIBLIOGRAPHY

Adair, J. *Leadership: A Modern Guide to Developing Leadership Skills.* Gower, London, 1983.

Adair, J. *Effective Team-Building.* Gower, London, 1987.

Bernstein A J. and Craft Rozen, S. *Dinosaur Brains: Dealing With all those Impossible People at Work.* Arrow Books, London, 1990.

Bettleheim, B. *On Uses of Enchantment.* Thames and Hudson, London, 1979.

Bohm, D. *Thought as a System.* Routledge, London, 1994.

Bohm, D. *On Dialogue.* Routledge, London, 1996.

Boot, R.L., Cowling, A.G. and Stanworth, J.K. *Behavioural Sciences for Managers.* Edward Arnold, London, 1982.

Brooks, F.P. *The Mythical Man-Month: Essays in Software Engineering.* Addison-Wesley, Reading, MA, 1975.

Capra, C. *'The Turning Point': Science, Society and the Rising Culture.* HarperCollins, London, 1983.

Clark, K.B and Fujimoto, T. *Product Development Performance.* Harvard Business School Press, Cambridge, MA, 1991.

Copper, J. *Louis Agassiz as Teacher,* Comstock, New York, 1945.

Deal, T. and Kennedy, A. *Corporate Cultures: The Rites and Rituals of Corporate Life.* Penguin, London, 1982.

Drucker, P.F. *Management: Tasks, Responsibilities, Practice.* Butterworth Heinemann, Oxford, 1988.

Hamel, G. *Competing for the Future.* Harvard Business School Press, Cambridge, MA, 1994.

Hamel, G. *Leading the Revolution.* Harvard Business School Press, Cambridge, MA, 2000.

Homans, G.C. *The Human Group,* New York, Harcourt Brace and World, 1950.

Horbie, F. *Creating the Innovation Culture: Leveraging Visionaries, Dissenters and Other Useful Troublemakers in Your Organisation.* John Wiley & Sons, Ontario, 2001.

Johnson-Laird, P.N. *Small Scale Models.* MIT Press, Cambridge, MA, 1993.

Katzenbach, J.R. and Dougless, K. *Wisdom of Teams: Creating the High-performance Organization.* Harvard Business School Press, Cambridge, MA, 1995.

Kauffman, S.A. *The Origins of Order: Self-organisation and Selection in Evolution.* Oxford University Press, Oxford, 1993.

Kelly, K. *Out of Control: The New Biology of Machines.* Addison-Wesley, Reading, MA, 1994.

Kosko, B. *Fuzzy Thinking: The New Science of Fuzzy Logic.* Flamingo, London, 1994.

Mathews, R. and Wacker, W. *The Deviant's Advantage.* Crown, New York, 2002.

Minsky, M. *Society of Mind.* Simon & Schuster, New York, 1985.

Mito, S. *The Honda Book of Management: A Leadership Philosophy for High Industrial Success.* Kogan Page, London, 1990.

Nolan, N. *The Innovators Hand Book: The Skills of Innovative Management: Problem Solving, Communication and Teamwork.* Sphere Books, London, 1990.

Peters, T.J. *Liberation Management: The Necessary Disorganisation for the Nanosecond 90s.* Pan Macmillan, London, 1992.

Rheingold, H. *Virtual Reality: The Revolutionary Technology of Computer-generated Artificial Worlds – and How it Promises to Transform Society.* Touchstone, New York, 1992.

Schaffer, R. and Thomson, H. 'Successful Change Begins with Results'. *Harvard Business Review*, Jan–Feb, 1992.

Senge, P.M. *The Fifth Discipline: The Art and Practice of the Learning Organisation.* Random House, London, 1993.

Senge, P.M. *The Fifth Discipline Field Book: Strategies and Tools for Building a Learning Organisation.* Nicholas Brealey, London, 1994.

Sherwood, D. *Unlock Your Mind: A Practical Guide to Deliberate and Systematic Innovation.* Gower, Aldershot, 1998.

Toffler, A. *Future Shock.* Bantam Books, London, 1970.

Utterback, J. *Mastering the Dynamics of Innovation: How Companies can Seize Opportunities in the Face of Technological Change.* Harvard Business School Press, Boston, 1994.

Wood, L.E. *Thinking Strategies: Exercises for Mental Fitness.* Prentice Hall, New Jersey, 1986.